LONGMAN CRITICAL READERS

General Editors:

RAMAN SELDEN, late Emeritus Professor of English,
Lancaster University and late Professor of English,
Sunderland Polytechnic;

STAN SMITH, Professor of English, University of Dundee

Published titles:

K. M. NEWTON, *George Eliot*

MARY EAGLETON, *Feminist Literary Criticism*

GARY WALLER, *Shakespeare's Comedies*

JOHN DRAKAKIS, *Shakespearean Tragedy*

RICHARD WILSON AND RICHARD DUTTON *New Historicism and Renaissance
Drama*

PETER BROOKER, *Modernism/Postmodernism*

PETER WIDDOWSON, *D. H. Lawrence*

RACHEL BOWLBY, *Virginia Woolf*

FRANCIS MULHERN, *Contemporary Marxist Literary Criticism*

ANNABEL PATTERSON, *John Milton*

JOHN MILTON

Edited and Introduced by

ANNABEL PATTERSON

LONGMAN
LONDON AND NEW YORK

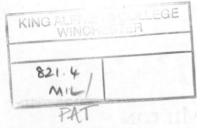
Longman Group UK Limited,
Longman House, Burnt Mill,
Harlow, Essex CM20 2JE, England
and Associated Companies throughout the world.

Published in the United States of America
by Longman Publishing, New York

© Longman Group UK Limited 1992

First published 1992

ISBN 0 582 04550 9 CSD
ISBN 0 582 04539 8 PPR

British Library Cataloguing-in-Publication Data
A catalogue record for this book is
available from the British Library

Library of Congress Cataloging in Publication Data
John Milton / edited and introduced by Annabel Patterson.
    p. cm. – (Longman critical readers)
  Includes bibliographical references and index.
    ISBN 0–582–04550–9 (csd). – ISBN 0–582-04539-8 (ppr)
    1. Milton, John, 1608–1674 – Criticism and interpretation.
  I. Patterson, Annabel M. II. Series.
PR3588.J64   1992
821'.4 – dc20   92–12385
                                                CIP

Set 9k in 9/11½ pt Palatino
Produced by Longman Singapore Publisher (Pte) Ltd.
Printed in Singapore

Contents

General Editors' Preface

The outlines of contemporary critical theory are now often taught as a standard feature of a degree in literary studies. The development of particular theories has seen a thorough transformation of literary criticism. For example, Marxist and Foucauldian theories have revolutionized Shakespeare studies, and 'deconstruction' has led to a complete reassessment of Romantic poetry. Feminist criticism has left scarcely any period of literature unaffected by its searching critiques. Teachers of literary studies can no longer fall back on a standardized, received, methodology.

Lecturers and teachers are now urgently looking for guidance in a rapidly changing critical environment. They need help in understanding the latest revisions in literary theory, and especially in grasping the practical effects of the new theories in the form of theoretically sensitized new readings. A number of volumes in the series anthologize important essays on particular theories. However, in order to grasp the full implication and possible uses of particular theories it is essential to see them put to work. This series provides substantial volumes of new readings, presented in an accessible form and with a significant amount of editorial guidance.

Each volume includes a substantial introduction which explores the theoretical issues and conflicts embodied in the essays selected and locates areas of disagreement between positions. The pluralism of theories has to be put on the agenda of literary studies. We can no longer pretend that we all tacitly accept the same practices in literary studies. Neither is a *laissez-faire* attitude any longer tenable. Literature departments need to go beyond the mere toleration of theoretical differences: it is not enough merely to agree to differ; they need actually to 'stage' the differences, not necessarily with a view to resolving them but in order to foreground the choices presented by different theories or to argue for a particular route through the impasses the differences present.

The theory 'revolution' has had real effects. It has loosened the grip of traditional empiricist and romantic assumptions about language and literature. It is not always clear what is being proposed as the new agenda for literary studies, and indeed the very notion of 'literature' is questioned by the post-structuralist strain in theory. However, the uncertainties and obscurities of contemporary theories appear much less worrying when we see what the best critics have been able to do with them in practice. This series aims to disseminate the best of recent criticism, and to show that it is possible to re-read the canonical texts of literature in new and challenging ways.

RAMAN SELDEN AND STAN SMITH

The Publishers and fellow Series Editor regret to record that Raman Selden died after a short illness in May 1991 at the age of fifty-three. Ray Selden was a fine scholar and a lovely man. All those he has worked with will remember him with much affection and respect.

Acknowledgements

We are grateful to the following for permission to reproduce copyright material:

The author, Francis Barker for extracts from 'A Challenged Spectacle: *Areopagitica*' in *The Tremulous Private Body: Essays on Subjection* (Methuen, 1984); Cambridge University Press for extracts from 'Fallen differences, phallogocentric discourses: losing *Paradise Lost* to history' by Mary Nyquist in *Post-Structuralism and the Question of History* ed. Derek Attridge *et al* (1987) and '"No meer amatorious novel?": *The Doctrine and Discipline of Divorce*' by Annabel Patterson in *Politics, Poetics, and Hermeneutics in Milton's Prose* ed. David Loewnstein and James Grantham Turner (1990); the author, Victoria Kahn for her article 'Allegory and the Sublime in *Paradise Lost*'; Oxford University Press for extracts from 'The Intelligible Flame' by James Grantham Turner in *One Flesh: Paradisal Marriage and Sexual Relations in the Age of Milton* (Oxford: Clarendon Press, 1987) and 'Milton's Early Radicalism' by Michael Wilding in *Dragon's Teeth: Literature in the English Revolution* (Oxford: Clarendon Press, 1987); Routledge for extracts from 'The Father's House: *Samson Agonistes* in its historical moment' by John Guillory in *Re-Membering Milton: Essays on the Texts and Traditions* ed. Mary Nyquist and Margaret W. Ferguson (Methuen, 1987), William Myers, 'The Spirit of Difference' in *Milton and Free Will: An Essay in Criticism and Philosophy* (Croom Helm, 1987) and David Norbrook, 'The Politics of Milton's Early Poetry' in *Poetry and Politics in the English Renaissance* (Routledge, 1984); University of California Press for extracts from 'The Politics of *Paradise Lost*' by Mary Ann Radzinowicz in *Politics of Discourse: The Literature and History of Seventeenth-Century England* ed. Kevin Sharpe and Steven Zwicker. Copyright © 1987 The Regents of the University of California; The University of Chicago Press for extracts from 'When Eve Reads Milton: Undoing the Canonical Economy' by Christine Froula in *Critical Inquiry* 10 (1983) and 'Dating Milton' by Jonathan Goldberg in *Soliciting Interpretation* ed. Elizabeth Harvey and Katherine Maus (1990); University of Pittsburgh Press for adapted extracts from 'What It's Like to Read *L'Allegro* and *Il Penseroso*' by Stanley Fish in *Milton Studies* (Volume VII: '"Eyes Fast Fix't": Current Perspectives in Milton Methodology') ed. Albert C. Labriola and Michael Lieb. © 1975 by University of Pittsburgh Press.

My primary debt of gratitude is, of course, to the twelve good men and women who agreed to participate in this project; not least because their participation was more active than is usually the case in such collections. Each author wrote his/her own headnote summarizing the argument that follows, and locating it within the shape of a larger work or a whole career; thereby relieving me of a delicate task and an awesome responsibility.

All of the essays reprinted here have had to be, to a greater or lesser extent, shortened and stripped of material extraneous to the purpose for which the selection was made. The authors have courteously agreed to the necessary, and in some places, minor additions needed to clarify allusions. To smooth the reading process, these changes have been made in typographical silence, though the authors have agreed to such changes. Readers are urged eventually to consult the whole of the works from which these excerpts have been taken.

All quotations of Milton's poetry are from *John Milton: Complete Shorter Poems*, ed. John Carey (London: Longman, 1971) and *John Milton: Paradise Lost*, ed. Alastair Fowler (London: Longman, 1971). All quotations from his prose are from *Complete Prose*, ed. D.M. Wolfe *et al*. 8 vols. (Newhaven: Yale University Press, 1953–80).

AP

1 Introduction

Caught in the cross-fire between the market appeal of a 'great' author and the strictures of postmodernism against a 'humanist' or author-centred literary theory, Catherine Belsey asks the question, 'Why Milton?'[1] and, in answering, understandably attempts to have it both ways by claiming that significance lies not in the man but in the era. Milton's canonical poems chart, she claims:

> some of the struggles and transformations which brought into being the world we now inhabit. They also constitute an intervention in those struggles and transformations. They record and participate in the historical turning-point which marks the installation of the modern epoch.
>
> (p. 8)

In introducing the essays in this volume, I naturally also assert Milton's significance as an object of advanced and intensive study, even and especially at the end of the twentieth century. The claim on our attention of an English writer of three centuries ago may seen tenuous compared with the demands by or on behalf of those who represent the enormously expanded and conflicted world we now inhabit. Yet the fact is that Milton's writings, though comparatively without influence on his immediate contemporaries, have been either a touchstone for ideas or a battleground of beliefs ever since his death in 1674, and he has been a symbolic figure in the evolution of at least three different disciplines. Readily constructed as a hero of the Whigs, not least by the eighteenth-century biography of John Toland, on the grounds of the political pamphlets written from 1649 to 1660 in defence of the English republic and the execution of Charles I, Milton has had a place comparable to that of John Harrington or John Locke in the history of political thought, particularly in the arenas of constitutional theory and individual liberties. In a looser sense he became a name in the canon of liberalism or libertarianism by way of his attack, in *Areopagitica*, on the Long Parliament's return to censorship.

For the same reasons (Milton's authorship of polemical tracts that in their own way chart the history of England from 1640 to 1660), supplemented by the fact that he held an official position in Oliver Cromwell's civil service, as Latin Secretary responsible for much international correspondence, Milton has always been a figure of some interest to historians. Towards the end of the twentieth century, this interest has intensified as a result of internecine struggles among British historians over the events of 1640–60, as to whether those events did indeed constitute a sociopolitical revolution with profound and definable causes and principles (including religion) or whether what happened was merely a civil war that occurred more or less by accident, through bad management on the side of both King Charles and his parliamentary critics, most of whom had never intended to bring about major structural changes in the government. In that debate Milton has acquired a new prominence, specifically in the work of Christopher Hill, the great Marxist historian of seventeenth-century nonconformity and sectarianism, to whose biography of Milton we shall return.

Most of the readers of this volume will, of course, be literary critics, who will approach Milton primarily as a poet and as the author of *Paradise Lost*. Nevertheless, much of this introduction will be dedicated to showing that it is impossible (though it has been tried) to separate the author of *Paradise Lost* from the Milton of seventeenth-century politics and history. Indeed, the shape of Milton's career has itself determined to some extent the trajectory both of earlier literary criticism and of the contemporary literary theory to which this series is dedicated. Whereas contemporary approaches to George Eliot, to cite the inaugural volume in this series, fall into the broad categories of debates on representation, language theory and deconstruction; politics and ideology; feminism; and psychoanalysis, in that order of importance, recent approaches to Milton have been dominated by two of these categories – the national politics that shaped both his career and his reception as a poet, and the sexual politics that unites *Paradise Lost* with his own pamphlets on divorce and that, ever since Sandra Gilbert defined him as an egregious representative of patriarchalism, has made him one of the monuments of feminist criticism.[2] By comparison, deconstruction has hitherto affected Milton criticism primarily, as we shall see, by way of his theology. Although a case could very well be made that Adam's conversations with Raphael in *Paradise Lost* are themselves debates about representation and problems of signification, most of the followers of Jacques Derrida have had difficulty in demonstrating the presence of metaphysical or epistemological aporias in a writer so confident that Truth, though fumbled together on earth, has divine guarantees elsewhere. Thus R. A.

Shoaf, in a study of Milton's philosphical assumptions that consistently uses the language of deconstruction, concluded that 'to deconstruct his text would necessarily be to transgress his intention', a caveat which, while some deconstructionists would find it laughable, nevertheless goes to the heart of a procedural dilemma.[3]

As for psychoanalytic criticism, its systematic application is almost solely represented by William Kerrigan's *The Sacred Complex*, which reads the Miltonic career, and especially the epic with its emphasis on the Father/Son relationship, as an Oedipal drama. But here too, interestingly, Milton's theology dominates the interpretation and gives it a very different twist to that normally expected from Freudian or Lacanian influences. 'I would like,' Kerrigan wrote in his introduction, 'to recover something of the original urgency of the encounter between religion and psychoanalysis. If psychoanalysis would guard us against the primitive illusions of religion, perhaps religious affirmations of the superego would guard us gainst the civilized illusions of a self-authenticating ego.'[4] The central insight here – that Milton was obsessed with a superego derived from his own relation to his father, and that he transferred his Oedipal feelings to his religious mythology – seems, now that Kerrigan has brought it to our attention, inarguable. But there are other aspects of the Miltonic psyche – as, for example, his obsessive attitude to work – that have not yet received sustained psychoanalytic attention.[5]

Fortunately, some of the best practitioners of the new critical theories cannot simply be constrained by the categories just outlined, but are skilled eclecticists and syncretists. In this volume I have tried to represent equitably the major models or brands of contemporary criticism and literary theory by using examples that are easily intelligible yet which avoid simple 'applications' of a single method. Few of the essays included are 'pure' instances of any one contemporary approach or theory, and several, especially the concluding piece by John Guillory, are masterly syntheses of approaches – in this case psychoanalysis and socioeconomic theory – normally thought of as incompatible. And the careful reader will discover many unforeseen connections and conversations *between* these essays, which suggests that the new 'theories' are not ranged so sharply *against* each other as some have supposed.

The beginnings of critical theory

In the case of Milton, the emergence of 'new' theoretical approaches cannot be fully understood and was to some extent determined by his earlier history of reception. While Milton *scholarship* has proceeded throughout this century more or less unmoved by critical fashion (I refer to the Columbia edition of the *Works*,[6] which began to appear in the 1930s, the Yale edition of the *Prose Works*, a project begun in the 1950s,[7] the founding of *Milton Studies* in 1968 and of the Milton *Variorum* under the editorship of Merritt Hughes in 1970[8]), the theoretical narrative begins with the moment – unusual in literary history – of Milton's *removal* from the literary canon. This was by authority of T.S. Eliot and F.R. Leavis, who together provoked a controversy among British intelligentsia that spanned two decades. In 1936 Eliot published an essay that began, provocatively: 'While it must be admitted that Milton is a very great poet indeed, it is something of a puzzle to decide in what his greatness consists.' Milton was subjected to the 'serious charge' of being a bad influence on poets; of indulging in 'rhetoric', as opposed to the conversational style which was carried forward by Dryden, to the extent of creating a barrier of style between his meaning and his reader. 'So far as I perceive anything,' Eliot continued, 'it is a glimpse of a theology that I find in large part repellent, expressed through a mythology which would have been better left in the Book of Genesis, upon which Milton has not improved.'[9] In 1947, however, Eliot delivered another statement on Milton, supposedly to correct the misjudgements of his previous one. Milton was, after all, a great poet whose influence might be less noxious than he had supposed, the 'remoteness of his language from ordinary speech' now appearing 'one of the marks of his greatness'.[10] Understandably, modern poets like himself, who had been carrying out 'another revolution in idiom', had been biased. Their bias depreciated Milton while contributing to the 'taste' for Donne; but a decade later, Eliot felt, 'we cannot, in literature, any more than in the rest of life, live in a perpetual state of revolution' (p. 148). This political language, as we shall see, was scarcely coincidental. But what Eliot gave back with one hand he took away with the other. Milton's language is now seen as 'a perpetual sequence of original acts of lawlessness' (p. 141) (another not-so-dead political metaphor); and Milton is praised for 'his inerrancy, conscious or unconscious, in writing so as to make the best display of his talents, and the best concealment of his weakness' (p. 142).

The significance of this episode resides in its paradigmatic relation to the history of modern literary criticism, including the ideological implications of an exclusive focus on style, language, or the 'text itself'. As the founding fathers of the movement that, when it spread to the United States, came to be called New Criticism, Eliot and Leavis were, indeed, rebuked by some of their sons for their attitude to Milton. New Critics like Cleanth Brooks, as much as traditional Milton scholars like Douglas Bush, set about demonstrating how extremely readable Milton's poetry was. And it seemed that, if Milton was to be unequivocally restored to canonical status, it would have to be in the same terms that had been used to unseat him. In the early 1960s this feat was accomplished by two critics, J.B. Broadbent[11] and Christopher Ricks,[12] whose views on Milton were as closely related as those of Eliot and Leavis, which they symmetrically reversed. Ricks, in particular, restored the idea of the 'Grand Style' as an honorific, rather than a stigma; but he did so by exploiting every nuance in Milton's language, especially his latinisms, and by privileging that most New Critical of values, ambiguity. It was only in his very last pages that Ricks wondered whether there was not 'something dangerously exclusive in concentrating on Milton's *style* alone', and raised the question of content; and then he significantly failed to answer it. Instead, he closed his case with the extraordinary statement that 'Milton writes at his very best only when something prevents him from writing with total directness.' Milton's 'greatest effects are produced when he is compelled to be oblique as well as direct' (pp. 147–8). What such an inhibition might be, precisely, New Critical methods were unable to suggest.

In fact, Eliot himself was more revelatory, at least in 1947, about the issues so obscured, even though part of his candor was unintentional, the product of an attempt to establish his own scientific perspective in contrast to Dr Johnson's more primitive cognitive tools.

There is one prejudice against Milton, apparent on almost every page of Johnson's *Life of Milton*, which I imagine is still general: we, however, with a longer historical perspective, are in a better position than was Johnson to recognize it and to make allowance for it. This is a prejudice which I share myself: an antipathy towards Milton the man. . . . But this prejudice is often involved with another, more obscure: and I do not think that Johnson had disengaged the two in his own mind. The fact is simply that the Civil War of the seventeenth century, in which Milton is a symbolic figure, has never been concluded. The Civil War is not ended: I question whether any serious civil war ever does end. . . . Reading Johnson's essay one is always aware that Johnson was obstinately and passionately of another party. No other English poet, not Wordsworth, or Shelley, lived through or took sides in such momentous events as did Milton; of no other poet is it so difficult to consider the poetry as poetry, without our theological and political dispositions, conscious and unconscious, inherited or acquired, making an unlawful entry.

(p. 134).

Given that Eliot wrote this statement two years after the British Labour Party took over the government of his adopted country, and proceeded to construct a social revolution, and knowing what we know from other sources of Eliot's 'theological and political dispositions', we may guess that, like Johnson, Eliot confused his 'antipathy towards Milton the man' with his antipathy towards Milton the hero of the Whigs.

The emergence of 'reading' as a theoretical enterprise

In Milton studies the moment of transition from New Criticism to something still newer was, perhaps, 1971, when there appeared a book which was simultaneously a consummate display of New Critical procedures and a defiance of Eliot's influential verdict that Milton's theology was 'repellent'. Stanley Fish's *Surprised by Sin: The Reader in Paradise Lost*[13] showed that New Critical methods could be deployed in the service of Miltonic content, and that they could assist in the task usually assumed by traditional Milton scholars – of deciding what, precisely, Milton intended his readers to learn about free will and obedience. Yet these issues inevitably brought back with them the author-centred, historically situated criticism that New Criticism, as a doctrine rather than a pedagogical practice, had supplanted. Fish's creatively self-contradictory project also assumed a curious position in the then-emergent debates about validity in interpretation, since he was one of the pioneers in the move to finesse the hermeneutical problem of authorial intention by locating all responsibility for literature's meaning in the reader. *Surprised by Sin*, however, had to posit *not* the untrammelled moves of reader response in a sentence-based exegesis, but rather a complicated pedagogical relationship between canny author (Milton) and unsuspecting, fallen yet basically intelligent, 'competent' reader (not Fish himself but *his* audience), the former laying in *Paradise Lost* a series of linguistic traps for the latter, who is led by the discovery of his own waywardness and initially wrongful allegiances (dislike of Milton's God, for example) to remorse and religious submission. The result was a brilliant reprise of the entirely conventional position that Milton's epic meant exactly what it said (when its divinities were speaking), and that any ambiguities (such as those that Ricks had discovered) were only the strategies of a writer determined to bind the reader to his theological cause, to bend him to his will. 'And what does the reader who has reached this point discover at the end of his labors?' wrote Fish in his conclusion. 'The truth, of course, or Truth, as it awaits whose who have climbed the Platonic ladder' (pp. 351–2). *Surprised by Sin*, therefore, achieved a surprising mix between traditional history of thought, a residual but ideologically undefended New Criticism, and an emergent strain of hermeneutics that would increasingly be referred to as 'theory'.

I have chosen to illustrate Fish's reader-response theory, otherwise known as 'affective stylistics', not by an excerpt from *Surprised by Sin* but rather by part of a slightly later essay, originally entitled 'What It's Like to Read *L'Allegro* and *Il Penseroso'*. This appeared in a special volume of *Milton Studies*, itself an attempt to demonstrate 'what directions critical methodology is currently taking'.[14] Its editors concluded, in *their* preface, that 'what Milton scholarship [was] up to . . . is what criticism itself has always been up to'. It is no longer clear that that statement holds; and in the case of Fish it seems, in hindsight, imperceptive, since his account of *L'Allegro* trembles on the brink between reader-response theory and the emergence of deconstruction, especially in its more libertine moments, its belief in free textual play.

Deconstruction and the dissolution of the subject

I began this introduction with Catherine Belsey's question 'Why Milton?' – a problem posed to an author-centred pedagogy by certain tendencies in poststructural thought which have tended to be grouped, in popular parlance, under the term 'deconstruction'. Belsey herself was influenced equally by Jacques Derrida's critique of meaning as 'presence' and Michel Foucault's attack on the concept of individual authorship, for which he wished to substitute the story of institutions and the anonymous 'on dit' that produces 'discourse' at any historical moment. Yet the fact remains that anyone reading *Paradise Lost* (let alone the autobiographical poems like *Ad Patrem* or the highly self-interested interpolations in the pamphlets) runs up against the irreducible and insistent presence of Milton the author, 'presence', 'Milton' and 'author' all, of course, being subject to our inference that Milton was (carefully or anxiously) constructing them for us and for himself. This resistance of Milton's canon to poststructuralism results, as I have said, in a peculiar version of deconstruction, whereby the epistemological problems are shifted to the terrain of theology. Belsey stresses those moments where the question of what authorizes human speech – an unproblematic, original Logos that guarantees truth – becomes itself the theme (as in *An Ode on the Morning of Christ's Nativity*) or the problem (as in *Lycidas*, where the presumably authoritative voices of Apollo and St Peter are only recorded by the 'I' who produces the elegy, but who himself, we learn in the last four lines, is only an 'uncouth swain', a construct of still another speaker who remains unknown, not present to the reader[15]).

In other words, the philosophical critique of truth and guaranteed meaning is not only *applicable to* Milton's writings but was within his own range of pious yet daring response to the question of what he believed, and on whose authority. This position was more rigorously argued by William Myers, whose chapter on 'The Spirit of Différance' in *Milton and Free Will* (included in this anthology) not only pursues the implications of

Derrida's thought through the sign system of *Paradise Lost* but also
provides a reliable summary of Derrida's argument about meaning, as it
derived from Saussure's linguistics.

This is a long leap from Fish's conclusion in *Surprised by Sin* (which
appeared only three years before Derrida's thought made its first major
appearance on the Anglo-American literary stage). Indeed, it may well be
discovered that contemporary deconstruction, with its attack on
logocentricity, is itself a child of the Reformation, when the relation
between the Logos and its textual transmission was so decisively put in
question that original meaning could never again be secured. But Fish
himself is the one major exception to my claim that deconstruction does
not work well on Milton except as an account of his own deliberate
exploration of the inadequacies of human knowledge in relation to divine
truths. For Fish has been able to adapt his own affective stylistics or very
close reading to a series of studies of Milton, and especially of the prose
tracts, that discover Milton's Protestant exegesis to be aporetic after all.
Thus the little-read tract *Of Prelaticall Episcopacy* is found to be an exercise
about the Protestant dilemma that the Word of God, as distinct from the
traditions of commentary upon it, is deemed entirely sufficient for
salvation, that it would be an impiety to think that the 'divine Scripture
wanted a supplement' (1:626), and yet here is Milton supplying that
supplement. It is a happy coincidence that Milton here employed that
very term, 'supplement', that Derrida found in Rousseau and made the
centre of a critique of writing as forever marking the presence of an
originary absence or deficiency of meaning. Fish remains, however,
elusive on the question of whether Milton himself was aware of the
dilemma. In relation to *Of Prelaticall Episcopacy* Fish wrote: 'The question
of the "status of his own discourse" is not one he evades or dodges or
misses, but one he raises and raises with all of the rigor to which a
deconstructionist might lay claim.' But in relation to certain details of
spelling in the *Doctrine and Discipline of Divorce* that Fish takes to be
significant, he insists that he is 'not claiming that these double meanings
are to be regarded as the product of Milton's intention, that they appear
in his text by design . . . the evidence is inconclusive . . . these and other
moments are signs of the extent to which he is the site of intentions that
pull against one another'.[16]

The return to explicit political interpretation
I Neo-Marxist or materialist criticism

Like deconstruction, when contemporary Marxist theory is turned on
Milton it produces a serious dilemma. On the one hand, academic

Marxists must necessarily look with favour on Milton for the sake of his twenty-year participation in the English revolution; on the other, his continual assertion of what is generally castigated as the 'bourgeois ideology' of individual self-determination must be something of an embarrassment. To continue to admire Milton as the free, speaking, and *hence* revolutionary subject (even after discounting his inconsistencies and self-deceptions) flies in the face of Louis Althusser's pronouncements that such beliefs in self-determination are the greatest self-deceptions of all, imposed on us by ideologies that in turn are constructed by governments.

It is therefore not entirely surprising that the first major attempt to read Milton in the light of Marxist theory, Christopher Kendrick's *Milton: A Study in Ideology and Form*, seems self-conflicted. While Kendrick's framework for understanding Milton and his environment is Marx's historical materialism, his abstract and difficult analysis leaves intact, finally, the notion of Milton as author, individual and person. Kendrick begins with Marx's paradoxical axiom: 'Men make their own history, but . . . under the given and inherited circumstances with which they are directly confronted.'[17] This venerable compromise between individual self-determination and environmental determinism allows Kendrick to develop an eccentric version of the theory of possessive individualism, deemed by some contemporary Marxists to come into existence only in late sixteenth or early seventeenth century England, along with the predominance of wage-labour. But by the time Kendrick has reworked the theory in the light of Milton's own preoccupations, it remains very much individualism after all. Marxist economics may have a 'superior explanatory power' when applied to the seventeenth century, but when facing Milton's interest in will and choice, and behind them in predestination, Kendrick finds a still greater explanatory power in the doctrine of monism, or the unity of body and soul, which allows him to generate an account of Milton's thought that is simultaneously materialist and ethico-religious. 'It was by identifying the soul's powers with those of the free commodity,' Kendrick argues, 'that Milton felt himself free' (p. 13). *Areopagitica*, his chief exhibit, is for Kendrick therefore not what we have long believed and celebrated, a monument of liberal thought – indeed, he regards this as a misreading (p. 23). Rather, its deep structure reveals Milton's materialist awareness of his era as one of economic transformation, of the conflation of categories represented by the phrase 'the marketplace of ideas' which, in extension to the notion of free trade, requires that truth, as our most valuable commodity, must not be monopolized (p. 40).

II The claims for Milton's early radicalism
Another branch of literary Marxism has tried to deal with the shape of Milton's career, and to tackle the question of when and how his political

theories developed. One of the central problems facing a student of
Milton today is how to interpret what he wrote between 1628, the year of
his *Ode on the Morning of Christ's Nativity*, and 1641, when the first of his
excitedly reformist pamphlets appeared. One might easily think that the
poems in English and Latin that he subsequently published in his two-
volume *Poems of Mr John Milton* in 1645 were indistinguishable, except in
the bite and power of some of them, from the products of the gentleman
poets and courtiers of Charles I and Henrietta Maria; and the fact that
they were published by Humphrey Moseley, a stationer of known
royalist sympathies, makes it difficult to argue that they were *really*
expressions of alienation from the same court culture, a critique posed
from within. Yet such arguments had indeed been made, and made with
such frequency in the last decade that the effort constitutes a noteworthy
phenomenon in the history of Milton's reception.

A pioneer in this effort has been Christopher Hill, whose *Milton and the
English Revolution* appeared in 1977.[18] Adopting the form of a traditional
literary biography for a redefinition of Milton's milieu as neither courtly
nor academic but as nonconformist and sectarian, Hill found relief from
the apparent conventionality of the early poetry in Milton's radical
associations, as, for example, with Alexander Gill, who was imprisoned
for libelling Buckingham in 1628 (p. 28). But the problem of the early
poems had to be faced. 'A masque,' wrote Hill, contemplating the text
we now call *Comus*, 'appears at first sight rather a surprising thing for a
Puritan to write – if we can properly call Milton a Puritan at this time'
(p. 45). The solution, which Hill himself evidently found incompletely
satisfying, was to create a micro-criticism in which the detail, such as the
Lady's plea 'for greater economic equality' as against 'lewdly-pampered
Luxury' (p. 47), acquires more weight than the social connotations of the
genre, while at the same time redefining Milton's version of the masque
in the Puritan – individualist tradition of successfully resisted
temptation.[19]

The theory of Milton's early radicalism is represented here not by Hill
himself, whose historian's approach to Milton's poetry has sometimes
been criticized for its lack of nuance, but by two younger literary critics
strongly influenced by Hill. Each of these has argued that some of the
early poems abandon or challenge the norms of Caroline court poetry.
Michael Wilding's account of *L'Allegro*, more coherent than his longer
essay on *Comus*, has the added advantage of providing a striking contrast
to Fish's position on *L'Allegro*. Where Fish argues that the poem's
(careless) joy '. . . is precisely reflected in the absence of any pressure on
us', Wilding puts pressure on the poem to reveal a socioeconomic
subtext. The second is David Norbrook's placement of *Lycidas* in a
tradition of prophetic, oppositionist writing that stretched from the
Lollard *Plowman's Tale* through Spenser's *Shepheardes Calender* to Milton.

Like Hill, Norbrook assumes that *Lycidas* was a blocked response to Laudian censorship; unlike Hill, he situates Milton also in the milieu of other Jacobean and Caroline poets, against whom, as analytical controls, the tone of his poetry can be measured. By comparing *Lycidas* with the elegies for Ben Jonson in 1638, or the statements of William Drummond, a neo-Spenserian who disliked Laud but feared social upheaval even more, Norbrook concluded that 'Milton's early poetry is radical not only in its explicit political comments but in its underlying visionary utopianism' (p. 62).

Paradoxically, Norbrook's discovery of an alternative, radical poetic tradition was supported, along with an unusual attention to the historical context, by conventional literary – critical methods and assumptions, including a 'real' author, an intentionalist theory of meaning, and 'literary' schools and milieux. In contrast, there is a branch of poststructuralism deriving more from Marx via Althusser and Foucault than Derrida which is also interested in Milton for explicitly political reasons. This is represented here by Francis Barker's essay on *Areopagitica*, an iconoclastic piece which finds the pamphlet the obverse of what the liberal tradition has believed it to be. Instead of honouring *Areopagitica* as a significant document in the long fight for intellectual freedom, or even, in Kendrick's terms, as a site on which that ideal jostled with new perceptions of economic change, Barker, deeply influenced both by Althusser's theory of ideology, state apparatuses and their 'interpellation' of the subject and by Michel Foucault's emphasis on discipline and punishment, sees Milton's pamphlet as the marker of an early modern era in which the individual, that invention of bourgeois ideology, will cease to exist. In his larger argument, *Areopagitica* is the 'call into being [of] a new state form' of discourse, and the creation, by its writing, of 'a novel citizen-subject' whose salient characteristic is unfreedom and whose substitute for it is the retreat into sexuality, or the tremulous private body.

III Reclaiming Paradise Lost: *problems of representation and intention*

The last two decades have likewise witnessed a fairly determined effort to rescue *Paradise Lost*, *Paradise Regained* and *Samson Agonistes* from the critical assumption most widely held since Coleridge – namely, that the late, great poems were *deliberately* apolitical, the product of Milton's disillusionment with the aims and achievements of the revolution, and that the rejection of his earlier plans to write an *Arthuriad*, a national epic, confirmed the move to transcendence. 'Finding it impossible,' wrote Coleridge, 'to realize his own aspirations, either in religion, or in politics, or society, [Milton] gave up his heart to the living spirit and light within him, and avenged himself on the world by enriching it with this record of his own transcendent ideal.'[20] Apart from a general tendency in contemporary criticism to reject 'transcendence' as a useful critical term, a new theoretical issue has emerged. Given that *Paradise Lost* is, unarguably, a story of a failed rebellion, what relation, if any, does its quasi-biblical plot have to the 'real' historical events that preceded its composition, and to which Milton had dedicated twenty years of his life? If there is a reference, what form precisely does the representation of those events assume?

There are a few signs that early readers believed that the poem did indeed refer to the English revolutionary experiment, but they are tantalizingly incomplete. Christopher Hill relates the incident of 1686–87, when Milton's friend Theodore Haak, who had translated the first three books of *Paradise Lost* into German, read them aloud to the Hanoverian pastor K.L. Benthem, who understood them as a commentary on Restoration politics in England. As Benthem recorded this experience, he mentioned that when Milton's friends had been told of the poem's title before it appeared, they assumed it would be a lament for the Good Old Cause and feared for his safety. When they actually read it they were reassured and withdrew their objections to the poem's publication. But, continued Benthem, when Haak read the early books to him, he realized that in fact 'this very wily politician [*'dieser sehr schlau Politicus'*] had concealed under this disguise exactly the sort of lament his friends had originally suspected'.[21] We may infer that Haak was engaged in some form of allegorization. In 1698 the Whig editor John Toland asserted in his *Life of John Milton* that 'to display the different Effects of Liberty and Tyranny, is the chief design of his *Paradise Lost*', a statement whose truth would probably be conceded by all but the most determined transcendentalist, but which does not take us beyond generalities to the vexed question of what Liberty and Tyranny were supposed to mean to a Restoration audience.

It is uncomfortable for readers of left-wing inclinations to recognize that Milton's rebel leader has himself many of the attributes of a tyrant. In consequence, some contemporary Miltonists, including Fredric Jameson, have turned the allegorical tables and proposed that neither Cromwell nor Milton himself but rather Charles I is the referent of the Satanic personality and programme. But a more important strategy for saving *Paradise Lost* for neo-Marxist theory was Jameson's argument about the 'political unconscious' of the poem. Extending his Durkheimian theory that religion was the 'master code' in which class conflict was played out in England in the seventeenth century, Jameson posited an 'overlap' between the structures of Calvinism and Marxism – both of them, obviously, determinisms.[22] The idea has formidable analytical potential, not least since the unmistakable intent of Milton's theological arguments in *Paradise Lost*, Book III, was to replace the determinism of orthodox Calvinism with an emphasis on personal choice that the history of Christianity would label Arminianism but which, if translated into sociopolitical terms, we would recognize as liberalism. Jameson, however, took this thought in quite another direction. Following Althusser and Pierre Macherey in *A Theory of Literary Production*, he argued that *Paradise Lost* unintentionally brings out the contradictions inherent in Calvinist ideology, not by conceptual analysis but by giving it *literary* representation (p. 46). In other words, *Paradise Lost* succeeds because Milton fails, because his poem 'ends up by producing the opposite of what it originally intended' (p. 48). Yet Jameson was unable to account for the fact that even figuratively a middle-class revolution (with religion as its symbolic language) nowhere 'seems to be present in the text' (p. 49). Instead of an image of class praxis, of a collective actor, the figure of Satan more resembled, Jameson thought, a great feudal baron, a fact explicable only by the reversed allegory mentioned above.[23]

For Christopher Hill the problem of representation, though it may not have been felt as a problem, produced two incompatible solutions. Hill's own allegiances and earlier historiographical decisions made him read the Restoration as the experience of defeat for the Nonconformists. On the one hand, therefore, he need posit no large philosophical schema as did Jameson, no such gap between Milton's intentions and his poem's independent subversion of them. *Paradise Lost* was indeed *about* a failed revolution, but it argued acceptance of a superior wisdom that frustrates human intervention. 'I see Milton,' Hill wrote, 'bitterly – because he must – accepting the Father whose will is Fate.' It is only the thought of *spiritual* regeneration that 'salvages something of man's dignity, freedom and responsibility from the wreckage of 1660'. In general Hill believed that 'the character of Satan alludes to some of the ways in which the Good Old Cause had gone wrong' (p. 366) and that the second half of the poem teaches the same lesson, with Eve now the figure of the mistaken rebels, whether in their intransigence or in their capitulation. Thus a primarily religious reading of the poem, though it posits a political–historical cause – Milton, taught by failure, justifies the ways of God to men and turns to the paradise within – is also a simple political allegory, whose valence is finally rather conservative.

This reading is, however, inconsistent with Hill's frequent allusions to censorship, his theory that in *Paradise Lost*, as with the early poems, Milton was unable to write with the freedom he would have chosen and so encoded his views. Hill cites Christopher Ricks on the subject of Milton's enforced indirection (p. 356) without observing the absolute disparity between Ricks's approach to the poem and his own. But one must wonder why such a penitential argument would have needed the protection of indirection in the first place. Would not the Restoration government have been pleased to sponsor so submissive an announcement from one of its old enemies, just as Cromwell had permitted publication of Abraham Cowley's *Poems* in 1656, with its conciliatory advice to the royalists: 'When the event of battel, and the unaccountable Will of God has determined the controversie . . . we must lay down our Pens as well as Arms, we must march out of our Cause itself'?[24] The defeatism Hill attributes to Milton scarcely squares with the hints of defiance he found in the occasional phrase within *Paradise Lost* – not merely the reference to an eclipse which 'with fear of change/ Perplexes monarchs' (1:598–9), which we know the censor objected to, but to the 'parsimonious emmet', the ant which Milton called a 'Pattern of just equality perhaps' (7:484–6) and which Hill saw as a gesture towards a future republic, Milton 'covering himself by an ambiguous "perhaps"' (p. 408).

The conflict between these two notions, of Milton as the chief literary spokesman of the experience of defeat, and of Milton as the poet of republican defiance, has been observed by Mary Ann Radzinowicz, whose cogent attempt to mediate a compromise between them is reprinted here on the grounds that it illuminates the procedural problem. Radzinowicz claims that, while the poem will support both the theory of 'politics abandoned' and that of 'politics encrypted', it does so in order to teach its readers to avoid simple solutions. The poem is a textbook in political education. Like Hill, Radzinowicz cites the 'parsimonious emmet' as an ideologeme of Milton's programme. Unlike Hill, she continues Milton's statement about the ant, to note that what immediately follows the word 'perhaps' is 'hereafter', which Radzinowicz reads as deferral. A failed revolution is to be replaced by a better-educated future – men progressively (in the tradition of Christian rationalism) 'gaining illumination'. Fixed meanings and single interpretations are coercive.

Radzinowicz's project can therefore be recognized as the rewriting of Fish's *Surprised by Sin* in the aftermath of both deconstruction and the political criticisms of Milton. In her hermeneutics the poem's resistance to clear political solution, its linguistic ambiguity, are wielded by Milton as his tools rather than, as in Jameson's argument, thrown up by the poem and, behind it, the society, in defiance of its author's wishes. Her Truth, being political science with religious foundations, is necessarily a little less Platonic than Fish's before he encountered deconstruction; but in the last analysis Christian rationalism and literary theory merge to produce a new version of the disengagement theory. Praxis is displaced not merely into a better-educated future but into the philosophical space that is ultimately only lexis. And whereas Jameson must posit Milton's failure in order that the poem may succeed, Radzinowicz must posit that Milton 'successfully resisted' the temptation to keep his political convictions current, instead transferring the Good Old Cause to the past of nostalgia and the future of wishful thinking, to 'perhaps' and 'hereafter' only.

IV *The radical sublime*

Some signs of intentionality, presumably consistent with Milton's wishes, appear in the preliminaries to the poem as published in 1674. Most important of these was Andrew Marvell's ambiguous verse account of Milton's 'project', 'On *Paradise Lost*', which presented him as a latter-day Samson braced to bring down the pillars of his society upon the heads of its leaders, an act, moreover, of revenge. When Milton himself actually developed the Samson story in *Samson Agonistes*, revenge has been sublimated; but Marvell's poem still reverberates oddly with Coleridge's statement that 'Milton avenged himself upon the world by enriching it with this record of his own transcendent ideal.' What connects those metaphors of violence to Marvell's pioneering definition of Milton's style, 'Thy Verse created like thy Theme sublime', which we must recognize as contemporary theory *avant la lettre*? As Victoria Kahn argues here, in a subtle and profound essay that represents the very best of poststructural language theory, we are now in a position to see what were and are the psychological roots and the metaphysical dimensions of the idea of sublimity, which is always in some sense both threatening to the reader and a challenge to her capacity to 'think hard' and so reimagine free will. Given the fascination of the conservative Edmund Burke with Milton's sublime, and Eliot's reference to his style as 'a perpetual sequence of original acts of lawlessness', we may be on the verge of discovering, also, that the sublime was itself always to some extent associated with ideas of supreme power and resistance to it. As Peter de Bolla has pointed out, Burke added to the second edition of his *Philosophical Enquiry into the Origin of our Ideas of the Sublime and Beautiful* a new section on power whose ultimate source is the godhead, which had the effect of 'transforming a partial account of the content or substance of sublime sensation into a coherent and all-encompassing theoretical model'.[25] The crucial notion at the heart of the sublime, that there is a primal excess to which reason, imagination and language all in different ways testify by their incapacity to grasp it, may be perceived as the converse of a deconstructive metaphysics, which posits an originary deficiency. But when 'power' is invoked at this theoretical centre, it is but a short step to Burke's anti-Jacobin writings, which suggest that his thinking on the sublime was inseparable from his horror at the French

Revolution.[26] Conversely, Immanuel Kant, as Jean-François Lyotard has argued, merged the experience of the sublime with his theory that the French Revolution, or rather the painful enthusiasm of those who were spectators to it, was a historical sign that man was capable of being the cause of his own improvement. As Geoffrey Bennington explicates Lyotard's commentary on Kant, 'the affect of enthusiasm marks this reaction as coming under, not the aesthetic of the beautiful (marked according to Kant by disinterested pleasure . . .) but the aesthetic of the sublime, which involves a "negative" pleasure, or an oscillation of attraction and repulsion, pleasure and pain. In the sublime, the imagination struggles and fails to find a direct presentation for the Idea [of progress]: that failure produces the pain, but the pleasure comes from the realisation of a capacity to conceive of ideas precisely beyond any intuitive presentation.'[27] Marvell wrote of *Paradise Lost* in terms that aesthetically anticipate Kant.

> That Majesty which through thy Work doth Reign
> Draws the Devout, deterring the Profane . . .

> At once delight and horror on us seize,
> Thou sing'st with so much gravity and ease.

And since one of Kant's examples in the *Critique of Judgement* of the sublimely unpresentable is the Jewish law forbidding representation, it is doubly pertinent to the *verbal* anthropomorphism of Milton's poem, that drawing away the veil of the unpresentable supreme power, to whose scandal Marvell draws attention by claiming that it needs no apology.

But it may be that the links between the aesthetic and the political are more direct. De Bolla himself includes, almost parenthetically, a very short chapter on 'The Voice of Liberty' whose topic is the oratory of William Pitt, as described by, among others, William Godwin: 'Sublimity, upon his tongue, sat, so enveloped in beauty, that it seemed, unconscious of itself . . . like the fearful whirlpool, it drew understanding, and every heart, into its vortex.'[28] Godwin thereby claimed Pitt for what might be thought of as a republican tradition. After Marvell's poem, which concludes by relating the sublime to the freedom of blank verse, there appeared in 1674 a note on 'The Verse', whose last lines were:

> This neglect then of rhyme so little is to be taken for a defect, though it may seem so perhaps to vulgar readers, that it rather is to be esteemed an example set, the first in English, of *ancient liberty* recovered to heroic poem from the troublesome and modern bondage of rhyming.

This not only set Milton apart from the royalist poets of the Restoration, who had made rhyme their mark of modernity, with Dryden as the chief exemplar and polemicist, but, by way of the phrase 'ancient liberty', placed *Paradise Lost* and its refusal to rhyme in a political vocabulary of opposition that had been continuous since at least the parliament of 1610.[29]

Feminist criticism

It is also possible that the two halves of Milton's poem are more closely related in a utopian programme than some of the critics I have so far cited would suggest. If the first half of the poem relates a failed rebellion, the second half recounts a process that we might call the raising in both Adam and Eve of political consciousness. And there is one crucial speech in Book 12 where Adam articulates, in response to the story of Nimrod, what he has learned about human relations.

> O execrable son so to aspire
> Above his brethren, to himself assuming
> Authority usurped, from God not given:
> He gave us only over beast, fish, fowl,
> Dominion absolute; that right we hold
> By his donation; but man over men
> He made not Lord; such title to himself
> Reserving, human left from human free.
> (12:64–71)

On the one hand we can read this passage as Milton's rejection of the absolute monarchist theories of Robert Filmer's *Patriarcha*.[30] On the other, we might reasonably see it as a rejection also of that version of patriarchalism against which feminist theory has erected its standard.

Like the debate over the 'real' politics, present or absent, of *Paradise Lost*, that over the sexual politics of the poem has been polarized in ways that the poem has provoked but is not entirely responsible for. To declare, on the basis of what happens or what is said in *Paradise Lost* (neither of which can be surely summarized), that Milton was either a misogynist or a proto-feminist is risking the charge of over-simplification and/or selective quotation; and, as Joseph Wittreich has argued in *Feminist Milton*, [31] such arguments ignore the long history of the poem's reception which during the late seventeenth century and the eighteenth shows that *both* readings were discoverable in the text. The reception of *Paradise Lost*, however, must include its scholarly treatment. Until recently Milton scholars avoided the topic of Milton's relations with or attitudes to women (the notable exceptions are John Halkett on the divorce pamphlets[32] and the deliberately shocking *Milton and Sex* by Edward Le Comte[33]); but with the development of academic feminism, and specifically, as I have said, due to the intervention of Sandra Gilbert, the sexual politics of *Paradise Lost* has become a battle ground on which are fought out professional struggles that have less to do with Milton than with the place of women in the late twentieth-century academy. It is perhaps significant, too, that Milton's strongest accusers have come from outside Milton studies, whereas women scholars who have worked with Milton over the long haul, such as Barbara Lewalski, Joan Webber and Diane McColley, have found his representation of Eve quite generous and even in advance of his contemporaries.[34]

From the long list of contributions to this debate I have selected, however, two striking essays which offer the reader more useful material than polemic. The first, Christine Froula's attack on Milton for his treatment of Eve in the scene where she remembers her creation, was a pioneering example of how small textual details that an earlier criticism might have ignored or seen only in the terms of Milton's classical learning – the Narcissus-like moment in which Eve gazes at her image in the water and becomes enamoured of it – can instead be seen as representing complex psychological ideas of subject construction. But the essay has the added advantage of introducing, via Elaine Pagels's *The Gnostic Gospels*, the relevance to Milton studies of feminist biblical criticism, with its ardent focus on the two versions of Genesis. The second, Mary Nyquist's essay 'Fall Differences, Phallogocentric Discourses: Losing *Paradise Lost* to History', both gives access (in bibliographical footnotes) to the already developed feminist literature on the poem and extends the problem of misogyny into an analysis of Milton's male readers and critics. In addition to these two essays, since most feminist criticism of Milton focuses exclusively on *Paradise Lost* and thereby loses the opportunity to consider the *biographical* origins of Milton's attitudes to women, I have included two approaches to the sexual politics of the divorce pamphlets: part of James Turner's learned study of Renaissance attitudes towards marriage and sexuality,[35] as these are refracted in Milton's polemic; and my own piece on the *Doctrine and Discipline of Divorce* as an unconfessedly autobiographical 'novel'. The last is included also in the hope that, given Milton's irremediable seriousness, it might serve as light relief.

If there is a relation between the divorce pamphlets and *Paradise Lost*, it must include the fact that Milton did not, after all, divorce Mary Powell or accept the second-best choice of a separation *a mensa et thoro*, which would not have permitted remarriage. Instead, the early biographies recount a reconciliation scene between husband and wife whose image reappears in the tenth book of the poem. It is worth noting that Milton's Adam does *not* assert, as under Michael's tutelage in Book 12 he reaches full knowledge about human potential and the structure of history and society, his absolute dominion over Woman. And if the second half of the poem, as I have suggested, can be read as Milton's resistance, rather than submission, to the experience of defeat, this allows us to notice also (along with Eve's consciousness raising) a semiphilosophical argument about how we learn, with the relation between Adam and Eve standing as a model for the reciprocity of masculine theory and female empiricism ('experience') in cognition. If Milton's Eve is not felt the equal of Adam by the time the reading process is concluded, she is certainly, to use her own words, 'more equal' (9:823), a formula that might be transferable back to the poem's *other* political agenda, reminding us that we need to pursue Milton's remarks about that parsimonious emmet beyond what either Hill or Radzinowicz chose to cite.

> The parsimonious emmet, provident
> Of future, in small room large heart enclosed,
> Pattern of just equality perhaps
> Hereafter, joined in her popular tribes
> Of commonalty: swarming next appeared
> The female bee that feeds her husband drone
> Deliciously.
>
> (7:485–491)

These are the last creatures named in the book of Creation, with the exception of the serpent, 'subtlest beast of all the field', a description that might well be applied to Milton himself, who in these few lines managed to suggest a complex argument about the intersections between class and gender before those somewhat reductive terms were ever invented.

Poststructuralism and the shape of Milton's career

My opening sentence mentioned postmodernist strictures against a humanist concept of the subject. This theoretical rejection of the centred or unified self, of the self-determining individual, and of the humanist studies that depend on those concepts, inevitably conflicts not only with the hitherto unquestioned notion of Milton-as-author, but also with the assumption so dear to literary history that copious writers have *oeuvres*, and that a chronological ordering of their works (the chronology, of course, depending on that of their lives) is not only the simplest but the most revealing. Milton hiself believed that the date of composition or occasion of a poem was important, and he sometimes (but not always) included that information in the *Poems of Mr John Milton* whose ordering and publication he carefully supervised in 1645. Sometimes, as in the famous Sonnet 19, 'When I consider how my light is spent', he included only so much information ('ere half my days') as would keep his readers guessing ever after. These hints provoked intense speculation about the dating of poems where the missing information would have been of vital importance. The case of *Ad patrem*, crucial to a psychoanalytic study of Milton, is one instance, and the question of whether *Samson Agonistes* is an early work or Milton's last words on the Restoration of the Stuarts, on his blindness and on failed marriages, is another. I myself am a believer in the usefulness of chronology, and even of arguments about it; and the essays or parts of essays in this volume are arranged, roughly speaking, so as to indicate that Milton began as a small-scale lyric or elegiac poet, moved (for twenty years) into the role of polemical pamphleteer, and then, with the coming of the Restoration, became the large-scale architect of the three great poems (though *Paradise Regained* is not represented here). Three essays (Fish, Wilding and Norbrook) deal with early poems; three (Barker, Turner and Patterson) with prose tracts; and five contributions (Myers, Radzinowicz, Froula, Myquist and Kahn) represent the dominance of *Paradise Lost* in the Miltonic canon. Nevertheless, on the theoretical issue of the *oeuvre* and chronology I have tried to be fair to poststructuralism. The collection begins with Jonathan Goldberg's essay on 'Dating Milton' wherein, in relation to the problem of dating Sonnet 19, Derrida is used to critique both the biographical impulse of traditional historical criticism (as exemplified by William Riley Parker) and the neo-Marxist criticism that, while claiming to unmask the bourgeois notion of individualism, cannot, Goldberg claims, liberate itself from its critical premises. At the other end of the anthology, however, I have placed John Guillory's strikingly original account of *Samson Agonistes* which, while it exemplifies an inspired eclecticism with respect to contemporary theory, in its blend of Freud with Weber and Bourdieu, also remains committed to the usefulness of thinking of *oeuvres* as 'life-narratives', and, by connecting Sonnet 19 to *Samson Agonistes*, reassures us that all writing (and reading) has a beginning, a middle and an end.

Notes

1. CATHERINE BELSEY, *John Milton: Language, Gender, Power* (Oxford: Basil Blackwell, 1988), p. 7.

2. SANDRA GILBERT, 'Patriarchal Poetry and Women Readers: Reflections on Milton's Bogey', *PLMA* **93** (1987): 368–82.

3. R.A. Shoaf, *Milton, Poet of Duality* (New Haven: Yale University Press, 1985), p. 57.

4. William Kerrigan, *The Sacred Complex: On the Psychogenesis of* Paradise Lost (Cambridge, Mass.: Harvard University Press, 1983), pp. 7–8.

5. The *theme* of work in Milton, as a concept poised somewhere between a classical idea derived from Virgil, social history and personal vocation, has, however, been discussed by Anthony Low, *The Georgic Revolution* (Princeton: Princeton University Press, 1985), pp. 296–352. In contrast to this conventional recourse to theme and intellectual history on an issue about which Milton was evidently anxious, psychoanalytic interpretation can sometimes be forced upon him without symptomatic provocation. See, for example, Richard Halpern, 'The Great Instauration: Imaginary Narratives in Milton's "Nativity Ode"' in *Re-membering Milton: Essays on the Texts and Traditions*, ed. Mary Nyquist and Margaret W. Ferguson (New York and London: Methuen, 1987), pp. 3–21, which reads the ode in terms of Lacan's theory of the Imaginary and the 'specific prematurity of birth'.

6. *The works of John Milton*, ed. Frank Patterson *et al.*, 18 vols (New York: Columbia University Press, 1931–8).

7. *The Complete Prose Works of John Milton*, ed. D. M. Wolfe *et al.*, 8 vols (New Haven: Yale University Press, 1953–82).

8. *A Variorum Commentary on the Poems of John Milton* (New York: Columbia University Press, 1970–   ).

9. T.S. Eliot, 'A Note on the Verse of John Milton', *Essays and Studies of the English Association* (Oxford, 1936). Cited from T. S. Eliot, *Selected Prose*, ed. John Hayward (Harmondsworth: Penguin, 1953), pp. 123, 130. These iconoclastic verdicts had been anticipated by F. R. Leavis in 'Milton's Verse', first published in *Scrutiny* in 1933 and reprinted in the influential *Revaluation: Tradition and Development in English Poetry* (London, 1936, 1964), pp. 42–61.

10. T.S. Eliot, 'Milton', Annual Lecture on a Master Mind, read 26 March 1947 before the British Academy; *Proceedings of the British Academy* **33**, cited from *Selected Prose*, p. 142.

11. J.B. Broadbent, *Some Graver Subject* (New York: Shocken Books, 1960).

12. Christopher Ricks, *Milton's Grand Style* (Oxford: Oxford University Press, 1963).

13. Stanley Fish, *Surprised by Sin: The Argument of Paradise Lost* (Berkeley: University of California Press, 1971).

14. *'Eyes Fast Fixt': Current Perspectives in Milton Methodology*, guest eds Albert C. Labriola and Michael Lieb (Pittsburgh: University of Pittsburgh Press, 1975), p. vi.

15. Belsey, pp. 23–33.

16. Stanley Fish, 'Wanting a Supplement: The Question of Interpretation in Milton's Early Prose' in *Politics, Poetics, and Hermeneutics in Milton's Prose*, ed. David Loewenstein and James Turner (Cambridge: Cambridge University Press, 1990), pp. 45, 61.

17. Karl Marx, *The Eighteenth Brumaire of Louis Bonaparte* in *Surveys from Exile*, ed. David Fernbach (New York: Random House, 1973), 2:146, cited in Kendrick, p. 3.

18. Christopher Hill, *Milton and the English Revolution* (New York: Viking, 1977).

19. On the topic of *Comus*, Hill has had several followers who have attempted to dismantle its courtly resonance. Though not all of them share his political convictions, these include: Maryann McGuire, *Milton's Puritan Masque* (Athens, GA: University of Georgia Press, 1983); Leah Marcus, 'Milton's Anti-Laudian Masque' in *The Politics of Mirth: Jonson, Herrick, Milton, Marvell and the Defense of Old Holiday Pastimes* (Chicago and London: University of Chicago Press, 1986), pp. 169–212; David Norbrook, 'The Reformation of the Masque' in *The Court Masque*, ed. David Lindley (Dover NH: Manchester University Press, 1984), pp. 94–110; Norbrook, *Poetry and Politics in the English Renaissance* (London: Routledge & Kegan Paul, 1984), pp. 253–65; Michael Wilding, 'Comus, Camus, Commerce: Theatre and Politics on the Border' in *Dragon's Teeth: Literature in the English Revolution* (Oxford: Clarendon Press, 1987), pp. 28–88.

20. Samuel Taylor Coleridge, Lecture X, *Literary Remains* (London, 1836), quoted from James Thorpe (ed.), *Milton Criticism: Selections from Four Centuries* (London: Routledge & Kegan Paul, 1951), p. 97.

21. H.L. Benthem, *Engelandischer Kirch-und Schelen-Staat* (Luneberg, 1694), p. 58, cited in Hill, p. 391.

22. Fredric Jameson, 'Religion and Ideology: A Political Reading of *Paradise Lost*', a paper occasioned by reflection on the rise of religious extremism in Iran, delivered at a conference at the University of Essex in 1980 and subsequently published in *Literature, Politics & Theory*, ed. Francis Barker *et al.* (London: Methuen, 1986), pp. 3–56.

23. A similar argument, but with very different theoretical underpinnings, is to be found in Joan Bennett, 'Satan and King Charles: Milton's Royal Portraits' in *Reliving Liberty: Radical Christian Humanism in Milton's Great Poems* (Cambridge, Mass.: Harvard University Press, 1989).

24. Abraham Cowley, *Poems* (London, 1656), a4.

25. Peter de Bolla, *The Discourse of the Sublime: Readings in History, Aesthetics and the Subject* (Oxford: Basil Blackwell, 1989), p. 65.

26. Compare Ronald Paulson, *Representations of Revolution* (New Haven: Yale University Press, 1983), pp. 68–73.

27. See Geoffrey Bennington, *Lyotard; Writing the Event* (Manchester: Manchester University Press, 1988), p. 166. I owe this reference to Jonathan Lamb, whose work on commentaries on Job and the politics of the sublime will be an important corollary to de Bolla.

28. William Godwin, *The History of the Life of William Pitt* (London, 1783), p. 301, cited in de Bolla, p. 145.

29. For an account of this vocabulary, see my essay on 'The Good Old Cause' in *Reading Between the Lines* (forthcoming). Compare Leonard Goldstein, 'The Good Old Cause and Milton's Blank Verse', *Zeitschrift für Anglistik und Amerikanistik* **23** (1975): 133–42, who argues that neo-classical literary theory, 'with its emphasis on restraint, decorum, order, reason, the rules . . . constitutes counter-revolution in the form of literary criticism' (p. 134). Goldstein's analysis is conducted, however, in terms of the history of prosody, not in terms of the political semantics of 'ancient liberty'.

30. Although Filmer's *Patriarcha* was not published until 1680, his *Observations upon Aristotle's Politiques* had been in print since 1652 and were therefore available to Milton. The Preface of Filmer's *Observations* already contains the crucial statement that Milton, through *his* Adam, was to deny: 'The first

government in the world was monarchical, in the father of all flesh. Adam . . . having dominion given him over all creatures, was thereby the monarch of the whole world; none of his posterity had any right to possess anything, but by his grant or permission. . . . There was never any such thing as an independent multitude who at first had a natural right to a community.' Cited from *Divine Right and Democracy*, ed. David Wootton (Harmondsworth: Penguin, 1986), p. 110.

31. JOSEPH WITTREICH, *Feminist Milton* (Ithaca and London: Cornell University Press, 1987).

32. JOHN HALKETT, *Milton and the idea of Matrimony: A Study of the Divorce Tracts and Paradise Lost* (New Haven: Yale University Press, 1970).

33. EDWARD LE COMTE, *Milton and Sex* (New York: Columbia University Press, 1978).

34. See BARBARA K. LEWALSKI, 'Milton on Women – Yet Once More', *Milton Studies* **6** (1974): 3–20; JOAN WEBBER, 'The Politics of Poetry: Feminism and Paradise Lost', *Milton Studies* **14** (1980): 3–24; DIANE McCOLLEY, *Milton's Eve* (Urbana, 1983). Lewalski's essay obviously preceded and (as Webber observes) obviated Gilbert's. To these should be added, as a fine early example of male feminist criticism, David Aers and Bob Hodge, '"Rational Burning": Milton on Sex and Marriage', *Milton Studies* **13** (1979): 3–23.

35. JAMES TURNER, *One Flesh: Paradisal Marriage and Sexual Relations in the Age of Milton* (Oxford: Clarendon Press, 1987).

2 Dating Milton*

JONATHAN GOLDBERG

The mention of Jacques Derrida towards the end of this excerpt from 'Dating Milton' points to its theoretical position: an attempt to call into question the grounds of traditional scholarship, here the supposedly natural and neutral question of chronology. How facts are produced is one question asked. Although the work of traditional Miltonists is scrutinized in the essay, its larger aim is to suggest complicities between various historicist approaches, new and old, by pointing to the transcendental function of historical narratives, especially when they are used to secure the identity of a canonical author. As opposed to this view, shared by traditional Miltonists but also, the essay argues, by advanced critics, the essay advocates a more contingent and revisionary sense of Milton by problematizing the notion of the self-identity of the historical moment or of the historical subject. Although the approach might be called deconstructive, it also insists on a materiality that will not succumb to determinate narrativizations, a resistance in writing. The focus in this excerpt is on Milton's sonnet 'When I consider how my light is spent' and on various attempts to date the poem, but the argument has consequences for the ways in which Milton's career has been written – as is argued in the Introduction to the Oxford Authors' *John Milton*. The project here, as in *Endless Worke, James I and the Politics of Literature* and *Voice Terminal Echo*, is to rethink the terrains of history and of literary history.

In a footnote to his biography of Milton, William Riley Parker pauses to make a confession: 'In this entire book there is no question of dating on

---

* Reprinted from *Soliciting Interpretation*, ed. Elizabeth Harvey and Katherine Maus (Chicago: University of Chicago Press, 1990).

which I have changed my mind so many times as that of *When I consider*.[1] Confession is Parker's word: 'this chapter, I confess, was the last to be typed in its final form.' As a glance at the commentaries gathered in the Milton Variorum or at the footnotes in Merritt Hughes's edition would show, Parker is hardly alone in his guilty irresolution in the face of the conflicting evidence about the date of the poem. Thanks to one phrase in the sonnet, 'ere half my days,' the poem apparently dates itself some time before Milton reached the age of thirty-five (in 1643); but because the poem did not appear in the 1645 *Poems*, and because the poem is assumed to refer to Milton's blindness (complete in 1651–52), it is presumed to be later (and much ingenuity has been spent to explain away the troubling self-dating the poem offers). Yet, when the poem was published (in 1673), it was placed after the sonnet on the Piedmont massacre of 1655. Like 'half my days,' this placement of the poem also appears to date it, but the 1655 date (for which Parker finally opted) disturbs scholars, who, like Parker earlier, assign the poem to 1651–52, and read (and date) it as a record of, as Parker puts it, Milton's 'fresh reaction to his blindness.'

When was sonnet 19 written? What impels historical scholarship to resolve the multiple and contradictory pieces of evidence about *When I consider* into a single and determinate moment of composition, a moment remarkable for its 'freshness' and for the presumed presence of Milton writing at that very moment? To ask the question that way begins to suggest some answers, and in the pages that follow, the question of dating is engaged in order to raise some fundamental questions about the kinds of narrativizations that produce conventional literary history. We may believe that we go to Parker or to the Variorum for facts, but what we encounter instead are narratives of value that need to be read historically. In the reading I propose (which is *not* a reading of the sonnet), a different sense of history from that which informs historical scholarship (or, it will be suggested, a variety of kinds of new historicisms) will be advanced. It calls into question the self-presence of the moment.

Rather than seeking the single, determinate, present moment of composition of the sonnet, the argument here depends upon the irresolvability of the evidence sketched above. In place of a narrative which imagines a Milton who was always the same, always himself (and in which the dating of the poem is part of that self-unfolding), I would offer a different account, one that refuses self-sameness either to 'Milton' or to the supposed regularities of a temporal progression. Opening itself to chance, contingency, and revision, the narrative I would offer can scarcely be contained by the economies of a conventional historical account; indeed, as much as this essay seeks to disrupt standard ways of reading the sonnet, so too it opens the possibility of a different way of engaging history. The irresolvable temporalities which mark the poem are, I will argue, legible through acts of intercalation, situating the poem and its speaker (neither of which, however, are assumed to be self-unified, self-identical, or immediately present) against a range of Miltonic self-productions. . . .

The Wordsworthian title of Mary Ann Radzinowicz's *Toward Samson Agonistes: The Growth of Milton's Mind* conveniently summarizes the informing narrative of historical scholarship. For all the arguments about dating sonnet 19 recorded in the Variorum, no matter which date of composition is advanced, depend upon the shared supposition that the 'correct' date of the poem will best explain how Milton became (and therefore always was) himself. When Parker, for example, changed his mind, it was to show the 'biographical *rightness*' of his new dating; the poem revealed Milton ready to write *Paradise Lost*, and the expended light of sonnet 19 referred back to the years when 'the poet' (for Parker, the essential Milton) had been writing prose. The poet, however, within the same essentializing construction, is no less the subject of the sonnet in the reading that A.S.P. Woodhouse offers (against the later Parker) in support of a 1651–52 dating of the poem in the Variorum. From an initial 'mood of depression, frustration, even impatience' in the initial lines, the sonnet, Woodhouse contends, 'is not so much resolved as lifted to a plane where self-regarding thoughts become irrelevant'.[2] Woodhouse's *Aufhebung* is explicitly transcendental; to date the poem properly enables it to be 'lifted' out of history.

'The main argument for dating *Sonnet 19* in 1652 has always been the state of mind it expresses' (p. 449) the Variorum editors contend. So saying, they point to the shared suppositions of historical scholarship; 'always' here (like Woodhouse's higher plane) reveals the teleological imperatives that produce 'biographical *rightness*.' Whatever date is argued for the poem, it is always in the service of this same story. Radzinowicz's account makes this perfectly clear; she dates the poem 1652, but considers it along with sonnets written in 1655 and later because, she argues, with them it 'records calm of mind,' 'spiritual progress.'[3] The 'growth of Milton's mind' is 'a dialectic leading to resolution, internal drama leading to integration, conflict leading to harmony' (p. 4).

This 'dialectic' serves a double dating; chronology submits not only to higher designs, the poet is imagined as always 'growing' into himself, never changed, or split, by historical experience. There is another way to read the conflicting evidence, however, one that would not efface the tension between 'ere half my days' and the placement of the poem in the 1673 volume by resolving the contradictory evidence in the transcendental 'rightness' of a life whose every moment is part of some transhistorical schema. It is that reading I would advance here. In that account, 'When I consider' would have been written and rewritten over a number of years, and would not be resolved into a singular chronological placement. Closest to this argument is E.A.J. Honigmann's willingness to make a case for dating the poem either in 1644 or 1651–52 or 1655. To admit the possibility of any of these dates, however, is nonetheless not to admit the possibility that I am imagining, of revision and rewriting across these dozen years. That is resisted because it would involve denying that the poem dates from a single and fully saturated moment in the Miltonic career. (Revision is generally accepted when it can be shown as part of the process of growth towards self-sameness.) But if the poem was written well before, at the same time, and several years after Milton became totally blind – during years, too, in which plans for what became *Paradise Lost* varied enormously, and in which Milton's political engagement moved from Presbyterian to Independent and beyond party identification – it will hardly deliver the 'always' that historical critics desire, nor that single 'state of mind' that would accompany it. Revision of this sort would deny the author his transcendental status. It would imbed the lyric in a history that refuses the teleological imperatives of historicism. For in such accounts, as the complicities between teleological narrativization and transcendental identification suggest, the attempt to date and place a poem definitively does not aim at putting the poem in history but in removing it from history. The self-realization of the author, the translation of the events from life into texts, produces texts which have been delivered from the conditions of their production.

It was precisely the conditions of his own production of the life of Milton that provoked Parker's guilty confession: 'this chapter, I confess, was the last to be typed in its final form.' Indecisiveness is shameful, and perhaps even more shameful the admission that the biography was not written straight through, in chronological order. Guilt attaches itself to second thoughts and revisions. And, I would argue, what is guilty in the practice of the biographer (committed, after all, to the truth of chronological unfolding), is, given a commitment to Milton's growth towards dialectical resolution, simply unthinkable when the question of dating Milton arises. These narratives of artistic transcendence tell the story of the timeless subjectivity of the modern subject: in his Wordsworthian 'growth,' Milton grows into, is always already, a modern poet.

If traditional historical scholarship has this story to tell, it is one that more recent historical analysis has *uncovered* in Milton's poem. Whereas traditional historical accounts claim to be finding the historical Milton, but instead produce the timeless modern Milton, Anthony Easthope, for instance, argues that Milton attempts to efface history in his sonnet in order to produce the illusory effect of the modern subject. For Easthope, the sonnet does not make present Milton-the-man in the throes of a devastating experience, nor does it offer an instance of Milton-the-transcendental-author behind the text; rather, the only Milton there is arises as an effect of textualization; 'the subject,' Easthope writes, 'is constituted as an effect of discourse.'[4] Looking at relations between signifier and signified, in terms of polysemy as well as syntactic deployment, and considering, especially, the relationship between enunciation and enounced in Milton's sonnet, Easthope charts Milton's position between Shakespeare and Dryden, concluding that the sonnet on his blindness – because of its controlled polysemy, its resolution of any disturbance in its syntax and, especially, because of its movement towards a resolution of the 'I' of the text into a structure of enunciation that has effaced the 'I' – is a 'transitional' text within a history of modern poetry (p. 311–). Quoting Christopher Caudwell's dictum, 'Modern poetry is *capitalist* poetry' (p. 302), Easthope argues that Milton's poem delivers a recognizable bourgeois subject. The mark of that subject-position lies in the effacement of the materiality of the speaker, producing the effect of the transparence and autonomy of the speaking subject.

From Easthope's perspective, then, what both Parker and Radzinowicz respond to is a particular discursive effect, a certain mode of constructing the subject that is recognizable from the vantage point of their modernity because Milton's is a relatively early version of the modern subject. In Easthope's view, which I share, to historicize historical scholarship would necessitate a recognition of historical difference and distance even within modernity. Historical scholarship would not seek to repeat the ideological effects of the earlier text but to locate them within a history that attended to the materiality of writing. Parker, guiltily, admits his use of a typewriter, acts of revision, even a change of mind, in his practice; less openly, Radzinowicz attempts to date the poem twice, thereby revealing the refusal to admit change that might not be assimilated to a pattern of growth and self-sameness.

Easthope is committed to a reading of the poem within a history of the subject. Nonetheless, his account *confirms* the traditional historicist reading of the poem. Although he demystifies that reading, he offers one that still depends entirely on it. He finds it 'convincing' (p. 301), for instance, that Milton's sonnets offer a chronological sequence charting Milton's growth from youth to maturity and retirement. Proving that the poem's polysemy is not radical, he repeats New Critical readings of the poem that show, of course, that its ambiguities do not go beyond resolvable double meanings. These resolutions, that narrative of growth, may be writing-effects produced in the service of a suspect bourgeois ideology. Nonetheless the difference between Easthope and a traditional historicist account has to do with whether the designs of the poem are repudiated or embraced.

Easthope places Milton's text in a 'transitional' position, and the
narrative he produces, with Shakespeare's radical polysemy on one
side and Dryden's transparency on the other, is another version of
the Hegelian 'dialectic' that also informs traditional historicism,
although here infected with a Marxist critique, as well as a Lacanian
account of the subject. In this history of the emergence of
the capitalist subject in modern poetry, Easthope charts a movement
from desire to demand, from a poetry inextricably connected to the
body to a poetry that registers the split that signals entrance into the
Symbolic. Although its terms are different, this is a very familiar history
of English poetry in the seventeenth century; it is T.S. Eliot's modernist
account of the dissociation of sensibility, now translated into a narrative
of the development of the subject from Imaginary unity to Symbolic
division.[5]

To tell the vital story that impels him, Easthope cannot be bothered
with the finicky questions that trouble traditional historical scholarship.
'Milton's sonnet *On his Blindness* (the title added by Newton) is usually
dated 1652 or 1655' (p. 307), he begins. Dating is apparently
inconsequential and an eighteenth-century title for the poem is
acceptable too. From these indications, there would apear to be no
history of modernity. Nor could the poem betray signs of the
compositional history that I have been suggesting. Of the poem itself,
Easthope writes, 'Any dislocation is temporary, is fully resolved, and
only confirms the decisive and unequivocal closure of the syntagmatic
chain strung across fourteen lines and two sentences' (p. 308). One
might be reading Woodhouse. Closure, resolution, and the like, there
exalted, here exposed, are nonetheless in the service of narratives which
share the same teleological imperatives.

The poem, I am suggesting – and this hypothesis is no more acceptable
to traditional historicists than it is to Marxist historiography – can neither
be determinately dated, nor can it be an instance in a history that seems
to have no need of dates. The counterevidence of 'ere half my days' and
the seemingly chronological placement of the poem after the one about
the 1655 Piedmont massacre is evidence nonetheless even if it cannot be
easily homogenized. So, too, within the poem. It records a voice which is
allowed articulation only to be silenced, retrospectively, by another voice
which is, only afterwards, said to have come before the first voice
speaking:

> Doth God exact day-labour, light denied,
> I fondly ask; but patience, to *prevent*
> That murmur, soon replies . . .
>   (italics added)

29

The temporality of such voicing not only refuses an empiricist chronology, ownership of voices in the poem is also thrown into question. The line before the ones just quoted could prepare for the entrance of the divine voice into the text, 'lest he returning chide,' while the voice marked as that of 'patience' does not only retrospectively supervene in this double marked voice-within-quotation; there is also no mark that makes clear whether that voice ever stops speaking in the poem or whether the 'I' of the first line of the poem ever recurs. The poem remains unresolved, resisting those designs which would lift it out of history.[6]

Like Easthope, I have no desire to repeat the claims of traditional historical criticism; but I believe that an ideological critique must resist the complicities revealed in Easthope's essay. If a history of the subject is to be written, I would argue, it will need to take into account the irresolvable temporality that affects the dating of Milton's sonnet and the complex temporality of projection and retrospection that marks, and remarks, its voice. These do not merely produce the split subject; they make resolution the illusory effects of a reading that has moved too quickly in its historization. To let history into this poem – to let this poem be in history – a history that acknowledged difference would have to be practiced. It would be based on quite different assumptions about the text – positing, for instance, its lack of empirical unity, its refusal to situate itself in a moment that submits to the concept of self-sameness; hence it would be impossible to describe the poem as the utterance of a subject-position characterized by the ability to own a moment, own itself, or transform self and moment into a linguistic object of transcendent value. These assumptions are not opposed to Easthope's, but they also refuse the possibility that one could misrecognize a putatively 'autonomous' subject-position in sonnet 19.

The ungroundedness of this position may help to identify the false grounds of traditional historical scholarship or the too easy assumption that one can demystify such accounts while, at the same time, accepting their premises. As such, this notion of dating also would be anathema to the New Historicism, whose great strength in showing the imbeddedness of aritistic production within its cultural situation nonetheless rests upon the same empiricist ground as traditional historical accounts. From the position of any of the historicisms, new or old, that I have outlined here, the dating of the sonnet that I have suggested would be unacceptable, since the temporality it claims has eschewed the *a priori* truth of teleological chronology or the possibility that the historic moment is present-to-itself, that it is outside of subsequent narrativization. (The temporality sketched here could be called, after Freud, Nachträglichkeit, and would insist that what is retrospectively constructed is not necessarily, is necessarily *not* what was;

rather, in Derrida's elegant phrase, it would be 'a past that has never been present,'[7] nor would it be present in its rewriting.)

If we were to go on 'dating Milton' (and making good on the pun that titles this essay), we would want to turn to the last sonnet and its vexed question of dating and identification (which wife is the 'late espoused Saint,' the critics ask and argue, and I would, again, answer: both wives dead by 1658), and to pursue the construction of the autobiographical into the field of the Other inevitably also constructed in a history of the discontinuities of the subject. The autobiographical in the divorce tracts would have to be read. The vexed dating of *Samson Agonistes* (immediate response to the first marriage? final poem?) would have to be raised, and the production of yet other Miltons would be implicated in these questions of temporality and writing. These must remain for another date. So, perhaps this essay ought, retrospectively, to be retitled. We could call it 'Blind Dating.'

Notes

1. WILLIAM RILEY PARKER, *Milton: A Biography*, 2 vols (Oxford: Clarendon Press, 1968), 2:1042.

2. A.S.P. WOODHOUSE and DOUGLAS BUSH, *A Variorum Commentary on the Poems of John Milton* (New York: Columbia University Press, 1970–), 2:2:469.

3. MARY ANN RADZINOWICZ, *Toward Samson Agonistes; The Growth of Milton's Mind* (Princeton: Princeton University Press, 1978), pp. 142, 144.

4. ANTHONY EASTHOPE, 'Towards the Autonomous Subject in Poetry: *Milton on his Blindness*' in *1642: Literature and Power in the Seventeenth Century*, ed. Francis Barker (University of Essex, 1981), p. 301.

5. This is the version of literary history that is repeated, too, in Francis Barker's otherwise compelling *The Tremulous Private Body* (London: Methuen, 1986).

6. The reader who wishes a reading of the poem based on these premises may turn to my *Voice Terminal Echo: Postmodernism and English Renaissance Texts* (London: Methuen, 1986), pp. 130ff.

7. JACQUES DERRIDA, 'Différance' in *Margins of Philosophy*, tr. Alan Bass (Chicago: University of Chicago Press, 1982), p. 21.

3 What It's Like to Read *L'Allegro* and *Il Penseroso**

STANLEY FISH

'What It's Like to Read *L'Allegro* and *Il Penseroso*' is, along with the
essay on Bacon's essays in *Self-Consuming Artifacts*, a relatively pure
instance of early reader-response criticism. Part of its purity inheres
in its claim to provide an instance of the methodological superiority
of reader-response criticism. Indeed in the second half of the essay
(not reprinted here) I claim that the analysis of temporal experience
rather than of spatial structure 'provides a firm basis for the resolving
of critical controversies'. In short, I was claiming objectivity for the
method and only later did I come to see that it was no method at all
but a practice that depended as much as any other on a set of largely
unarticulated assumptions about the nature of mind, the structure of
time, the operations of consciousness, etc. In some ways I would
now think of the presentation as, if not dishonest, at least staged.
The suggestion, for example, is that readings of pastoral by Tuve and
Rosenmeyer merely confirmed the independent findings of my analysis. But I suspect that the truth is that those readings were very
much in my mind, and therefore directing my mind when the analysis
was undertaken, and that therefore the entire enterprise was much
less new than I wanted to believe. What was new and remains
valuable, I think, was the asking of another question about two
poems that had been interrogated by countless others before me.
Today were I to return to the poems, I would ask still other questions
and they would be generated by my recent interest in Milton's corpus
as a working out of the implications of an antinomian theology. In
the context of that theology, questions of freedom and constraint,
feminine and masculine postures, theories of political action, etc.,
would now come to the foreground; whereas in the essay written

---

* Reprinted from *Milton Studies* 7 (1975): 77ff.

over twenty years ago, they are slighted in favour of a passion for theory that has happily abated.

I have only one point to make and everything else follows from it: *L'Allegro* is easier to read than *Il Penseroso*. This I assume is hardly news, but if one were a subscriber to the *Times Literary Supplement* in 1934, the matter might seem to be shrouded in considerable doubt, for on October 18 of that year J.P. Curgenven initiated a remarkable correspondence by asking and answering the question, 'Who comes to the window in *L'Allegro*, line 46?' [After many weeks in which different candidates are proposed], the controversy ends on November 29 with a letter from W.A. Jones, The County School, Cardiganshire, who reports that his classes of schoolchildren 'invariably and without noticing any difficulty understand the lines' (p. 856). Whether or not the editors took this as a comment on the entire affair is a matter of conjecture, but at any rate they append a footnote to Jones's letter: 'We cannot continue this correspondence.'

The point is, of course, that this correspondence could have been continued indefinitely, but even in its abbreviated form, it allows us to make some observations.
1.   The proponent of each reading makes concessions, usually by acknowledging that there *is* evidence for the readings he opposes.
2.   Each critic is able to point to details which do in fact support his position.
3.   But in order fully to support his respective position every one of the critics is moved to make *sense* of the lines by supplying connections more firm and delimiting than the connections available in the text.
4.   The making of sense always involves an attempt to arrange the images and events of the passage into a sequence of logical action.

What are we to make of all this? If the entire exchange proves anything, it is that Milton does not wish to bind us to any one of these interpretations. I do not mean that he left us free to choose whatever interpretation we might prefer, but that he left us free *not* to choose, or more simply, that he left us free. As Brooks and Hardy observe, the reader of these lines 'is hurried through a series of infinitives . . . the last of which is completely ambiguous in its subject.'[1] I would only add that the ambiguity is *so* complete that unless someone asks us to, we do not worry about it, and we do not worry about it (or even notice it) because while no subject is specified for 'come,' any number of subjects – lark, poet, Mirth, Dawn, Night – are available. What is *not* available is the connecting word or sustained syntactical unit which would pressure us to decide between them, and in the absence of that pressure, we are not obliged to decide. Nor are we obliged to decide between the different

(and plausible) sequences which choosing any one of these subjects
would generate.
1. If it is the lark who comes to the window, he does so while the cock
'with lively din' scatters the rear of darkness thin and the two birds thus
perform complementary actions.
2. If it is the Dawn that comes to the window, she does so while the
cock with lively din scatters the rear of darkness thin and is thus faithful
to our understanding of the relationship between cock's crowing and
dawn.
3. If it is the poet (L'Allegro) who comes to the window, he does so in
response to lark, cock, and dawn: that is, while they are performing their
related functions.
4. And if it is Mirth who comes to the window, the action allies her
with lark, cock, and dawn in the awakening of L'Allegro.

All of these readings hang on the word 'while' in line 49, but since
'while' is less time-specific than other temporal adverbs, it does not
firmly call for any of these and, more to the point, it functions equally
well, that is, equally *loosely*, in all of them. Rather than insisting on a
clear temporal relationship among the events it connects, 'while' acts as a
fulcrum around which those events swirl, supplying just enough of a
sense of order to allow us to continue, but not so much that we feel
compelled to arrange the components of the passage into an intelligible
sequence. In short, 'while' neither directs nor requires choice; instead, it
frees us from choice and allows us – and I mean this literally – to be
careless. This is also the effect of the two 'ors' in the preceding couplet:
'Through the sweetbriar or the vine,/Or the twisted eglantine.' The 'ors'
divide alternative images, each of which registers only for a split second
before it is supplanted by the next. We are neither committed to any one
of them, nor required to combine them into a single coherent picture.
The effect of the couplet extends both backward – softening the outline of
the window and of *who*ever or *what*ever has come to it – and forward –
removing the pressure of specificity from the weakly transitional 'while'.

I intend the phrase 'weakly transitional' precisely; for it exactly
captures the balance Milton achieves by deploying his connectives. If
there were no transitions, the freedom of the poem's experience would
become a burden, since a reader would first notice it and then worry
about it; and if the transitions were firmly directing, a reading would be
obliged to follow the directions they gave.[2] Milton has it both ways, just
as he does with a syntax that is not so much ambiguous as it is loose.
Twentieth-century criticism has taught us to value ambiguities because
they are meaningful, but these ambiguities, if they can be called that,
protect us from meaning by protecting us from working. They are there,
not to be noticed, but to assure that whatever track a reader happens to
come in on, he will have no trouble keeping to it; no choice that he

makes (of lark, poet, Goddess, etc.) will conflict with a word or a phrase that he meets later. Anything fits with anything else, so that it is never necessary to go back and retrace one's effortless steps.

Rosemond Tuve has written that the pleasures enumerated in *L'Allegro* all have 'the flat absence of any relation to responsibility which we sometimes call innocence.'[3] What I am suggesting is that the experience of *reading* the poem is itself such a pleasure, involving just that absence; for at no point are we held responsible for an action or an image beyond the moment of its fleeting appearance in a line or a couplet. Moreover it is a *flat* absence in the sense that we are not even aware of having been relieved of it. That is why Cleanth Brooks is not quite right when he declares that the unreproved pleasures of *L'Allegro* 'can be had for the asking';[4] they can be had *without* asking.

Critics have always been aware of the curious discreteness that characterizes *L'Allegro*, both as an object and as an experience, but in general they have responded either by downgrading the poem, so capable, as D.C. Allen observes, of 'desultory rearrangement,'[5] or by attempting to rescue it from the charge of disunity and fragmentation. In 1958 Robert Graves went so far as to suggest that in the course of composing *L'Allegro* Milton misplaced sixteen lines, probably over the weekend. The lines beginning 'Oft listening' (53) and ending with every shepherd telling his tale under the hawthorn in the dale (68) originally followed the account of the Lubber fiend as 'Crop full out of the door he flings,/Ere the first cock his matins rings' (113–14). By restoring the original order, Graves asserts, we make the poem very much less of a 'muddle' (that is, we make *sense* of it). Otherwise, he points out, we are left with this improbable sequence of events:

> While distractedly bidding good-morrow, at the window, to Mirth,
> with one ear cocked for the hounds and horn . . . [he] sometimes, we
> are told, *'goes walking, not unseen, by hedgerow elms, on hillocks green.'*
> Either Milton had forgotten that he was still supposedly standing
> naked at the open window – (the Jacobeans always slept raw) – or the
> subject of 'walking' is the cock, who escapes from the barnyard,
> deserts his dames, ceases to strut, and anxiously aware of the distant
> hunt, trudges far afield among ploughmen and shepherds in the dale.
> But why should Milton give twenty lines to the adventures of the
> neighbor's wandering cock? And why, *'walking not unseen'*? Not unseen
> by whom?[6]

Graves is not unaware of the impression he is making. 'Please do not think I am joking,' he implores, and at least one critic has taken him seriously. Herbert F. West, Jr., admits that such an accident of misplacement is 'possible' and that Graves's emendation 'does little apparent danger to the text' and even seems to 'smooth over some difficult spots.'⁷ And so it does. The poet now looks out of his window to say, quite naturally, 'Straight mine eye hath caught new pleasures,' and it is the Lubber fiend who walks not unseen on hillocks green where he is espied, one assumes, by plowman, milkmaid, mower, and shepherd. The sequence ends as he listens to each shepherd tell his tale under the hawthorn in the dale, making for a perfect transition to the next section, which begins with line 115: 'Thus done the tales, to bed they creep.' Yet Graves's emendation should, I think, be rejected and rejected precisely *because* of its advantages; for by providing continuity to the plot line of the poem, it gives us something to keep track of, and therefore it gives us *care*. It is Milton's wish, however, to liberate us from care, and the nonsequiturs that bother Graves are meant to prevent us from searching after the kind of sense he wants to make. 'Not unseen by whom' he asks, and he might well have asked, why *not* unseen, a formula which neither relates the figure of the walker to other figures nor declares categorically the absence of such a relation, leaving the matter not so much ambiguous as unexamined. Or he might have asked (perhaps did ask) what precisely is the 'it' that in line 77 'sees'? This question would only lead to another, for the pronoun subject is no more indeterminate than the object of 'its' seeing – the beauty who is the cynosure of neighboring eyes. Is she there or is she not? 'Perhaps,' answers Milton in line 79, relieving us of any responsibility to her or even to her existence. This in turn removes the specificity from the adverbial of place which introduces the following line: 'Hard by, a Cottage chimney smokes.' Hard by what? Graves might well ask. In this context or noncontext the phrase has no pointing function at all. It merely gets us unburdened into the next line and into the next *discrete* scene, where with Corydon and Thyrsis we rest in 'secure delight' (91) that is, in delight *se cura*, delight without, or free from, care.

It is the promise of 'secure delight,' of course, that is at the heart of the pastoral vision, although it is the literary strength of the pastoral always to default on that promise by failing to exclude from its landscape the concerns of the real world. Milton, however, chooses to sacrifice that strength in order to secure the peculiar flatness of effect that makes reading *L'Allegro* so effortless. The details of this landscape are without resonance; they refer to nothing beyond themselves and they ask from us no response beyond the *minimal* and literary response of recognition. This lack of resonance is attributable in part to the swift succession of images, no one of which claims our attention for more than a couplet. Each couplet is self-enclosed by ringing monosyllabic rhymes, and the enclosures remain discrete. Continuity is provided by patterns of alliteration and assonance which carry us along but do not move us to acts of association or reflection. The 'new Pleasures' which the eyes of both speaker and reader catch are new in the sense of novel, *continually* new, following one another but not firmly related to one another. From lawns to mountains to meadows and then to towers, the sequence is so arranged as to discourage us from extrapolating from it a composite scene, the details of which would then be interpretable. Neither time's winged chariot nor anything else is at the back of these shepherds, and the verse in no way compels us to translate them into figures for the young poet or the weary courtier or the faithful feeder of a Christian flock. In other words, we know and understand the quality of their untroubled (careless) joy because it is precisely reflected in the absence of any pressure on us to make more of their landscape than its surfaces present. This introduces the interesting possibility that while *L'Allegro* is the easier of the two poems to read, it was the more difficult to write. In *Il Penseroso* Milton can exploit the traditions his verse invades; in *L'Allegro* he must simultaneously introduce them and denude them of their implications, employing a diction and vocabulary rich in complex associations without the slightest gesture in the direction of that complexity. In *L'Allegro* it is not so much what the images do but what they do not do. The poem is a triumph of absence.

The figure of Orpheus as he appears in lines 145–50 is thus a perfect surrogate for the reader; the music he hears calls him to nothing, as we have been called to nothing by the verse. He is enwrapped in harmonies, resting on 'heaped Elysian flowers' (147) as we rest, unexercised, on the heaped (not arranged) flowers of the poem's images and scenes, insulated from the resonances and complications which might be activated in another context (the context, in fact, of *Il Penseroso*). This music *merely* meets the ear and the ear it meets has no answering responsibility (of which there is the 'flat absence') beyond the passive responsibility of involuntary delight. When Graves discovered that *L'Allegro* was 'rather a muddle,' it was after many years of reading the poem. 'I had however,' he explains, never before 'read it so carefully.'[8] The point that I have been making is that no one asked him to, and that his period of *mis*reading began when he decided to accord the poem the kind of careful attention from which it was Milton's gift to set us free.

It is this freedom which is banished when *Il Penseroso* opens by declaring 'Hence vain deluding joys.' 'Vain' here is to be taken as fruitless or without purpose, and it refers not to an abstraction, but to a mode of experiencing, a mode in which the brain is quite literally 'idle' because it is 'possessed' by a succession of 'gaudy shapes' and fancies 'which ere we see them come are gone.' This is of course the experiential mode of

John Milton

L'Allegro, and it should not surprise us to find that the experience of reading *Il Penseroso* is quite different.

Notes

1. Cleanth Brooks and John E. Hardy, *Poems of Mr John Milton* (New York: Gordian, 1951), p. 136.

2. For a similar point, see Leslie Brisman, '"All Before Them Where to Choose": *L'Allegro* and *Il Penseroso*', *JEGP* **71** (1972): 239.

3. Rosemond Tuve, 'Structural Figures of *L'Allegro* and *Il Penseroso*' in *Milton: Modern Essays in Criticism*, ed. Arthur E. Barker (New York, 1965), p. 61.

4. Cleanth Brooks, *The Well Wrought Urn* (New York: Harcourt Brace Jovanovich, 1947), p. 54.

5. D.C. Allen, *The Harmonious Vision* (Baltimore: Johns Hopkins University Press, 1954), p. 6.

6. Robert Graves, *Five Pens in Hand* (New York: Ayer Co. Publishers, 1958), p. 59.

7. Herbert J. West, Jr, '"Here's a Miltonic Discovery . . ."', *Renaissance Papers, 1958–1961*, p. 73.

8. Robert Graves, 'John Milton Muddles Through', *New Republic* (27 May 1957), p. 17.

4 Milton's Early Radicalism*

MICHAEL WILDING

For years now the blandly disseminated view of the pre-revolutionary decades of the early seventeenth century has held that the works of English literature of those years belong to a non-political world. It was a depoliticized reading made possible by an awareness of the extent and effects of censorship and a consequent refusal to decode political meanings from the literary texts. But the revolution did not suddenly appear from nowhere. And if we look at Milton's poetry of the 1630s we can see evidence of the social tensions and unmistakable assertions of revolutionary sentiments.

How radical was the young Milton? Can we find evidence of a political commitment in the poetry associated with his Cambridge years? Is there anything in the early work that looks forward to the revolutionary?

Milton's *Poems* of 1645 has generally been seen as an unpolitical or apolitical volume, as embodying Milton's youthful poems of the age before revolution . . . The 'New Critical' reading of the 1645 volume offered in the commentary by Cleanth Brooks and John E. Hardy presented a poet shorn of the political.[1] The New Critical, depoliticizing approach to Milton was never as critically exciting as the application of the approach to the metaphysical poets. Milton never became a central figure in new critical practice, despite the earlier essay on *L'Allegro* and *Il Penseroso* in Brooks's *The Well Wrought Urn*.[2] But the negative aspects of the approach, the removal of the socio-political context, had their effect and the Brooks and Hardy readings achieved a pervasive influence.

Louis Martz developed the approach in his elegant essay, The Rising Poet, 1645:

* Extracts reprinted from *Dragon's Teeth: Literature in the English Revolution* (Oxford: Clarendon Press, 1987.

Here is the picture of a youthful poet, free from adult cares, sometimes wandering alone, amusing himself, sometimes making music for his friends or acquaintances, sometimes writing in his native vein, sometimes evoking a strain from idealized antiquity – but with a light and dancing posture that we do not usually associate with John Milton: *et humum vix tetigit pede.* It is clear, from many indications, that Milton has designed his book with great care to create this impression.

The entire volume strives to create a tribute to a youthful era now past – not only the poet's own youth, but a state of mind, a point of view, ways of writing, an old culture and outlook now shattered by the pressures of maturity and by the actions of political man.[3]

But whereas Brooks and Hardy had essentially ignored the political, Martz argues that the volume [as published by Humphrey Moseley and stressing royalist associations] is contrived to present an unpolitical impression, a commitment to 'the transcendent value of art.'

Immediately certain separations need to be made in Martz's account between Milton's activitites and those of his publisher Milton may have tacitly accepted the image Moseley was creating. At the same time, the head-notes to the poems themselves and the arrangement of the volume allow a radical theme to be perceived. Both Moseley as publisher and Milton as writer would have been aware of the advantages of appealing both to Protestant radicals and to royalist aesthetes; a larger audience than appealing to only one sectarian group. Moseley may have endured Milton's radicalism as Milton may have endured Moseley's conservatism. The permutations are multiple. My point is to stress the multifaceted nature of the 1645 volume. Thomas Corns has argued that the 1645 *Poems* show Milton engaged in 'a further attempt to dissociate himself from the archetypal sectary,' an image with which his polemical writings had identified him.[4] 'It contains a number of poems which in no way square with his ideological position by 1645, but which serve to restate his social status and aspirations.' And Corns concludes:

Milton's volume of poetry indicates clearly enough in its maturer items the Puritanism of the poet. Milton draws attention to it. *Lycidas* is introduced as foretelling 'the ruin of our corrupted clergy then in their height'. . . . The abiding impression, however, of any browser selecting this volume in Moseley's bookshop early in 1646 must surely have been of the eminent respectability of its author. Over and over again the volume declares his wealth, his establishment connections, his contact with European culture, and his scholarship.

Dr Corns is surely right in pointing to the contradictions within the 1645 volume between Milton's gestures at respectability and his gestures at radicalism. In part the contradictions may have been tactical, in part they may have expressed contradictions within Milton's own thinking. But in exploring these contradictions it is necessary that both the conservative and the radical implications should be explored.

To find political radicalism in the non-prophetic early poems as well as in the prophetic ones would strengthen our case. *L'Allegro* seems an initially unlikely locus for the political; but the force with which the political has been denied here suggests a significant repression:

> Come, and trip it as you go
> On the light fantastic toe,
> And in thy right hand lead with thee,
> The mountain nymph, sweet Liberty;
> And if I give thee honour due,
> Mirth, admit me of thy crew
> To live with her, and live with thee,
> In unreproved pleasures free . . .
>   (33–40)

It is hard to see how sweet Liberty could be construed as anything other than liberty. It is not luxury or licence or anything pejorative. It is a positive value that has an unavoidable political meaning. Switzerland, that Protestant mountainous stronghold of religious freedom, may be implied. Yet Cleanth Brooks in his influential essay in *The Well Wrought Urn* dismisses this natural reading:

If, under the influence of Milton's later political career, we tend to give Liberty any political significance, we find her in *L'Allegro* in very strange company, consorting with

> Jest and youthful jollity
> Quips and cranks, and wanton wiles
> Nods, and becks, and wreathed smiles . . .
> Sport that wrinkled Care derides
> And Laughter holding both his sides.[5]

But the passage Brooks quotes precedes the introduction of Liberty; jest, jollity, quips, and cranks are presented as the qualities or companions of Mirth. Liberty is a more serious quality that Milton distinguishes from Mirth. Brooks offers no argument for his rejection of the political reading of liberty here. He implies that a knowledge of Milton's later political career pollutes the reading, but liberty would have meant liberty whatever Milton's later career.

Brooks went on to make another distortion that has proved remarkably influential in later readings:

> The first scene is a dawn scene – sunrise and people going to work: the ploughman, the milkmaid, the mower, and the shepherd. But though we see people going to work, we never see them *at* their work.
>
> (p. 44)

But when we turn to that first scene, Brooks's case simply falls down:

> While the ploughman near at hand
> Whistles o'er the furrowed land,
> And the milkmaid singeth blithe
> And the mower whets his scythe,
> And every shepherd tells his tale
> Under the hawthorn in the dale
> (63–68)

Stanley Fish has pointed to the pervasive ambiguity of syntax and image and reference in *L'Allegro* and *Il Penseroso*. What Brooks did was to accentuate one aspect of the ambiguous and repress the other. The phrases in the poem that can be read as indicating people going to work can as readily be interpreted as accounts of their being engaged in work. The ploughman who 'whistles o'er the furrowed land' may be whistling across a ploughed field on his way to work; or the whistles may express the song of his labour and the speed with which he is ploughing. The milkmaid who 'singeth blithe' may as readily be singing while she works as not. The shepherd who 'tells his tale' can be telling a tale while keeping an eye on the sheep; or he may be counting them, telling his sheep, keeping tally. The clinching case is the mower who 'whets his scythe.' Cleanth Brooks writes as if the sharpening of the scythe was not work, but some relaxed occupation of the mower's leisure time. But the scythe has to be constantly resharpened, and the whetting is part of the rhythm and activity of mowing as much as the strokes cutting the grass.

The work is present and is joyous. In *L'Allegro* labour is delight. It is a vision, like William Morris's haymaking in *News from Nowhere*, fulfilling, enjoyable.[6] Yet the exhausting quality of the labour is not repressed: this is not a false or purely decorative pastoral. To read of:

> Mountains on whose barren breast
> The labouring clouds do often rest
> (73–74)

is to be reminded of the hardship of physical rural labour, of the need for rest, of the harshness of the places of rest available to the labourer. When we are shown the cottage 'hard by' the towers and battlements, the 'hard' picks up the 'barren breast' of the mountains on which the 'labouring clouds . . . rest' to remind us of the hard life of the cottager; its implications spread into cottage life, not the castle or crenellated manor-house. And it is not easy to see how labour can be evacuated from the picture of the cottagers:

> Hard by, a cottage chimney smokes,
> From betwixt two aged oaks,
> Where Corydon and Thyrsis met,
> Are at their savoury dinner set
> Of herbs, and other country messes,
> Which the neat-handed Phyllis dresses;
> And then in haste her bower she leaves,
> With Thestylis to bind the sheaves,
> Or if the earlier season lead
> To the tanned haycock in the mead. . . .
>
> (81–90)

Brooks comments 'we do not accompany them to the haycock, nor do we feel the sun which "tans" it' (p. 49). But the demands of labour cannot that easily be denied. The emphatic present tense stresses the present activity of dressing the dinner and rushing off to work; the 'haste' with which Phyllis leaves the bower to bind the sheaves emphatically stresses a hurried meal, hurried because of the pressing demand of labour; and the alternative 'or if the earlier season lead' similarly stresses that whatever season there is pressing work. There is always some demand.

As a result of his case, Brooks has to distort the poem further by treating unambiguous images of labour as somehow exceptions. He writes:

Nobody sweats in the world of *L'Allegro* – except the goblin:

> Tells how the drudging Goblin sweat
> To earn his cream-bowl duly set,
> When in one night, ere glimpse of morn,
> His shadow flail hath threshed the corn. . . .

Perhaps it is overingenious to suggest that in this scene – the only depiction of strenuous activity in the poem – Milton has 'cooled' it off by making the flail 'shadowy', by presenting it as part of a night scene, and by making the labourer, not a flesh-and-blood man, but a goblin.

> And yet the scene has been carefully patterned: it is balanced by the
> passage in *Il Penseroso*, where the spectator having taken refuge from
> the sun listens 'While the bee with honeyed thigh, . . . at her flowery
> work doth sing. . . .' Goblins and bees are the only creatures
> presented 'at work' in the two poems.
>
> (pp. 49–50)

But rather than excepting goblins and bees, we might more profitably see
them as thematic reinforcements of the image of labour. All nature
labours: human male and female – ploughman and milkmaid; the
labouring clouds; the insect world, the bee, type and reminder of human
social labour here as in Marvell's *The Garden*; and the supernatural world.
Labour is not something separate from life, either here, or in Adam and
Eve's gardening labour in Eden, or in the description of God as 'my great
taskmaster', in Sonnet 7.

The significance of Brooks's denial of the presence of labouring activity
in *L'Allegro* is brought into political focus by some comments of Raymond
Williams in *The Country and the City*:

> The whole result of the fall from paradise was not that instead of
> picking easily from an all-providing nature, man had to earn his bread
> in the sweat of his brow; that he incurred, as a common fate, the curse
> of labour. What is really happening, in Jonson's and Carew's
> celebrations of a rural order, is an extraction of just this curse, by the
> power of art: a magical recreation of what can be seen as a natural
> bounty and then a willing charity: both serving to ratify and bless the
> country landowner, or, by a characteristic reification, his house. Yet
> this magical extraction of the curse of labour is in fact achieved by a
> simple extraction of the existence of the labourers. The actual men and
> women who rear the animals and drive them to the house and kill
> them and prepare them for meat; who trap the pheasants and
> partridges and catch the fish; who plant and manure and prune and
> harvest the fruit trees, these are not present; their work is all done for
> them by a natural order . . .[7]

It is this extraction of the existence of the rural labourers in the
representative rural poetry of the early seventeenth century that Milton
confronts and resists. Brooks attempts to subsume *L'Allegro* to this
dominant, quasi-pastoral, patrician, landowning vision. And his attempt
to do so when detected reveals the politics of Milton's vision more
clearly. The labourers are present; indeed, the labourers are introduced
before the landowners, gentry and aristocrats are encountered in the
poem. The labour of the rural workers is recognized, given a dignity and
an aesthetic beauty in commemoration, and its hardships acknowledged.

The human basis for Milton's stand against the forces of oppression – bishops, monarchs, all the figures of power and authority that he confronted – lies here in a recognition and sympathy for the labouring class.

Notes

1. CLEANTH BROOKS and JOHN E. HARDY (eds), *Poems of Mr John Milton: The 1645 Edition with Essays in Analysis* (New York: Gordian, 1951).

2. CLEANTH BROOKS, *The Well Wrought Urn: Studies in the Structure of Poetry* (1947) (London, 1968).

3. LOUIS MARTZ, 'The Rising Poet, 1645' in Joseph H. Summers (ed.), *The Lyric and Dramatic Milton* (New York, 1965), p. 5. Reprinted in Martz, *Poet of Exile: A Study of Milton's Poetry* (New Haven: Yale University Press, 1980).

4. THOMAS N. CORNS, 'Milton's Quest for Respectability', *Modern Language Review* 77 (1982): 778.

5. BROOKS, *The Well Wrought Urn*, p. 43.

6. MICHAEL WILDING, *Political Fictions* (London: Routledge, 1980), p. 59.

7. RAYMOND WILLIAMS, *The Country and the City* (1973; repr. New York: Oxford University Press, 1975), p. 32.

5 The Politics of Milton's Early Poetry*

DAVID NORBROOK

The English Revolution and John Milton have often been constructed
in comparable ways in English cultural history, as republican aberra-
tions forming an 'Interregnum' in a naturally hierarchical and monarchist order. The attempted 'dislodging' of Milton by Eliot and
Leavis was also an attempt to dislodge certain modes of oppositional
political discourse. *Poetry and Politics in the English Renaissance* re-
examines the origins of that tradition of radical poetry from Milton to
Shelley which Eliot and Leavis had discredited. The book was written
at the high point of the 'revisionist' movement in seventeenth-century
historiography, which restated an organicist and traditionalist analysis of English society. At the same time, the first wave of the 'New
Historicism', by demolishing conventional notions of political agency
and intentionality, was producing a somewhat comparable picture of
the political community as masochistically submissive to images of
royal power, with occasional transitory outbursts of 'subversion'. An
attempt is made here to offer a more long-term analysis of the poet's
and intellectual's public role: if poetry often glorified those in power,
it could also mobilize cultural memories that went much further back
than short-term personal quarrels and could encourage resistance
rather than submission. The concluding chapter analyses *Lycidas* as a
culmination of the more radical traditions of public poetry on formal
as well as conceptual levels, systematically challenging organicist
models of form and unity, whether in the spheres of historical
temporality, of the state, or of poetic tradition and formal structure.
Walter Benjamin and Harold Bloom (in a politicized version) are
evident points of reference; the analysis of fissures in English national
identity is particularly indebted to Tom Nairn's *The Break-Up of Britain*.

---

* Reprinted from *Poetry and Politics in the English Renaissance* (London: RKP, 1984).

In his political pamphlets of the 1640s Milton viewed the development of English history in terms that mirrored his own self-development. The visible church, he argued, had come to be dominated by time-serving prelates while the truly godly had lived in silence and obscurity. What appeared to the apologists for the Church of England to have been its steady growth in prosperity had in fact been a process of stagnation. Milton admired Edward VI, looking back nostalgically in one of his sonnets to the days when Cheke gave him a humanist education; he felt an immediate sense of spiritual kinship when he read Bucer's Christian utopia, 'De regno Christi.' But the king had died young and political difficulties had impeded the reformation. About the reign of Elizabeth Milton had little positive to say: he admired Archbishop Grindal, but regarded the Elizabethan settlement as an unsatisfactory, 'lukewarm' compromise. Since then there had been a steady reaction. The bishops' obsession with tradition had prevented the 'renovating and re-ingendering Spirit of God' (1:703) from taking its course. England had been the first country to 'set up a standard for the recovery of lost Truth' but was now the last to enjoy the benefits of reformation (1:525). But the time was at last to be redeemed, the long wait of the godly would be rewarded by 'the long-deferred, but much more wonderful and happy reformation of the Church in these latter days' (1:519). In his increasing apocalyptic enthusiasm Milton went beyond traditional Protestant symbolism, arguing that Truth was 'the daughter not of Time, but of Heaven' (1:639). There was an absolute opposition between the secular realm of time and the 'dateless and irrevoluble circle of eternity' (1:616). What was at hand was not a 'revolution' in the old sense of a return to a previous state of purity but something completely without precedent: the New Jerusalem 'without your admired link of succession descends from Heaven' (1:703). Milton hoped in the 1640s that poetic and political expectations would converge, that he would be able to produce a great celebration of the nation's apocalyptic renewal. His pamphlets were full of references to the tradition of prophetic poetry – to Dante, Petrarch, *The Plowman's Tale*, and Spenser. His prose tracts were themselves rhapsodic and linguistically inventive; but he insisted that they were not yet his major achievement, that they were only 'abortive and foredated' (1:820). In the end, of course, his great poem was to celebrate a lost paradise rather than a reformed commonwealth, but the extent of his early hopes helps to explain his later disillusion. At the height of the tumults of the 1640s, however, he did find time to bring out a collection of his early poems, and he made prophetic claims for *Lycidas*, which, he said, had foretold the ruin of the Anglican church.

Recent historians have warned that it is misleading to read the polarisation of the 1640s back into the 1630s. Rather than seething with pre-revolutionary ferment, it is argued, the England of that period was fundamentally tranquil, and only a tiny and unrepresentative minority cared very much about censorship or religious reaction. Certainly the religious and social radicals of the 1640s never succeeded in finding a broad political base in a country where traditionalism was still very strong, and where loyalties to local country communities were often more powerful than allegiance either to the central government or to religious ideologies. Many people were very reluctant to fight for either side in the Civil War.[1] Some critics have argued that Milton's own radicalism came very late, and have made a sharp separation between the poet of the 1630s and the Puritan of the 1640s[2]. It has been argued that Milton's publication of his poems in 1645 was an attempt to demonstrate his social respectability at a time when he was coming under heavy attack for the alleged democratic tendencies of his political writings.[3]

There are undoubtedly discontinuities and inconsistencies in Milton's canon: there is not a simple, steadfast march towards Puritan revolution. But it is possible to exaggerate the discontinuities. The political tracts are of course rhetorically very different from the early poems; but they are also different from many more conventional tracts, being marked by exceptional subtlety of rhetorical strategy, modifying and subverting conventional responses.[4] Their method is indeed sometimes so oblique that their immediate political effectiveness may have been blunted. Milton's early poems use comparable strategies: they make their political points not so much by direct comment as by modification of generic expectations. The lack of explicit political statement need not be too surprising. After the dissolution of Parliament in 1629, orthodox channels of political debate were still more strictly controlled; through the 1630s ecclesiastical censorship was tightened. The period of the 'king's peace' can be seen as the most determined attempt in English history to 'aestheticise politics', to suppress articulate discussion and to try to force the realm into a harmonious pattern of ritualised submission. Advocates of a militant foreign policy continued throughout the 1630s to press for a change in direction, but had to do so by very indirect means since public discussion of foreign policy in or out of Parliament was no longer possible. Champions of British intervention in the Thirty Years' War were still looking to Elizabeth of Bohemia, in her exile in the Netherlands, and even wishing that she, rather than her brother, were on the British throne.[5] The Dutch envoy complained that whenever he tried to raise urgent political and military issues the Earl of Arundel, the king's negotiator, tried to distract him by talking about pictures and galleries.[6] There can be little doubt that substantial parts of the political nation, exhausted by the turbulence of recent years, welcomed the new peace and stability. But there were undercurrents of dissent. Charles and Laud would not have acted so firmly had they not believed that the political situation in the 1620s, under Abbot's lax regime, had been getting out of hand, that without firmer discipline radical sects would have continued to multiply until they became politically dangerous. Milton had come to political maturity in the 1620s, at a time when poets as well as radical dissenters had been growing irreverent about established authority. There were cracks in the elegant facade of religious and social uniformity, and Milton was unusually sensitive to these points of tension. His brief phase of responsiveness to Caroline aestheticised politics gave way to an increasingly emphatic politicisation of aesthetics. Rather than stating his opinions explicitly he built into his poems a distrust of specious harmony obtained at the expense of repression. In the 1640s he was to elaborate this distrust into a political theory influenced by the Florentine republicans; like the Machiavelli of the *Discourses*, he believed that an element of disorder and dissension was essential to the maintenance of liberty, that to try to achieve complete, static harmony was to invite stagnation.[7] When he used aesthetic analogies in his political works he modified their traditional associations. If building the reformed church was like carving a statue, it was necessary to acknowledge that this task was bound to produce an element of waste matter, the sects that could not be harmonised with the main church: here Milton's emphasis was on the process, the 'struggle of contrarieties', not on the finished product (1:795). When he compared the church or state to a temple, he emphasized that a building made up of human beings could never be 'united into a continuity, it can but be contiguous in this world' (2:555). Even if he had not yet fully articulated them in his own mind, such ideas are implicit in the major works of the 1630s.

In some respects the young Milton appeared a stylistically conservative poet, remaining faithful to literary modes that were being rejected by many fashionable writers. In the political climate of the 1630s it was the poetry of the politically traditionalist Jonson and his followers that seemed most modern, most emancipated from old-fashioned Puritan pieties. George Wither had responded to the pioneering role of the court in patronising new artistic modes by attacking all literary artifice as politically suspect; but Milton's position was more complex. The Spenserian tradition by the 1630s had become worthy but dull, lacking any responsiveness to artistic innovation; and a spirit of religious and political innovation could not really be encouraged by artistic conservatism. The adventurous, experimental quality of Milton's early poetry has often been underestimated. He viewed poetic history, like political history, in apocalyptic terms: rather than envisaging a smooth, steady progression towards perfection, he sought, in his own poetry, to make the last first and the first last. He revived elements in the old prophetic tradition that were currently unfashionable. He was also willing, however, to imitate the formal experiments of more courtly writers, and to push these innovations even further, thus exposing the ultimate political conservatism behind the superficial modernity of the courtiers. His underlying commitment was to the prophetic tradition. The idea that the purification of religion would lead to the purification of poetry was implicit in the apocalyptic tradition. Bale and other writers had Protestantised the humanist attack on scholasticism, arguing that the authoritarianism of the Roman church led to the decay of learning and of poetry. George Hakewill, whose refutation of the ideal of universal decay may have influenced Milton, cited Mantuan to the effect that monks and friars did not delight in verse and gave examples of Sidney, Spenser and Buchanan as part of his proof that a renewal of learning was in progress. His friend John Jonston praised Spenser in a book which prophesied that the millennium might begin before the end of the century.[8] Such ideas were encouraging for a young prophetic poet. His verse could express in symbolic form the underlying apocalyptic implications of the reform of learning as a whole.

But apocalyptic ideas were not viewed with enthusiasm at the Caroline court. At a time when the government was moving closer to Spain the strident identifications of the Pope with Antichrist in the Protestant tradition became somewhat embarrassing. Bacon had been careful to combine his apocalyptic rhetoric with frequent panegyrics of learned monarchs, and some of his works were published with official approval in Charles's reign. But millennialist writers considered it prudent to withhold publication. Belief in a future millennium had been associated in the previous century with popular radicalism. The theorists of the 1630s were certainly not advocating egalitarianism, but their ideas were suspect because they implied the need for Britain to take part in the general European crusade against Antichrist. The leadership of the Protestant cause had passed to Gustavus Adolphus; Joseph Mede identified his military victories with the opening of the fourth vial (Revelation xvi.8), a decisive step towards the defeat of Antichrist. In one of his eclogues Francis Quarles presented the apocalyptic hopes that Gustavus Adolphus had aroused in England and the despair caused by his death in 1632 – a despair frequently compared to the emotion caused by Prince Henry's death.[9] Knevett ended the eighth book of his supplement to 'The Faerie Queene' with a lament at his hero's death. Charles discouraged excessive enthusiasm for Gustavus Adolphus, however; far from defending Protestant military influence, he closely co-operated with the Spanish navy in their campaign against the Dutch. Laud discouraged the traditional links between British and Continental

Protestants and expelled foreign Protestants who did not conform to the rites of the Church of England.[10] Many apocalyptic works remained unpublished in the 1630s; the result was an explosion of millennarian publications after the collapse of censorship in the 1640s.

In 1637 Milton was presented with a new occasion for writing poetry, when members of his Cambridge college assembled a volume in memory of his friend Edward King, who had been drowned in the Irish Sea. Though *Lycidas* opens with formulae of unwillingness, of taking up the pen before the due time, the poem is written with the assurance of someone who has at last found the proper subject. The 'sad occasion' is also 'dear', and his words are indeed 'lucky'.

But why did King's death release Milton from his impasse? He does not seem to have kept up his college friendship with King, who had gravitated towards the Laudian group at Cambridge, and whose poetry, despite Milton's claim in *Lycidas*, was unambitious and undistinguished. Death would already have been on Milton's mind before he heard that King had been drowned: his mother had recently died and the plague had struck his village. The slow maturing of his poetic gifts, his conscious deferment of worldly advancement, meant that the sudden death of a young friend would have brought home to him the fact that his own life would seem to have been effectively wasted if he were now to die. *Lycidas*, as critics have long recognised, is about Milton, and about poetry, as much as it is about Edward King. But this does not mean that the poem is narrowly egotistical, or that it is concerned with the eternal ideals of art as opposed to the transient concerns of politics. It does not mean that he saw himself as contributing to a timeless essence called 'the pastoral tradition'. But in writing *Lycidas* Milton was able to define his position in a specific tradition of prophetic poetry, and to renew and transform that tradition in the light of changed political circumstances.

Milton's awareness of alternative poetic traditions in England would have been sharpened just before he began work on *Lycidas*. For just six days after King's death, on 16 August 1637, Ben Jonson died in London.[11] After a brief interregnum in the period immediately after Spenser's death, Jonson had effectively become poet laureate, relegating poets in the Spenserian tradition to secondary public roles. Who could now take his place? In the end it was the young cavalier poet Sir William Davenant who emerged as Jonson's successor (though he does not seem to have received an official title).[12] It was natural for the 'sons of Ben' to think of poetic 'succession' as analogous to royal succession: Jonson had constantly emphasised the analogies between poet and prince, and one elegist hailed him as 'King of *English Poetry*'.[13] The name 'tribe of Ben' was a witty allusion to Revelation (vii.8), but the playfulness indicated Jonson's wariness about taking claims to prophetic power too seriously.

Poetic tradition, like political tradition, was a matter of smooth continuity, with authority passing down through legitimate channels rather than being conferred by a sudden divine afflatus. Similar connections between literary excellence and religious conservatism were made in several of the elegies for Jonson which were published in 1638 under the title *Jonsonus Virbius*. The collection was edited by Brian Duppa, an Arminian who was Vice-Chancellor of Oxford University, and many of the contributors had links with Oxford.

Many of Jonson's elegists identified excessive emotion in poetry with religious enthusiasm, and hence tried to adopt a cool and composed tone. Jonson's friend Richard Corbett had ridiculed the extravagant outpourings with which the Puritans had greeted the death of their idol Prince Henry, and elaborate funerary effusions were increasingly becoming a mark of a Puritan outlook.

At the same time as this volume of restrained and conservative elegies was being assembled at Oxford, contributions were being requested for a tribute to an obscure don from Cambridge. Although the political and religious differences between the two universities – Oxford a centre of Arminianism and subsequently of royalism, Cambridge of Puritanism – were already visible, at least one poet wrote elegies for both men, and Milton could have done the same.[14] He had published a tribute to Shakespeare, and he recognised Jonson's stature. But he remained silent on Jonson's death and put all his linguistic resources into the poem for King. Whereas in *Comus* Milton had adopted a characteristically Jonsonian form and revised it, *Lycidas* marks a decisive and unambiguous commitment to the Spenserian tradition. Spenser was Milton's true poetic 'father', but it was Jonson, with his massive literary authority, who had caused a more immediate 'anxiety of influence'.[15] Milton had been struggling to avoid becoming just one more of the 'sons of Ben'; a powerful release came with his death – just as Dryden was to feel released by Milton's death. But in *Lycidas* Milton was laying claim to a literary authority that did not depend on respect for established religious institutions. The plants which the swain invokes at the beginning – laurel, myrtle, and ivy – were associated with the coronation of poets. At this time when the choice of a laureate was being considered, Milton paid tribute to the 'laureate hearse' of a King who lacked high office (several elegists made a political pun on King's name) and made a powerful critique of current poetic and political developments.

   Lycidas differs radically in tone and form from the tributes to Jonson; it differs also from the poems in the Cambridge volume, which revealed a certain caution about giving free rein to prophetic passion. King's brother Henry set the tone in the first English elegy:[16]

> No Death! I'le not examine Gods decree,
> Nor question providence, in chiding thee:

Some of the Cambridge elegists did try to give an effect of strong emotion by sub-'metaphysical' conceits, but the hyperboles were so numerous that the effect was diluted. There is some evidence that *Iusta Edovardo King* was planned as a whole and that Milton may have seen some of the other elegies before writing *Lycidas*. If so, he set out to distinguish himself from his contemporaries rather than subduing his own poetic voice to the tone of the whole. *Lycidas* was placed at the end of the volume; it was the longest poem, and the only eclogue, amongst the contributions in English. Far from refusing to question providence, Milton repeatedly does so. The poet's voice is never assimilated to urbane everyday speech; this enables the poem to rise to heights of prophetic zeal. But the formality of language does not permit a stately distancing and ritualising of grief: at moments when the poem seems to be moving towards some satisfactory closure, the ritual will suddenly be exposed as a vain attempt to obscure the truth by specious beauty. The pastoral framework clearly differentiates the poem from the currently fashionable conceits and 'strong lines'; but the hyperboles are there on a more submerged level. There is an undercurrent of restless wordplay, of half-realised paradoxes – leaves which are 'shattered' (the word could mean 'scattered' but the stronger sense is there too), blind mouths, enamelled eyes, sucking showers.[17] The effect is of excitement, even hysteria, only just contained. The disruptions of the rhyme-scheme reinforce this effect. Milton builds up expectations of formal completion which are then disrupted: for example, there are moments (11. 130–8, 163ff) when the poem seems to be about to fall into ottava rima stanzas, but not until the very last eight lines are these expectations fulfilled. Some critics have drawn analogies with the 'mannerist' art fashionable at Italian courts in which a conspicuous asymmetry was played against an underlying order; Alastair Fowler has detected an elaborate numerological structure in the poem, despite its apparent irregularity.[18] But even if this structure does enact some underlying analogy with the cosmic order, the point of the poem is to show how unconsoling the order of nature is in the face of death and the corruptions of the church. Milton's experiments in rhyme go beyond anything attempted by the Italian poets he imitated, such as Della Casa and Tasso.[19] It is as if he were trying to produce not an imitation of more recent courtly writers but an impression of the kind of poetry that might have been written in Italy had the prophetic tradition not been stifled by the Counter-Reformation (Della Casa and Tasso had both had problems with the Inquisition). There is a toughness in *Lycidas* that is closer to Dante, who was disdained by many Italian courtiers for his uncouthness, than to fashionable pastoralists.

The elegies in *Jonsonus Virbius* – and most of those in *Iusta Edovardo King* – indicate the growing hegemony of the closed couplet as a dominant metrical form, a development which Jonson had strongly influenced. This form was to become for the Augustans a symbol of political as well as poetic order; and within five years of the composition of *Lycidas* Sir John Denham was to make these analogies explicit in *Cooper's Hill*, where the couplet signifies the balance and harmony of the constitution, and it disciplines excessive enthusiasm in poetic imagination in much the same way as traditional political and religious forms curb Puritan enthusiasm. In *Lycidas* movements towards a closed couplet are constantly disrupted. A temporary resolution is reached at the end of Phoebus's speech:

> As he pronounces lastly on each deed,
> Of so much fame in heaven accept thy meed.

This consolation already distances the poet from the emphasis on earthly fame to be found in many Jonsonian elegies; but in the context of the poem's formal unevenness, the couplet appears too facile to offer a convincing resolution, and the poet's questions continue. Jonson had claimed that a short life could be seen as a harmonious poem; in *Lycidas* life and death constantly evade harmonious patterns. The immortality given to 'Virbius' is radically insufficient.

Milton's choice of the pastoral convention itself ran counter to current fashions. It is necessary, of course, to distinguish between different kinds of pastoral. The 'Arcadian' pastoral of Sannazaro and Tasso was in vogue in some court circles, though the 'sons of Ben' had little time for the fashion. In *Lycidas*. Milton indicates the dangers of escapism in this tradition. The long 'flower' passage (11. 132–51), in which the poet tries to divert his thoughts after the terror of St Peter's speech, may be felt to go on slightly too long, as if the poet were desperately trying to shut out unpleasant realities. And at 1. 153 he concedes that he has been dallying with 'false surmise', that no amount of pastoral embroidery can conceal the fact that King's corpse has been washed away to sea. Milton's pastoralism is less courtly than humanist and didactic, in the tradition of the eclogues of Petrarch, Mantuan and Spenser. The allegorical eclogue was already passing from fashion by the 1630s. For poets trying to achieve a more colloquial speaking voice, the genre seemed too elaborate and also too pedantic. After *Lycidas* no really important allegorical eclogues were produced in England until Shelley's *Adonais*. When Dr Johnson attacked the poem for its pedantry he probably sensed a connection between Milton's militant humanism and his political radicalism. He refused to conceal his erudition for the sake of social propriety. The artifice of his allegory is never naturalised: Milton makes it very clear that there is a dissociation between surface level and deeper meaning, between Lycidas and his friend battening their flocks with the dew of night and the activity of reading or discussing poetry. The rising and setting of the sun had become a stock symbol of life's transience and appeared frequently in the Oxford and Cambridge elegies; but in *Lycidas* the sun rises and sets three times, each time on a slightly different symbolic level. The juxtaposition of classical mythology with Christian symbolism had become standard in Renaissance eclogues but Jonson had always tried to avoid any violent clashes; his verse implies the smooth continuity of human experience from classical to Christian eras. Milton makes the discontinuities as conspicuous as possible. Self-conscious display of learning was of course appropriate in a volume of Cambridge elegies, and there is in *Lycidas* a level of academic wit. The description of Camus as 'footing slow' plays on the etymological sense of 'pedantic'. But this pun is immediately succeeded by the ferocious urgency of St Peter's speech; none of the other elegies has a comparable range of tones. Milton is not simply parading classical learning or engaging in literary jokes; his classical allusions are politically pointed. His most important classical model was Virgil's tenth eclogue, but he departs conspicuously from his original. Virgil's poem is a lament for Gallus, who is dying of unrequited love. The highly politicised commentaries of Renaissance humanists assumed that this 'love' was at least in part political, that what Gallus really lacked was courtly favour. In *The Shepheardes Calender* Spenser had contrasted the difficult and unequal 'love' of courtly relationships with more mutual friendship; in *Lycidas* Milton revises his classical model to make his hero someone who repudiated love both in erotic and political senses, who never sought courtly advancement and found fulfilment instead in personal friendships.[20] Several elegists pointed the contrast between this humble King and King Gustavus Adolphus of Sweden whose death had occasioned many poems in England.

If *Lycidas* affirms the value of the academic as opposed to the courtly life, this is only to be expected in an elegy for a college fellow. But the fact that Milton was contributing to a Cambridge volume had political significance in itself. Cambridge had special associations with the Spenserian tradition. As Phineas Fletcher indignantly pointed out in 1632, the low-church tradition, which in his mind was associated with Spenserian poetry, was now being denounced as seditious 'Puritanism'. Resistance to Laudianism had, however, been stronger at Cambridge than at Oxford. The Chancellor, the Earl of Holland, tended to side with the Calvinists against Laud, who postponed a visitation to enforce conformity in 1635. But tighter controls were being imposed, and in 1637 the satirist John Bastwicke, reviving the irreverent satire of the Marprelate tracts, imagined the Archbishop advancing on the universities 'with a rod in his hand . . . to whip those naughty scholars, that will not learne well their lesson of conformity'.[21] By the time Milton wrote *Lycidas*, Bastwicke was in prison and his ears had been cut off. Of course, Laud had supporters at Cambridge, and King seems to have been amongst them. One contributor to *Iusta Edovardo King* invoked Spenser to attack dissenting iconoclasts, equating them with the 'blatant beast'.[22] In *Lycidas* Milton recalled a very different element in the Spenserian tradition, the strong suspicion of clerical authoritarianism.

The anxieties felt by Cambridge Calvinists were shared elsewhere in the country. There had been some hopes in 1635–6 that the king might be persuaded to summon a Parliament and take a more militant stand against the Spanish, but in 1637 he was still co-operating with the Spanish navy. The ascendancy of the High Church party was revealed in June 1637 by the arrest of Bishop John Williams, one of Laud's enemies and a defender of the Calvinist tradition. Williams was not arrested for directly political reasons and his character was far from austere – he was no Archbishop Grindal – but his arrest increased the general resemblances between the political conjuncture in 1637 and the situation when Spenser published *The Shepheardes Calender*. Ecclesiastical reaction seemed to be in danger of stifling the voice of Protestant prophecy. The savage punishment of Prynne, Bastwicke and Leighton had disturbed even people who were not particularly sympathetic to religious dissent. A Star Chamber decree of July 1637 had introduced sweeping new restrictions in an attempt to block loopholes in the censorship law.[23] Foxe's *Acts and Monuments* had chronicled the attempts of Catholic bishops to suppress godly preachers; now it had, Milton wrote subsequently, 'almost come to be a prohibited book' (1:679). Fulke Greville's treatise on religion, with its derogatory remarks about bishops, had been cut from his collected poems; his highly oblique protests against the Caroline regime by means of Tacitean lectures had been quickly stopped. William Browne published nothing in the 1630s, but his opinion of what was happening was revealed in 1640 when he wrote an excited letter to Sir Benjamin Rudyerd in praise of a speech he had made in the Long Parliament. Rudyerd had denounced those who abused all the godly as 'Puritans'; Browne wrote that his speech had been infused with 'the spirit which inspired the Reformation and the genius which dictated the Magna Charta'.[24]

In this climate of increasing dislike of censorship, the apparent digressiveness of the most explicitly polemical passage in the poem, St Peter's attack on the clergy, takes on a particular significance. Milton marked off this passage both in the 1645 rubric – 'by occasion' – and by internal stylistic pointers: the speech threatens to break the poem's frame, to shrink the pastoral streams. On a rhetorical level the speech is in a strict sense digressive: the aim of the poem is to mourn Edward King. But the way in which Milton chose to mourn his friend was politically charged; in writing an elegy for someone who was both poet and priest he was led to ask questions about the state of the church as well as about poetry. Even if he had not included Peter's speech the poem would still be highly political. And this speech is carefully worked into the poem's structure. It is prepared for by Phoebus's speech which likewise raises the style to a higher level; St Peter's final 'smite no more' takes up the opening 'Yet once more' and will be echoed in the triumphant 'weep no more'. But by making Peter's speech stand out from its immediate context Milton is able to give the effect of truth bursting through censorship – an idea that was highly charged in 1637–8. Earlier in the poem there is an image of the blind Fury as a censor, cutting off the existence of a poet who hoped to 'burst out into sudden blaze'. Milton was to use this phrase in *Animadversions* to describe the collapse of censorship: 'the aggreev'd, and long persecuted Truth . . . burst out with some efficacy of words . . . after such an injurious strangle of silence' (1:669). St Peter's speech is a reminder that language can not only 'build the lofty rhyme', that it can have destructive as well as creative force. At the beginning of the poem the swain's words 'shatter' the leaves.

A concern with the power of language and of music unites the different charges made by 'the pilot of the Galilean lake'. The major allegations were conventional to the tradition of anti-ecclesiastical pastoral; Quarles made similar charges in *The Shepheardes Oracles*. But Milton gave the indictment an exceptional unity, concision and intensity. St Peter's complaint is vague enough to have evaded the Laudian censorship, but he hints at more than he says. The attack on shepherds who 'scramble at the shearers' feast' reflects the stock complaint that the Laudian bishops cared only about personal advancement. 'Blind mouths', Milton's brilliant pun on the etymologies of 'bishop' (person who sees) and 'pastor' (person who feeds), accuses the bishops of failing to encourage the preaching of the word and hence of encouraging ignorance and superstition. The Laudians argued that simple people were incapable of benefiting from the austerely intellectual atmosphere of Calvinist worship, that they needed the aid of ritual. Milton later wrote that to justify the suppression of Puritan lectureships on this basis was to put out the people's eyes and then complain that they were irredeemably blind (1:993). The figure of the blind mouths leads on to a further indictment of their incompetence at preaching, couched in musical terms: their songs grate on their scrannel pipes. The idolatry rife among the people is symbolised by the sheep-rot, by a grotesque swelling of wind that corresponds to the bishops' corrupt music. While the bishops' mouths are blind, the throat of the 'grim wolf' gapes to devour his prey. The wolf is clearly one of the Jesuits who were making converts at court, but his 'privy paw' implies consummate dissimulation and recalls the old Protestant satiric convention of the Anglican foxes who were wolves in disguise. The crucial factor is that nothing is said, that prophetic voices are being silenced.

The culminating image of this passage is the 'two-handed engine at the door'. An enormous amount of critical effort has gone into finding a precise referent for this 'dark conceit'. But its most likely referent is yet another rhetorical figure, the two-edged sword of Revelation i.16 and xix.15, which was commonly interpreted in the apocalyptic tradition as referring to the immense power of the prophetic Word. The threatening, almost surreal character of Milton's 'two-handed engine' recalls the illustrations in Bale's 'Image of Both Churches' and in many Protestant New Testaments of Christ standing with his arms apart and the two-edged sword issuing from his mouth. In this sense the trope is self-referential: its menacing indeterminacy, designed to inspire awe and repentance, embodies, as well as referring to, what Milton later called the 'quick and pearcing' force of the Christian message (1:827). Christ's 'reforming Spirit', wrote Milton, mounts a 'sudden assault' on human traditions (1:704). Earlier in the 1630s he had felt himself to be 'unweapon'd', but *Lycidas* reflects a growing confidence in his linguistic powers. He is also assimilating more fully than ever before the legacy of the Continental as well as English traditions of prophetic poetry. The combination of the extremely elliptical and the matter-of-fact in the phrase 'that two-handed engine' is reminiscent of Dante, whose presence can be felt at several points in *Lycidas*. In *Paradiso* ix St Peter vehemently denounces ecclesiastical corruption; and in *Paradiso* xxix Beatrice complains that preachers are telling idle stories instead of heeding Christ's injunction to go forth with the shield and lances of the Word. Fiacius had reproduced these passages in his catalogue of testimonies to the spirit of reform, which had opened with a lengthy discussion of St Peter's humility: he would never have interpreted the keys offered to him by Christ (Matthew xvi.18–19) as supreme temporal authority or abused the sword of the Spirit to fight for a temporal kingdom. Later Protestant writers like Duplessis-Mornay had popularised not only Dante's attacks on papal pretensions in the *De Monarchia* but also the polemical passages in the *Paradiso* ix and xxix, which embarrassed Catholic censors. At the time he wrote *Lycidas* Milton had been doing some research into Papal censorship of the *De Monarchia* (1:438). Such censorship, he believed, was ineffectual: his own allusion to Dante showed that the prophetic voices of preaching and poetry could never be completely silenced. Retribution, says St Peter, stands 'at the door'. This allusion to Revelation (iii.20) indicates that the apocalypse cannot be long deferred: in 1641 Milton was confidently to proclaim that 'thy Kingdome is now at hand, and thou standing at the dore' (1:707). Milton leaves it for history to give a full explanation of his 'two-handed engine', to reveal precisely what political form the triumph of the Word will take. Commentaries on Revelation themselves conceded that the process of interpretation was progressive and in some sense bound up with political action: to effect a decisive defeat of the forces of Antichrist would be to translate one of St John's prophecies into reality, to reach a new understanding of the text. Echoes of Revelation become more explicit in the later sections of *Lycidas*. The speaker invokes St Michael just before the consolation, and the vision of Lycidas in heaven draws heavily on apocalyptic prophecies. The cry that 'there shall be no more tears' (Revelation vii.17, xxi.4) provides the ultimate authority for the injunction to 'weep no more'. At the start of the poem, the speaker is locked into the cycle of natural recurrence – 'yet once more' – but by the end he has had a vision of the ending of time, and the word 'once' has taken on connotations of finality. In Hebrews xii.26–7 St Paul writes that 'once more' promises God's apocalyptic judgement.[25] The phrase modulates into 'no more', which is at once consoling for the elect and threatening to the unregenerate.

St Peter's speech is a call for religious reform; but how radical, in 1637, did Milton want those reforms to be? The 1645 rubric seems to claim that he had already anticipated the complete destruction of episcopacy; and some critics have found indications of a radically separatist programme in the poem's allegory. The ship was a traditional emblem of the visible church, and King's shipwreck may, on one reading of the poem, represent the corruption of the Laudian church: King can be saved from ecclesiastical shipwreck only by the direct intervention of Christ who walked the waves. On this reading the 'pilot' must be not St Peter, the first Bishop of Rome, but Christ, the only true head of the invisible church of the faithful, who is described as carrying keys in Revelation i.18.[26] But the allusions to the mitre and the keys make St Peter a more likely attribution; and there are significant qualifications in Milton's rhetoric. The 'pilot' condemns 'such as' are greedy, thus implying that the church is not entirely irredeemable. His complaint that nothing is said at court about the growing influence of Jesuit proselytising, the 'grim wolf with privy paw' was modified by Milton between November 1637 and the first publication of the poem in 1638: Laud had taken some steps against the Jesuits, and 'nothing said' was amended to 'little said'. A frontal attack on episcopacy would in any case have made little sense in 1637–8, at a time when opposition to Arminianism and to other aspects of royal policy was bringing together a broad front of political forces which were united in hostility to Laud but not in more specific religious programmes. Neither Prynne nor the majority of Puritans were at this stage completely opposed to episcopacy; on the other hand, Prynne was ready to co-operate politically with radical anti-episcopalians like Leighton and Bastwicke. Only after the collapse of Anglican authority was it to be fully revealed how much the unity of 'Puritanism' had been an illusion created by common hostility to Laud.[27] For his part, Milton was trying to speak with the authority of a whole tradition of prophetic poetry which went back to an era before the Reformation; and the more recent Spenserian tradition had been sympathetic to low-church episcopacy on the Grindalian model. That he still had hopes of possible reforms within the existing structures is indicated by his plans, after he had finished *Lycidas*, for an epic poem about King Arthur: such a poem would have implied panegyric of the Stuarts. As recently as 1636 there had been hopes that Charles might revert to more militantly Protestant domestic and foreign policies. *Lycidas* rises to epic tones at the point where Milton describes St Michael's Mount – a stronghold associated with the angel of apocalypse – looking towards the Spanish garrison at Bayona. In legend King Arthur had defeated a Spanish giant at St Michael's Mount.[28]

But such allegiance to the monarchy and to episcopacy was in Milton's case very much conditional on the king's pursuit of godly policies. In *Lycidas* the transforming authority of the divine Word has priority over all secular traditions. Whenever we date Milton's final rejection of any compromise with traditional Anglicanism, it can be argued that the poetry of the 1630s already constituted an emotional preparation for this decision. Milton was certainly not one to lag behind contemporary opinion. He was moved to publish his first pamphlet, *Of Reformation*, at a time when some kind of compromise, the 'reduced episcopacy', advocated by Ussher and supported by Quarles, seemed to be likely to prevail. Milton fiercely attacked such lukewarm compromises and urged the need for a radical break with the past. He was soon to become disillusioned with many features of the presbyterian programme, but in 1641 it provided the most immediately practicable means of achieving radical change. England must reject merely national traditions and bring herself in line with the 'best reformed churches' on the Continent. And that pressure was already being felt when Milton wrote *Lycidas*. In July 1637 Laud's attempts to impose a new prayer-book on the Scots had provoked riots in Edinburgh which were to develop into a full-scale rebellion. Charles's attempts to aestheticise politics foundered on the intensely politicised and rationalistic culture created by the Scottish Reformation. Already in the summer of King's death the Venetian ambassador was writing that Laud feared that this rebellion would spread to England: the English people, 'no less than the Scots seem greedy for an opportunity to extricate themselves from the yoke to which they are being subjected insensibly, little by little'.[29] . . . It did not necessarily require supernatural gifts to believe that though Laud was now at the height of his power, his fall might be at hand. God the master-dramatist would bring low the mighty and exalt the humble, just as Lycidas, though 'sunk low', had 'mounted high', just as the humble pastoral form had become in the hands of prophetic poets a vehicle for divine discourse.

Lycidas is not a call for revolution, but its tone is not exactly cautious and moderate. Milton's political outlook at this time can usefully be contrasted with the response to current events of another poet, William Drummond. A literary conservative, and admirer of the Spenserian poets, Drummond also published a pastoral elegy in 1638. As has been seen, he disliked Laud's policies and supported religious toleration. But he was extremely worried by the growing force of radical Protestant opinion in Scotland, rightly fearing that it would unleash forces as intolerant as Laud's reaction. Moreover, Drummond was socially conservative, afraid that Protestant zeal might overthrow the social hierarchy. Whereas Milton had revised and revalued the tradition of Spenserian pastoral, Drummond was content simply to preserve the tradition; and a similar conservatism informed his social thought. In his pamplet 'Irene', written in 1638, he warned the nobility who were leading the Scottish rebellion that 'the climactericke and period of the monarchicall Governmentes of Europe is not yet come, and when, or if ever, it shall come, yee who are Nobles shall perish with it'. Turning to the people, he urged them: 'Questione not the thrones of Kinges, revive not your old equalityes of Nature'.[30] This was a quotation cited for contradiction from the climactic scene in Greville's *Mustapha*, where the priest backs down after wanting to incite the people to revolution:[31]

> Question these Thrones of Tyrants;
> Reuiue your old equalities of Nature.

Before long, sections of the people were indeed to be demanding the revival of their old equalities, and radical questioning was to pass from Tacitist closet drama to uncensored pamphlets addressed to the general public. The prospect of such an event terrified Drummond. Milton, however, was to welcome the ferment of questioning and debate in *Areopagitica*, and *Lycidas* fuels, rather than quelling, the apocalyptic excitement that was soon to shatter the old order. About the time he wrote *Lycidas* Milton entered in his commonplace book a quotation from Sulpicius Severus: 'the name of kings has always been hateful to free peoples' (1:440).

But *Lycidas* is not merely a destructive poem, a prophecy of doom.

Milton's apocalyptic hopes involved not just the reformation of a reactionary church but also a renewal of all the arts, including the art of poetry. The prophetic voice of judgment is counterbalanced by visions of a new kind of harmony with nature. The fact that the bishops' songs are 'lean and flashy' implies the possibility of a newer, more ample and resonant kind of poetry. A radical change in political conditions would permit the release of the full potential of the English literary tradition. In *Of Reformation* Milton set his own, open and inventive style against the 'fantastick, and declamatory flashes' admired by the Laudian bishops (1:568). In *Lycidas* new developments in poetic style are symbolised by music and by clear water. When he called the work a 'monody' Milton was not only using a technical term for a particular kind of elegy but also alluding to the new music that revived a long-lost harmony with nature. This secular music is itself an echo of the apocalyptic music which Milton had already described in 'On the Morning of Christ's Nativity': he describes heaven in musical terms, making Lycidas hear the 'unexpressive nuptial song' while the saints 'sing, and singing in their glory move'. The fluid syntax (possibly echoing *Paradiso* xxxi 4–5) makes song and action interchangeable. The 'other streams' of the heavenly waters are shadowed on earth by the Muses' streams, and the heavenly harmony is adumbrated by the harmony with nature which Lycidas's musical skill permitted: like Orpheus, he made the trees fan 'their joyous leaves to thy soft lays'. The imagery of Arcadian pastoral can be 'false' if it is used simply to aestheticise, to block out awareness of pressing political and religious concerns; but it can also provide a vision of an apocalyptically redeemed secular existence. *Lycidas* ends not with doom and terror but with the swain's joyful song; his pipe with its 'tender stops' almost comes to life itself under the power of his Orphic song. His song is not insipidly Arcadian: it has confronted the realities of death and judgment. But it has gained a new energy from this confrontation; it leads him on to 'pastures new'. Milton's early poetry is radical not only in its explicit political comments but in its underlying visionary utopianism. The joy of poetic composition is bound up with the exercise of the political imagination. The early poems in fact heralded a period of unprecedented utopian speculation.

Notes

1. JOHN MORRILL, *The Revolt of the Provinces* (London, 1976). For the view of 1630s England as strongly polarized between 'court' and 'country', see P.W. Thomas, 'Two Cultures? Court and Country under Charles II' in Conrad Russell (ed.), *Origins of the English Civil War* (London, 1973), pp. 168–93, and Christopher Hill, *Milton and the English Revolution* (London, 1977), pp. 13–21;

for one of the more temperate counter-statements, Robert Ashton, *The English Civil War: Conservatism and Revolution* (London, 1978); Ch. 1.

2. JOHN SPENCER HILL, *John Milton: Poet, Priest and Prophet. A Study of Divine Vocation in Milton's Poetry and Prose* (London, 1979), pp. 44–5.

3. THOMAS N. CORNS, 'Milton's Quest for Respectability', *MLR* 77 (1982): 769–79.

4. See, for example, Joseph A. Wittreich, Jr. 'Milton's *Areopagitica*: Its Isocratic and Ironic Contexts', *Milton Studies* 4 (1972): 101–15.

5. *Diary of John Rous*, ed. M.A.E. Green (London: Camden Soc., 1856), p. 19.

6. *Calendar of State Papers Venetian* (1636–39), p. 79.

7. On Italian influence see Blair Worden, 'Classical Republicanism and the Puritan Revolution' in *History and Imagination: Essays in Honor of Hugh Trevor-Roper*, ed. Hugh Lloyd-Jones *et al.* (London, 1981), pp. 184, 190–1, and Zera S. Fink, *The Classical Republicans* (Evanston, 1945), pp. 90ff.

8. GEORGE HAKEWILL, *An Apologie or Declaration of the Power and Providence of God* (2nd edn, London, 1630), pp. 252–4; John Jonston, *An History of the Constancy of Nature* (London, 1657), pp. 67ff. (Jonston's book was first published in Latin in 1632.)

9. PAUL CHRISTIANSON, *Reformers and Babylon: English Apocalyptic Visions from the Reformation to the Eve of the Civil War* (Toronto, Buffalo and London, 1978), pp. 124–9; Francis Quarles, *Works* ed. A.B. Grosart, 3 vols. (Edinburgh, 1880–1), 3: 230–2.

10. On the severing of contacts with the Continent see H.R. Trevor-Roper, *Archbishop Laud 1573–1645* (2nd edn, London, 1962), pp. 197ff.

11. W.H. PHELPS, 'The Date of Ben Jonson's Death', *N&O* 225 (1980): 146–9.

12. E.K. BROADUS, *The Laureateship* (Oxford, 1921), pp. 53–7.

13. BEN JONSON, *Works*, ed. C.H. Herford and P. and E. Simpson, 11 vols (Oxford, 1925–52), 11:443.

14. The Cambridge poet Clement Paman published an elegy in *Jonsonus Virbius* and two elegies for King survive in manuscript though they were not published: Bodleian MS. Rawl. poet. 147, fols. 146–7, 147–51. There is another elegy on King, by Thomas Booth, in the same manuscript, fols. 61–2. I am indebted to Fram Dinshaw for these references.

15. Cf. HAROLD BLOOM, *The Anxiety of Influence* (London, 1973), pp. 11, 27.

16. *Iusta Edovardo King Naufrago* (Cambridge, 1638). sig. F2r. The English elegies are conveniently reproduced in Joseph Anthony Wittreich, Jr, *Visionary Poetics: Milton's Tradition and his Legacy* (San Marino, 1979), pp. 279ff. On numerological unity in the collection see Alastair Fowler, ' "To Shepherd's Ear": The Form of Milton's *Lycidas*' in *Silent Poetry: Essays in Numerological Analysis*, ed. Alastair Fowler (London, 1970), pp. 171, 181n., and on *Lycidas* as a critique of the other poems, Wittreich, pp. 89ff. One elegist compared King to Virbius (*Iusta Edovardo King*, sig. E4r).

17. JOHN CREASER, '*Lycidas*: The Power of Art', *Essays and Studies* 34: 134–5. Cf. Ellen Z. Lambert, *Placing Sorrow: A Study of the Pastoral Elegy Convention from Theocritus to Milton* (Chapel Hill, 1976), pp. 155ff.

18. FOWLER, 'To Shepherd's Ear'; on the rhyme-scheme see also Wittreich, *Visionary Poetics*, pp. 167–84, who shows some previously unsuspected regularities.

19. F.T. PRINCE, *The Italian Element in Milton's Verse* (Oxford, 1954), pp. 71–88.

20. J. MARTIN EVANS, 'Lycidas, Daphnis, and Gallus' in John Carey (ed.), *English Renaissance Studies: Presented to Dame Helen Gardner* (Oxford, 1980), pp. 22–44.

21. *The Letany of John Bastwicke* (London, 1637), p. 6; Hugh Trevor-Roper, *Archbishop Laud 1573–1645* (2nd edn, London, 1961), pp. 205–10.

22. *Iusta Edovardo King*, p. 17.

23. F.S. SIEBERT, *Freedom of the Press in England* (Urbana, 111, 1952), pp. 142ff.; F.B. Williams, Jr, 'The Laudian Imprimatur', *Library*, 5th series, 15 (1960), pp. 96–104; Christianson, *Reformers and Babylon*, pp. 136ff.

24. WILLIAM BROWNE, *Poems*, ed. G. Goodwin, 2 vols, (London, 1894), I: xxv.

25. On these apocalyptic echoes see Wittreich, *Visionary Poetics*, pp. 137ff.

26. D.S. BERKELEY, *Inwrought with Figures Dim: A Reading of Milton's 'Lycidas'* (The Hague, Paris, 1974), pp. 73ff, 197–8. Interestingly, the contrasts between Christ and Peter, and between different kinds of ecclesiastical vessel, are developed by Sir William Mure: see his *Works* ed. W. Tough, 2 vols, Edinburgh and London, Scottish Text Society, 1898, I, p. 305.

27. Nicholas Tyacke, 'Puritanism, Arminianism, and Counter-Revolution' in *The Origins of the English Civil War*, ed. Conrad Russell (London, 1973), pp. 135, 141–2. On Prynne's links with Bastwicke, and strategies for circumventing the censorship, see Stephen Foster, *Notes from the Caroline Underground: Alexander Leighton, the Puritan Triumvirate, and the Laudian Reaction to Nonconformity* (Hamden, Conn., 1978), esp. pp. 37, 42, 50.

28. CLAY HUNT, *'Lycidas' and the Italian Critics* (New Haven and London, 1979), pp. 143–4; Berkeley, *Inwrought with Figures Dim*, p. 70.

29. *Calendar of State Papers Venetian, 1636–9*, p. 273.

30. DRUMMOND, *Poems and Prose*, ed. R.H. MacDonald (Edinburgh and London, 1976), pp. 182–3. On Milton's interest in Drummond see Christopher Hill, *Milton and the English Revolution* (London, 1977), p. 490.

31. GREVILLE, *Mustapha*, V.iii.92–3. A reference to 'voluntarye servitude' in the next sentence of Drummond's pamphlet indicates that he recognizes the affinities between Greville and La Boetie.

6 *Areopagitica:* Subjectivity and the Moment of Censorship*

FRANCIS BARKER

Francis Barker's *The Tremulous Private Body: Essays on Subjection* was, when it appeared in 1984, one of the first literary-critical responses to what Barker himself calls 'the enormously suggestive work on discourse, power and the body carried out by Michel Foucault' (p. ix) during the late 1960s and 70s, and which, at least in its emphasis on the history of sexuality, Barker properly recognizes as a development out of Freud. The idea of the body as a site of a radically new kind of subjectivity is, in this elastic series of meditations on seventeenth-century 'texts', developed by way of Pepys's *Diary*, some Jacobean tragedies (especially *Hamlet*), Descartes's *Discourse on Method*, Rembrandt's *The Anatomy Lesson of Dr Nicolaas Tulp*, Marvell's 'To his Coy Mistress'. For Barker, modernity means the coming into focus of the body as a site of subjectivity, 'at the moment when the division between the public and the private is constructed in its modern form,' (p. 14) in the middle of the seventeenth century; and the eclectic series of objects that are thus combined into what Foucault might have called a 'discursive formation' is typical of the argumentative freedom distinctive of Foucault's legacy. The essay on *Areopagitica* draws less on theories of the modern body than on another strain in Foucault's thought, the critique of institutional control and surveillance of the individual, here represented by censorship; and because all of Barker's theoretical models are subsumed by the classic Marxist hypothesis of the transformation from feudalism to capitalism, and of the negative consequences of capitalism's product, the privatized bourgeois subject, Milton's appeal to the Long Parliament cannot be read as a classic document of liberalism, but rather as an instance of

---

* Reprinted from *The Tremulous Private Body: Essays on Subjection* (Methuen & Co. Ltd, London, New York, 1984.

the 'more directly ideological control implanted in the new subjectivity' (pp. 46–47).

And as for regulating the Presse, let no man think to have the honour of
advising ye better than your selves have done in that Order publisht next before
this, that no book be printed unless the Printers and the Author's name, or at
least the Printers be register. Those which otherwise come forth, if they be
found mischievous and libellous, the fire and the executioner will be the
timeliest and the most effectual remedy, that mans prevention can use.

(*Areopagitica*, 2: 569)

It is certainly an index of the depth of the crisis that these words, apart
from a few lines serving as an *envoi*, conclude what is otherwise regarded
as one of the great texts written against censorship. But that a writing
which sets itself that task should end by handing discourse over to the
executioner is only fully a paradox when viewed from the idealist
standpoint of a plenitude of human speech. It is skewed when seen from
the perspective of the principle of rarefaction which governs the actual
distribution of human discourse. A full speech stands above its
conditions, sufficient to itself, at once adequately grounded in its own
meanings and at the same time aspiring to, if not already extant in, a
universal and sacred realm of independent and discrete truths. But the
discursive position which wishes to escape the antinomies (purely
internal to a certain historicism) between the universal and the historical
will have to recognize that even where discourse is globally implicative it
is none the less locally relational, hollowed by the *strategic* character of its
deployment. For this reason to contemplate *Areopagitica* as a significant
document of some 'human freedom' would only be to assuage a
particular restlessness in respect of the truth, and then only
momentarily. To the extent that it has been thought in the past that
Milton conceived of liberty and censorship as antithesis, it is now
necessary to take his text's will to freedom at a little less than its face
value, and to exercise a critical decoding rather than the more familiar
appreciative summary. Discursively, *Areopagitica* operates to call into
being a new state-form, and to inscribe there a novel citizen-subject. And
it does this despite its argument. This is not to say that its substance is
beside the point; on the contrary, censorship was a decisive experience of
the seventeenth century, which has even managed to cover its own
traces and disappear from the standard histories of the literature of the
period which are silent on the subject; none the less, *Areopagitica* is a
document which arranged its arguments, its rhetoric and its metaphors –
its utterance – among and across relations which it inscribes within itself
without ever making them the evident object of its arguments or the

manifest content of its speech. To say that these distinctions operate behind the back of the text, or as its unconscious, would be to risk too far the temptation of a metaphysic of depth which we have been at pains to avoid so far, despite the fact that it is the history of its emergence which we are tracing here. But the transactions of the text, in the *discursive* register, are in a real sense unknown to the text itself.

While an anecdote (although in no way trivial for being such) will not by itself deprive *Areopagitica* of its 'literary' truth and return it to its discourse, it will serve to indicate a pathway to the issue: Milton was never opposed to censorship, in fact we know that in 1651 he served as a licenser of news books, a state censor. If this only signals, as many have argued, that Milton was prepared to make a division in the field of discourse between those daily words too promiscuous not to come under the scrutiny of the governing authority and the graver products of 'the industry of a life wholly dedicated to studious labours' (2:489–90) (and thus, no doubt, more docile), this is at least to have dislodged his pamphlet from its universality. This relocation can be further effected by replacing the text within the preceding development of the means of policing discourse which the office of state for which he worked inherited. From the early part of the previous century through to what was to be one of the last executive acts of the Caroline government, the authorities established, elaborated and consolidated increasingly fierce and attentive measures to bring the printing and distribution of books under their direct or delegated control. The detail of this history is accessible elsewhere, but here some description of its main tendency will serve to point out the structural contrast between Milton's text and the developments anterior to it. Whichever aspect of the mechanism of control we examine, whether it be the trade-off by which the Crown granted the Stationers' Company a virtual monopoly on printing in return for the acceptance of overt or implicit responsibility for regulating the issue of its presses, or the more formal provisions for pre-publication licensing by officers of Church and state, in either case the period saw a strengthening and increasing sophistication of the censoring machine. From the Elizabethan Injunctions of 1559 to the Star Chamber decree of 11 January 1637 which provided for a largely professional censorship dealing with printed matter under separate categories, procedures were built up to ensure an ever more vigilant and pervasive control: the scope of materials coming within their purview was progressively widened, as were the means of enforcement, until the censorship, in these corporal times, had at its disposal an almost unlimited power to punish. By the time that the Long Parliament abolished Star Chamber and the other prerogative courts, a high wall of prohibition, surveillance and punishment had been built up around the printed word in whose supervision the government was prepared to invest enormous quantities of time, labour and expertise.

It would be wrong, however, to conclude that with the accession of Parliamentary forces this machinery was dismantled. For a period after the abolition of the Caroline executive courts there was a brief and unprecedented freedom of the press in which printing shops and their products proliferated. But within a few years, shaken by the explosion of written discourse which attended the breakdown of censorship, the same Parliament was soon enacting its own regulatory measures, including the Order of 14 June 1643, against which Milton wrote *Areopagitica*. The reanimated censoring machine – which was met with widespread and sometimes armed popular resistance – was, in its essential outline, identical with the Star Chamber provisions. Although the personnel was changed and Parliamentary appointees substituted for the clerics and other delegates of the Caroline government, and the prerogative Crown authority to license was not reestablished, the machinery itself was refined still further. Now nine categories of books were designated, and an even more precisely organized battery of licensers established to deal with them.

A small but decisive incision in this structure is offered by *Areopagitica*. A feature common to all the preceding measures, whatever the degree of complexity of the censoring apparatus or the poignancy of its disposable violence, but which separates Milton's text from them, is that they each place the moment of state intervention before that of publication. *Areopagitica*, though also a call for censorship (slightly reduced in scope), places that moment in the production and distribution of discourse *after* it has 'come forth.' The pre-publication licensing of the Tudor, Stuart and early Parliamentary measures are those of a pre-emptive state designing to stop the publication of what were called, in a phrase surviving from the reign of Henry VIII, 'naughty books'; its powers were vengeful ones which bore down on the transgressions it had itself failed to prevent. The powers of the Miltonic 'provisions,' however, are essentially deterrent (although also punitive). They offer to the discoursing subject the image of an eventuality of punishment which will occur if the offending book comes out, while she or he remains 'free' to publish it. This crucial difference between the Miltonic text and the history of censorship which goes before it (and, indeed, after it, for *Areopagitica*'s proposals were not enacted immediately) encodes two distinctly separate versions of the state and its relation to social life. The pre-Miltonic state acknowledges its existence as state, but one could say, without investing the state with a spurious benevolence, that it also assumes an essential continuity between itself and the subjects it incorporates: the body of the king, the place of representation, and the correspondences of kinship, power and sense, are coterminous. This state knows no limits because in theory nothing is outside its domain. It is permissive only in the ungenerous sense that it seeks positively to supervise the production and the contents of discourse. Its paternalism is given in the fact that it assumes the father's role of a real and metaphysical authority which is all-pervasive, backed up by the angry recompense of punishment. But in the Miltonic 'state' – that set of relations marked out in *Areopagitica* – it is already possible to detect the outline of that modern settlement which founds itself on a separation of realms between the public arena of the state apparatus and another domain of civil life. Here a new liberty is encoded, although it is but a negative one. The subject, now emerging as a private citizen although not legally named as such in a constitution which is, to this day, unwritten, or – rather – 'inscribed elsewhere', may do as it pleases up to the point of transgression where its activity will be arrested by the agents of the apparatus who patrol the frontier between the two spaces.

But lest it be thought that this is simply a step along an even and uncomplex path from the old tyranny to a new and modern freedom, it is important to emphasize the extent to which what is proposed in *Areopagitica* represents a fresh form of control.

What is to become the meagre political insubordination of a classical liberalism can be discerned even at this stage when Milton's text defines liberty as what is in any case the basis of its own political practice: not the positive freedom of a just order, but the *ex post facto* redress of grievances. And as he says, the attack on licensing is not intended to introduce licence. On the contrary all of Milton's descriptions of social life emphasize the stability, maturity and sobriety of the English nation. Far from the 'untaught and irreligious gadding rout' (2:547) which a preemptive censorship must assume the people to be, they are in fact characterized by a remarkable degree of that *self-discipline* which, along with other qualities associated with it, is to become the linchpin of a move articulated by the text from the unmediated and overt violence of the older settlement to a more indirectly ideological control implanted in the new subjectivity. The text defines the principal problem for government, the 'great art', as discerning 'in what the law is to bid restraint and punishment, and in what things persuasion only is to work' (2:527), and in a similar way, to censure the population 'for a giddy, vicious and ungrounded people' would be 'to the disrepute of our ministers' whose 'exortations, and the benefiting of their hearers' are to be among the central means of securing the required tranquillity in what would otherwise be 'an unprincipled, unedifyed, and laic rabble' (2:537). The decisive moment of control is now to be not so clearly the sanction of punishment, as the inner discipline, the unwritten law, of the new subjection: for 'under pittance and prescription, and compulsion, what were virtue but a name, what praise could be then due to well-doing, what grammercy to be sober, just or continent?' (2:527). The state succeeds in penetrating to the very heart of the subject, or more accurately, in pre-constituting that subject as one which is already internally disciplined, censored, and thus an effective support of the emergent pattern of domination. As Milton reminds us again and again, the new subject becomes the location of the new drama of individual conscience which 'doth make cowards of us all,' or, as Hamlet might have said had he reflected in a different language on his political situation, ascertains each of us severally in obedience to a sovereignty whose head we dare not thus cut off. Conscience, assisted by that private reason, deliberation and judgement with which *Areopagitica* invests the bourgeois citizen, enters in the text into an essentially single battle with temptation (amongst whose 'objects of lust' (2:527), as Pepys discovered, are certain books) and in doing so interiorizes conflicts and dynamics which are newly encoded as belonging to subjectivity rather than to the social exterior.

It would, then, be a misplaced reception of *Areopagitica*'s separation of the old kingdom that succumbed to a euphoria of early liberation remembered (although bourgeois culture's self-universalization doubtless accounts for the timelessness of the text's alleged pertinence). At stake in Milton's call for 'civil liberty' is a control which is in some ways more profound than when such legislated or unlegislated rights are missing. In the settlement which begins to impinge here, the state secures its overall penetration on the basis of an apparent withdrawal and limitation of its pertinent domain: Milton accepts that in the realm of discourse at least, atheism and blasphemy might continue to be the state's concern, but allots the rest to the individual subject who 'searches, meditates, is industrious, and likely consults and confers with his judicious friends' (2:532), in short, to civil society. But by demarcating the public space of the state's competence from the private realm of individual freedoms, it has secured its domination there too, by securing the recto of its public verso. This is why *Areopagitica* remains the text of a new power despite its agonistic rhetoric of liberty. In addition, it is important that the essence of this power lies as much in the line of division between the public and the private as in the substantive contents of what lies to either side of it. It is not that in the establishment of a domain of public authority and another area of private freedom, domination has been confined to one, and liberation released into the other, but that the division itself is the very form of the new power, grounded as much in the apparent freedom of even the choices allowed by Milton's benign pluralism as in its more overt controls. It is counter-intuitive and defies every instinct of common sense to insist that the inception of specific and more or less well-defined freedoms – 'free consciences and Christian liberties' (2:554) – is the effect of a powerful new dominion; but, without impugning the sacrifices of the women and men who gave their lives for these freedoms, that is the outcome. In the division between the two spheres is encoded an essential settlement which allots civil liberty to the subject only on condition that it is indeed *civil*, with all the well-ordered Roman and juridical connotations which seventeenth-century classicism, to be reinforced in the eighteenth century, could add to the ideological registers of that word. The horror with which Milton contemplates the logical consequence of the principle of licensing books when he remarks that it would necessitate the extension of control to every area of social life, to all discourse and representation, all styles of dress, each country dance, every guitar in every bedroom (while it foreshadows the absolute *disciplinary* surveillance which will be consolidated later) is now counterposed to the intrinsic sobriety of the people which argues against the need for detailed state control. That sobriety is the condition, in the sense both of a central feature of, and a condition of granting, even the provisional civil liberty envisaged by the text.

A few moments with the *Diary* of Philip Henslowe show that despite the firm attachment of authors' names to Jacobean play-texts today, the actual construction of the works, in so far as it was a commercial enterprise carried out largely by jobbing writers whose remuneration for odd additional scenes, revision and initial composition is recorded in Henslowe's accounts of payment, was also a collaborative process. The firmness of the attachment of any author's name to text, let alone that of a single author who becomes, thus, fully and singly, the subject of that text, had then by no means an equal fixity with that which has been constructed subsequently, often by dint of elaborate and frequently wasted canonical scholarship. In Milton's discourse on discourse, however, an important step in the establishment of that fixity, and that writing subjectivity, is taken. *Areopagitica* twice refers approvingly to the Order of Parliament passed immediately before the licensing provisions against which it argues, which provided for the registration on publication of the names of author and printer, and for the protection of copyright vested, for the first time in English law, in the author. Although measures fully resembling modern copyright were only enacted by the so-called Statute of Anne at the beginning of the eighteenth century, the Miltonic evocation of the early measures is of great ideological significance. *Areopagitica* marks a shift in representative and central discourse from the performed writing of the early seventeenth-century stage to the more evidently 'written' writing of the later period: a transition from collaboration (of composition and performance) to individual production, and from visuality to script. And in the new discursivity, in which the text is fully in place for the first time, an essential relation of the author to that text is a property relation.

Of course, in order to preserve the idealism of *Areopagitica* it is necessary to construct an imaginary division within discourse (formally identical to that opening between body and soul) so that Truth, which Milton goes out of his way to insist should not be 'monopolised and traded in by tickets and statutes, and standards . . . like our broad cloths and our wool packs' (2:535–6), can be spoken of separately from the book-commodity which is thus left free, by rhetorical sleight of hand, to enter the market-place. At the same time as the discoursing subject is newly confirmed in the domain of private liberty, the material writing of discourse also enters the 'free' exchange of civil society. Truth, the conveniently ideal form, hovers, naturally, above it.

The marks of this economy of discourse are not, however, as emphatic in the text as those defining the conditions of that discoursing subject, who must now – in a phrase which would have been resonant for Pepys – 'in a private condition, write' (*Areopagitica*, 2:486). Whether it be 'him who from his private house wrote that discourse to the Parliament of *Athens*' (2:489), that 'private man' (2:522) to whom Plato forbade poets to read before their verse had been scrutinized by authority, or simply the phrase which adequately positions the subject in relation to the objects and the destination of discourse – 'When a man writes *to* the world' (2:532) – in each case the discursive location is clearly enunciated, and in addition the judicious and rational discrimination, imputed to the new subject in general, is the more insistently emphasized when it is overtly the subject of writing (or of reading). In seeking to extract the discoursing subject from state control, 'leaving it to each ones conscience to read or to lay by' (2:501), the text ever more clearly hands the subject over to that deeper control which we have already evoked. In doing so it signals the more graphically the profound implication of seventeenth-century discourse in the machinery of censorship, and in particular the imbrication of the founding moment of bourgeois discursivity, articulated as a socially hegemonic form, with that machinery.

That censorship was a constitutive experience for the seventeenth century – and for ourselves – needs stressing in view of the deletion of the entire problem from the history of writing. But if it is hardly possible to overemphasize its importance for the texts of the period, this should not be taken to refer only to the gross instances (although they should be identified and understood) where the censor's pen has left gaps in the text, but also to the *fullness* of the period's discourse. It has taken a historian writing on literature to notice what literary criticism has been studiously blind to. Christopher Hill shows that by a certain moment an entire literary mode – pastoral – could function as a set of coded symbols by which political statements could be enunciated in a form that would allow them to evade the censorship: with sufficient care in the manipulation of the stock conventions it could always be claimed that the poem was only about nymphs and shepherds after all. And centuries later literary 'critics' would agree. But this evasive coding is itself only a relatively simple and external instance of discourse being conditional on censorship not in its elisions but in its substantial articulation. In a still profounder sense the very structure of *all* bourgeois enunciation is governed by its relation to censorship as a determinant condition.

If this subjectivity is sketched in the seventeenth century, although perhaps not fully and ultimately consolidated as a phenomenon then, it is of crucial importance that its discourse, and the discourses in which it emerges, are censored ones. It is an essential link between the inner being of the subject, that interiority for which the pre-bourgeois polity had no role, and the outer dimension of the state. While censorship is a state function, an exterior apparatus of control, in so far as the domain it polices is the production, circulation and exchange of discourses, it is one that reaches into the subject itself. It thus has a double function here, at once representative and substantive: representative in as much as it stands cross-sectionally for a whole ensemble of other changes brought about by the long process of the bourgeois revolution in the relationship between state and civil society, state and citizen, and for the opening-up of that division, a caesura missing from the Jacobean spectacle, or if present, only so in promissory form; but substantive in as much as it is the articulating mode of the bourgeois subject in discourse. When Milton's persona replied peremptorily to an imagined opponent 'The State Sir . . . The State shall be my governors, but not my critics' (2:534), he offered a more consequential hostage to historical fortune than he imagined.

7 The Intelligible Flame*

James Grantham Turner

Turner's study of Milton and paradisal sexuality came about accidentally, during an attempt to write the history of libertinism; in a few deft strokes, he was to have defined the 'Christian tradition' against which emerged the secular and philosophical lusts of Rochester, Casanova and de Sade. This naive model could not survive the first reading of Milton's sulphurous and passionate divorce tracts, themselves branded 'libertine' by horrified contemporaries. Rake and 'Puritan' shared the same contradictions, the same unstable fusion of hypermasculine scorn for the female 'clog' and furious nostalgia for the sexual bond, promoted to the 'prime institution' of human identity. Milton recognized, quite explicitly, that the 'brood of Belial' will rejoice to find their own debaucheries sanctioned by these tracts, sweeping aside the fragile distinction of Liberty and Licence; he even declared, with ill-disguised envy, that promiscuous men 'by reason of their bold accustoming prove most successfull in their matches'. When Turner began this study in the early 1980s the divorce tracts were relatively neglected, having been treated as footnotes to *Paradise Lost* or episodes in intellectual history; it seemed innovative to treat both the tracts and the poem as emotive poetic discourses of sexuality and masculinity. Nevertheless, 'The Intelligible Flame' offers little new in the way of methodology or explicit theory. Compared with, say, the lighter touch of Annabel Patterson (next extract) it seems too literal-minded, too ready to extrapolate from the text to a developmental biography in which the same erotic themes are confronted, first in the 'ugly' or violent polemic and then in the 'mature' or harmonious epic. Still, three more-or-less dialectical and materialist assumptions can be discerned here. First, that phenomena manifest

---

* Reprinted from *One Flesh: Paradisal Marriage and Sexual Relations in the Age of Milton* (Oxford: Clarendon Press, 1987).

themselves most fully in contradiction. Second, that the text (whether literary or expository) signifies through its *working*, its operation or performance of an ideology expressed as much by gesture and weight as by idea. (At moments the divorce tracts carry this to an extreme, 'working' like the muscles of a face or a badly sealed bottle of plums.) And third, that the aesthetic is irreducibly political. For Milton, this means that the polemic 1640s should not be seen as an embarrassing distraction from his immortal verse, but as the crucible of his life work. The divorce issue, exploding with the Civil War, forced him to treat a personal episode as a national crisis, and it plunged him into a total engagement with the story of Genesis, which he was half inclined to dismiss as 'remote' or to convert into Platonic myth. Without the divorce tracts, Milton might have produced a turgid *Arthuriad* or *Cromwelliad* instead of *Paradise Lost*.

Patterning from the beginning: exegesis and the vision of perfect marriage

Milton approached the question of divorce with a strange combination of harsh practicality and exalted idealism. Though he despised 'empty dreams' and 'Utopian politics', his proposals are matched not in the tentative and circumscribed suggestions of his Protestant forebear Bucer, but in the Paradisal fantasies of the Spiritual Libertines and the divorce laws of More's Utopia. He bases his doctrine on fallen weakness and the impossibility of gaining 'lost Paradise', and yet he insists that unless a marriage recaptures the Paradisal bliss 'in some proportion' it is not a marriage at all but 'a daring phantasm, a meer toy of terror' – and should be immediately annulled.[1] Milton remains profoundly divided between two models of marital perfection: Old Testament patriarchy, and the inspiring but elusive ideal gained from immersion in the first chapters of Genesis.

Though Milton's proposals were denounced as the work of a scandalous libertine, their declared intention is to restore the institution of marriage by reclaiming its original essence as defined by Genesis – a process initiated by Christ himself. *Tetrachordon*, for example, begins by explicitly relating his own method to Christ's quotation of Genesis in Matthew 19:6: 'it will undoubtedly be safest, fairest, and most with our obedience, to enquire, as our Saviours direction is, how it was in the beginning'. To clarify the original state of creation will restore, to a degenerate age, a sense of 'the true dignity of man . . . especially in this prime institution of Matrimony, wherein his native pre-eminence ought most to shine' (2:586–7). Returning to the beginning thus provides not only the first principles of historical interpretation and Scriptural exegesis, but also a sense of primacy and loftiness suitable for the opening of a treatise on what is here defined as the highest form of human life. Milton claims the supreme authority of 'our Saviours direction' because Christ too, confronted with a marital problem by the Pharisees, had solved it by turning to the 'first institution' of marriage in Genesis; Deuteronomy may be an important support of the edifice of divorce law, but Genesis is its main pillar. Nevertheless *The Doctrine and Discipline of Divorce* and *Tetrachordon* aim to demolish the law of indissoluble marriage that took its authority from the very words that Christ spoke to the Pharisees on that occasion – 'they are no more twain, but one flesh; what therefore God hath joined together, let no man put asunder'.

Milton recognizes that 'the first institution will be objected to have ordain'd marriage inseparable' (2:244), but he answers not by abandoning the scrutiny of Genesis but by redefining that original institution more stringently – by seizing upon its first principle ('it is not good that man should be alone') and subordinating all subsequent purposes to that one. (Luther used a similar method, but he chose the procreative 'increase and multiply' as his master-verse.) Thus Milton will maintain 'that marriage, if we pattern from the beginning as our Saviour bids, was not properly the remedy of lust, but the fulfilling of conjugall love and helpfulness' (2:250); he will uphold Christ's method of 'patterning after the beginning' even if it means wresting Christ's own words into a contrary meaning.

Milton begins this apparently impossible reversal by co-opting the Saviour into his own dynamic and emotive vision. Christ and the 'adventuring' exegete are presented in identical terms, as liberators and healers, agents of warmth and life: Christ's words have been 'congeal'd into a stony rigor'; Milton's new reading will 'soften and dispell rooted and knotty sorrowes', and so enable his countrymen, unlike the stubborn Jews, 'to follow freely the charming pipe of him who sounded and proclaim'd liberty and reliefe to all distresses'. The heroic pamphleteer will 'ease and set free' the minds of men from the 'needlesse thraldome' of a bad marriage, and 'lend us the clue that windes out of this labyrinth of servitude' (2:237–41). He even claims that his legislation for divorce could lead the way back to Paradise, or establish contemporary marriage as the Paradise within: it would 'restore the much wrong'd and over-sorrow'd state of matrimony, not onely to those mercifull and life-giving remedies of *Moses*, but, as much as may be, to that serene and blisfull condition it was in at the beginning' (2:240). The crucial phrase, however, is 'as much as may be.'

Milton's interpretation of Genesis hesitates between optimism and pessimism. The story of the fall provides not only an authoritative (though cryptic) definition of human nature, but a 'way to perfection'; in our efforts to retrace that arduous route, however, we also discover the limits of human potential. Analysing Genesis will reveal the relative depth and strength of our most powerful constitutive drives, and this in turn will teach us how far we can expect to fulfil them. So the chronological order of God's words (as Milton reconstructs it) proves that the soul's longing for companionship is 'more deeply rooted' in human nature than is sexual desire, 'even in the faultless innocence', and must likewise take precedence in our marriage-laws; Milton's whole argument, that mental incompatibility should be grounds for divorce, is based on the primacy of this 'intelligible flame, not in Paradise to be resisted . . . which if it were so needful before the fall, when man was much more perfect in himself, how much more is it needful now against all the sorrows and casualties of life' (2:251–2). But this comparison of the fallen and the unfallen state may also teach us our weakness, and we might therefore conclude that we should *not* try to conform to the 'first institutions' of Paradise: 'while man and woman were both perfet to each other, there needed no divorce', but after the fall it was an act of mercy to establish divorce in the Mosaic law – and can the New Testament law of charity be less merciful than the Old? 'The Gospel, indeed, tending ever to that which is perfetest, aim'd at the restorement of all things as they were in the beginning'; but 'if . . . marriage must be as in the beginning, the persons that marry must be such as then were' (2:665–6). Using Genesis to solve the problem of divorce brings out a flaw in the scheme of redemption, for the impossibly high demands of the 'way to perfection' contradict the mildness and mercy of the Redeemer.

Milton solves this dilemma by making a crucial distinction, a dichotomy that reflects the tension in his own mind between the hard realist and the Utopian idealist, the agitator and the poet. 'In our intentions and desires' we must pursue the full Edenic ideal, but 'in execution' we must fight for such regulations 'as reason and present nature can bear' (2:666). In the inner realm we can still try to be 'persons such as then were', but in practice we must recover and obey the true spirit of the Mosaic law, to save us from the rage and exhaustion of the failed idealist. If God had meant us to imitate the life-long marital commitment of Adam and Eve, Milton argues, He would have said so in the books of law; instead the description of Paradisal marriage is 'set . . . out of place in another world at such a distance from tne whole Law, and not once mention'd there', and cannot be interpreted as a command. The story of the fall – hitherto assumed to provide the most intimate and authoritative definition of human nature – is now described as remote and other-worldly. In the case of a bad marriage we should not try to live up to the Edenic ideal: it is more humanly realistic 'to follow rather what moral *Sinai* prescribes equal to our strength, than fondly to think within our strength all that lost Paradise relates' (II:316). 'Strength', which elsewhere in the divorce tracts refers to the passive endurance of an irritating marriage, here describes the ability to live up to an imaginative response to the original text – an attempt which must inevitably crash against the practical limitations of fallen humanity.

But by recommending a pragmatic renunciation of the Paradise within, Milton does not abandon the idealism he derives from Genesis. By restoring the Mosaic divorce for hatred, which allowed for post-lapsarian imperfections, English legislators would paradoxically revive God's original conception of marriage, since spiritual compatibility would then be once again the primary factor. Moses may have enshrined fallen weakness in his written law, while letting the 'supernatural law' of lifelong fidelity 'vanish in silence . . . ev'n as the reason of it vanisht within Paradise', but he did this precisely *because* the bond of love is 'ancienter, and deeper engrav'n in blameless nature' (2:330). The text of 'lost Paradise' is thus both 'vanisht' and ever-present. Moses's legislation, and Milton's heroic endeavours to restore it, rest on a central contradiction: they will lead us back to the Paradisal happiness by pushing to its logical conclusion the fact that it is beyond our strength ever to return there.

Once this emanational hierarchy is established, the sexual act itself may become 'legitimate' and receive 'a human qualification'. Physical consummation is thus admitted among the ends of marriage, albeit grudgingly, when it is 'an effect of conjugal love . . . proceeding as it ought from intellective principles'.[2] If the sexual act is initiated by bodily passion or 'sensitive force' it is 'at best but an animal excretion, but more truly worse and more ignoble than that mute kindlyness among the herds and flocks'. But Milton is prepared to imagine a truly 'human' form of sexuality, 'holy' and 'pure', in which the delights of mental compatibility blend or flow over into the physical act of love – 'which act being kindly and voluntarie, as it ought, the Apostle . . . call'd . . . *Benevolence*, intimating the original thereof to be in the understanding and the will' (2:609, 270). Animal physicality can thereby be subsumed into the voluntary realm – an ideal that Augustine, and mainstream commentators after him, could only embody in fantastic speculations about the intercourse that Adam and Eve might have enjoyed if they had not fallen before their wedding night. Here it is the common expositors who locate Edenic sexuality 'in another world', and Milton who insists on establishing it in the present. But in the divorce tracts these tributes always come backhandedly, in concessional or contrastive clauses whose main target is the infamy of 'despis'd' copulation, compulsory 'benevolence' with a hated spouse.

The characteristic movement of the divorce tracts is one of oscillation: Milton ventures hesitantly into the complex implications of voluntary sexuality, only to take frequent refuge in the simplicities of dualism and ascetic denunciation of the flesh. Thus he sometimes assumes a wide gulf between sex and 'conversation', the social intercourse of properly compatible lovers, but in the next breath will bring them closer again: 'why then shall divorce be granted for want of bodily performance, and not for want of fitnes to intimate conversation, when as corporal benevolence cannot in any human fashion bee without this?' (2:609). Occasionally he goes even further: when he complains that the inexperienced suitor 'may easily chance to meet, if not with a body impenetrable, yet often with a minde to all other due conversation inaccessible' (2:250), he is assuming that sex is itself a form of conversation, and when he upholds the true love of male and female against the claims of male friendship made by the 'crabbed' and 'rustic' Augustine, he even suggests that the 'conversation' of the ideal couple will rekindle their sexual ardour: 'there is one society of grave friendship, and another amiable and attractive society of conjugal love, besides the deed of procreation, which of it self soon cloies, and is despis'd, unless it bee *cherisht and re-incited* with a pleasing conversation'. He even claims that the wife's adultery could make her a better companion.[3] At such moments we glimpse, however tantalizingly, a Milton who prides himself on his expansiveness and urbanity (neither 'crabbed' nor 'rustic'), and who projects into marriage an almost libertine fusion of erotic excitement and mental life.

The context for this attack on Augustine shows how vulnerable and defensive Milton was in this area. The coarse 'narrow-Augustinian' opinion had been used in the anonymous *Answer to . . . the Doctrine and Discipline of Divorce* (1644) to challenge Milton's ideal of 'conversation'. We should recall that 'conversation' was not only a general term for social intercourse but also a legal and colloquial term for copulation; the Answerer tries to trap Milton between these two meanings. On the one hand he snickers lewdly at Milton's claim – admittedly an astonishing one – that the experienced libertine is better than the sober man at finding out whether a bashful fiancée is really 'fit for conversation'; on the other hand he reiterates Augustine's denigration of female companionship – marriage cannot have been constituted in Genesis by 'the solace and content in the gifts of the minde of one another only', for then God would have made a male friend out of the rib. The bond of marriage is not 'delectableness of converse', which women cannot so much provide, much less to 'speak Hebrew, Greek, Latine, and French, and dispute against the Canon law as well as you'; it is rather 'a pleasant conversation' in the purely sexual sense.[4]

John Milton

Female usurpation: the act of bondage

Milton's doctrine and discipline of divorce may be summarized as
follows: marriage must retain its pre-lapsarian bliss 'in some proportion',
and to do this it must not be grounded in mere procreation – whereby
woman becomes a department of the domestic economy, a kind of brood
mare – but in a 'mutual fitnes to the final causes of wedlock, help and
society', in a 'due conversation' suffused with erotic gestures of the sort
that pass between the lovers in the Song of Songs. (The husband should
lie between the breasts of his wife, comfort her with apples, and drink of
the juice of her pomegranate, while the wife, if 'mutual fitness' has any
meaning, will rejoice in the kisses of his mouth, and perfumes will blow
from her garden.) Without this 'cheerful society of wedlock' man is
incomplete – she is 'another selfe, a second self, a very self itself'; within
it every facet of life, even the bestial genitals, receives 'a human
qualification' (2:251, 600, 606).

It seems, then, that *humanitas* is only properly forged in the reciprocal
delight of compatible lovers. When this ideal relationship breaks down or
proves illusory, however, the 'manly' course – far manlier than private
despair and manlier even than sexual adventurism – is to fight for
divorce, to expel the female in a heroic gesture of separation that at one
point is even compared to the primal act of Creation itself. We should
therefore enquire how Milton reconciles the obligations of mutuality and
manliness, and how he conceives the reciprocal relation of the sexes – the
'most resembling unlikeness and most unlike resemblance' that alone can
generate true marital delight.

Milton was obviously very moved by the ideal of equality. In *Tetrachordon*
'prime Nature made us all equall', in *The Tenure of Kings and Magistrates*
'all men naturally were born free, being the image and resemblance of
God himself, and were by privilege above all, the creatures born to
command, and not to obey' (3:198), and in *Paradise Lose* Adam demands a
companion of the same species – for no 'societie . . . harmonie or true
delight' can exist between 'unequals' (8:383–4). In his earlier writings,
however, Milton seems uncertain whether to include females in the
species 'man'. He embraces the harsh Pauline interpretation of Genesis
('he not for her, but she for him') without the subsequent qualification,
that man is 'by' woman and does not exist without her. He seizes upon
one aspect of a complex, braided text – male supremacy – and forces
every other strand into compliance with the single principle he has
promoted.

Every mention of 'man' or 'him' in Scripture is thus interpreted by
Milton as referring not to *homo*, the human being, but to *vir*, the male as
opposed to the female. This gives a querulous, tight-lipped tone to his

exposition – the 'peevishness' that Virginia Woolf detected, less justly, in *Paradise Lost*.

Milton is divided between two conceptions of subordination. He recognizes, with contemporary marriage-theorists, that the relation of man and wife is an inequality 'tempered with equality': 'man is not to hold her as a servant, but receives her into a part of that empire which God proclaims him to, though not equally, yet largely, as his own image and glory; for it is no small glory to him, that a creature so like him, should be made subject to him'.[5] This is consistent with his approval of 'the woman's just appeal against wrong and servitude' in Roman law. Elsewhere, however, we hear nothing of this temperate and accountable authority: any derogation of masculine power, any lapse of female duty, which for Milton consists in the constant voluptuous manifestation of her own subordination, is denounced in the harsh language of extremism. Marriage to a less than perfect wife, as we have seen, is an 'intolerable wrong and servitude above the patience of man to bear', 'a league [not] of love [but] of bondage and indignity', 'an enthrallment to one who either cannot, or will not bee mutual'. Man must therefore 'acquitt himself to freedom' by divorce, for 'all men naturally were born free . . . to command and not to obey'; woman apparently was born to the reverse. It is not clear what distinguishes this from 'servitude', from which the wife is supposedly exempt.

Milton's trouble with subordination should be related to the neurotic fear of sexual pollution, thraldom, and emasculation expressed not only in the virginal philosophy of *Comus*,[6] and in his dramatizations of marital failure, but in his attacks on political enemies. In *Of Reformation* (1641), for example, he accuses the bishops of sexually corrupting the youth of England; true Liberty 'consists in manly and honest labours, in sobriety and rigorous honour to the Marriage Bed, which in both Sexes should be bred up from chast hopes to loyal Enjoyments', but the bishops concentrate their designs on boys, conspiring to 'effeminate us' and to 'despoile us both of *manhood* and *grace*'.[7] In the works of the later 1640s and 1650s, the dangers of effeminacy are discovered not just in the narrow area of illicit sexuality but in the household and the state. Those books of the *History of Britain* written during his first marriage, as Edward Le Comte has shown, quiver with a coarse dismissive disdain of female rule that sometimes leads Milton to contradict his own sources.[8] In his anti-monarchist tracts he mocks Charles I's attempts to perform 'masculin coition' upon Parliament, and sneers at him for praising Henrietta Maria 'in straines that come almost to Sonnetting': this shows 'how great mischeif and dishonour hath befall'n to Nations under the Government of effeminate and Uxorious Magistrates, who being themselves govern'd and oversward at home under a Feminine usurpation, cannot be farr short of spirit and authority without dores, to govern a whole Nation'. Woman's task is evidently to infuse 'spirit and authority' into her husband by her amorous submissiveness, so that he can function in the world of men. In the *Defences*, again, he attacks Salmasius (and later More) as a submissive husband, a grovelling swine, a eunuch, and a hermaphrodite – apparently interchangeable terms. In contrast he points explicitly to his own manly efforts, in the divorce tracts and elsewhere, to restore liberty both political and domestic: 'in vain does he prattle about liberty in assembly and marketplace who at home endures the slavery most unworthy of man, slavery to an inferior'. The loathing that pervades Milton's battles over status and territory confirm the anthropologist's insight, that 'pollution ideas' are necessarily related to 'a total structure of thought whose key-stone, boundaries, margins and internal lines are held in relation by rituals of separation'.[9]

Milton may have steeped himself in chivalrous romance, as he claims in the *Apology*, but neither in the divorce tracts nor in the political tirades do we hear anything of the gentle sway of beauty, the courtly pretence that the realms of male and female power are absolute and complementary. He appears to share the fear of a later knight errant, that *la belle dame sans merci* might have him in thrall. The only power a woman can exercise, in Milton's view, is tyranny; and the sexual act, far from being the one area this side of heaven exempt from power relations, as St Paul would have it, is the very factory of female usurpation. Milton allows the husband no gracious surrender, no 'condescension' in its old non-pejorative sense; in bed he must redouble his efforts not to fall into the opposite of manliness, into thraldom, effeminacy and palpable uxoriousness. Indeed, marriage becomes the realm of Lilith, a sinister and magical power. Throughout the political pamphlets, the divorce tracts and *Samson Agonistes*, the female is endowed with associations of deceit and sorcery which confuse the boundaries of the whore, the wife, and the witch.

The *Apology* describes the Reformation as an Old Testament divorce subverted by the 'whoorish cunning' of the 'crafty adulteresse', who 'like a witch' leaves sentimental mementos and 'inticing words' behind her so that she can still exercise her power: 'thus did those tender hearted reformers dotingly suffer themselves to be overcome with harlots language' (1:942). *Eikonoklastes* denounces the followers of an uxorious king as 'men enchanted with the *Circaean* cup of servitude' (3:488). The divorce tracts address the case of the wise but inexperienced man, whose bad marriage-choice is sometimes described as an error in his own judgement but sometimes as a sinister beguilement – 'wisest men' have often been 'drawn . . . by suttle allurement within the train of an unhappy matrimony' (2:603); likewise the Chorus advises Samson to 'tax not divine disposal' (a temptation also for the unhappy husband, we recall) because 'wisest Men / Have err'd, and by bad Women been deceiv'd' (210–11). Samson himself in his tirade against Dalila denounces the 'arts of every woman false like thee', which have 'beguil'd' and even killed the 'Wisest and best men';[10] accusations of hastening death, which had also been made in the *Doctrine and Discipline*, are repeated throughout the interview with Dalila, and form Samson's last words on the subject (1009). The 'arts' of this 'sorceress' are clearly those of a Circe or a female Comus; she has tried to ensnare him with 'trains', 'ginns and toyls', a 'fair enchanted cup', and 'warbling charms'.[11] Anti-marital bitterness led Milton to apply the fate of Samson to the unhappy husband, grinding in the mill of an undelighted and servile copulation, and later to change Dalila from a strumpet to a wife in *Samson Agonistes* – though in the heat of fury Samson ceases to distinguish between the wife and the 'Concubine' or between sexual attraction and the 'venereal trains' of sorcery; he even suggests that it is post-coital sleep, rather than telling his secret, which has shorn him of his strength and 'Softened' him 'with pleasure and voluptuous life' (532–8). It is ironic that 'voluptuous life', as distinguished from contemplative or active, is precisely the area consigned to the wife in Milton's vision of ideal marriage, and relaxation is precisely the service she provides. And the liberation offered by divorce is itself described as a softening and a charm. The corruption of marriage, vividly portrayed in this central scene of *Samson Agonistes*, thus disturbingly retains features of its happiest state.

The overwhelming impression of the divorce tracts, like that of the Dalila episode in *Samson Agonistes*, is one of violence. We can certainly detect in both cases the bruised remains of an ideal vision of Paradisal happiness and love.[12] But when Samson expels Dalila we do not witness the 'beneficent and peaceful' dismissal required by the rule of charity, nor do we feel, as one critic has claimed, that we are in the presence of a man who has suddenly regained a vision of marriage as 'an image of a well-tempered human Soul'; we see an act of fundamental savagery, quite unlike the calm to which he is led at the end of his crisis of confidence in the Lord.[13] The rage of the divorce tracts likewise undermines their professed devotion to 'love and peace', and disrupts the calm and rational procedure of exegesis. In the closing books of *Paradise Lost* we follow the painstaking reconstruction of trust, forbearance, and mutual loyalty in the face of unprecedentedly destructive emotions, and we see two individuals struggling with but resisting the very desire that Milton so richly indulges in his other marital writings – the temptation to expel and annihilate the other. The divorce tracts and *Samson Agonistes*, on the other hand, seek the restitution of order in a great sundering, a solitary and destructive cataclysm.

The major problem of bad marriage, Milton believed, is that it forces the godly and sensitive young man to 'live a contentious and unchristian life'. The main problem of the divorce tracts, in turn, is this: how far can a contentious and unchristian book rectify this intolerable wrong? The radical in Milton of course believed that he was overthrowing Dagon, imitating the violence of God Himself when He takes reformation in hand;[14] and the artist in him also would recognize the need for an intensified mimesis or surrogate experience. But Milton's almost fascistic enthusiasm for violence surely clashes with the principle of temperance, which involves managing and shaping, rather than surrendering to, the forces of 'passion', 'paine', and 'experience'. This judgement of failure may seem to be inappropriately moralistic, but we should not forget that *Areopagitica* itself, and the activist poetics proclaimed throughout Milton's prose, forges a vital link between ethics, aesthetics, and the reader's response.

We conclude, then, that though they are suffused with theoretical eroticism and Utopian dreaming, and illuminated by moments of 'poetical enthusiasm', at the core the divorce tracts are authentically ugly. They lack the fair-mindedness of Milton's later summary of the divorce question in *De Doctrina Christiana*, and their Old Testament sense of pollution is not redeemed by the miraculous presence of real love, as it is in the sonnet 'Methought I saw my late espoused saint'. These tracts claim to bring 'love and peace', a 'divine touch' that 'in one instant hushes outrageous tempests into a sudden stilnesse and peacefull calm'; but they are distorted by rage, petulant accusation, and violent disdain. Theirs is not the ugliness of Rembrandt's Adam and Eve, shot through with an almost Kierkegaardian compassion,[15] not the lyric grief over human failure that runs through *Paradise Lost*, but the shapeless and incoherent vehemence of a man who considered himself 'unspeakably wrong'd'. If the bond or 'conversation' between reader and text were regarded as a marriage and subjected to the criteria of these tracts, Milton himself would be expelled.

The divorce tracts are still a necessary state in the dialectic of Milton's development, however; they belong to his 'growth', if not his 'compleating'. In the terms of *Areopagitica*, conflict is a mark of authenticity. A rational and coherent text would not have been true to Milton's ideology of sex and gender, nor would it have been an adequate vehicle for his fractured response to the Paradisal ideal. He refuses to abandon 'experience', but he also refuses to lose hold of the idea that 'some proportion' must obtain between squalid reality and the myth of perfection. In these tracts his sense of proportion is uncertain, often submerged in the struggles of the moment or pulled apart by contradictory responses to the fall; but it is precisely these tensions that propel him towards *Paradise Lost*.

Notes

1. *PL*, VII:39; *Prose*, 2: 253, 316, 526, 667; cf. *Utopia*, II, where the Utopians provide divorce for incompatibility, by mutual consent and after serious deliberation (though only when both partners have found alternate spouses, as Stephen Fallon points out in a private communication).

2. 2:606, 609; cf. *De Doctrina*, 6:355: pre-lapsarian sexuality was 'an effect or natural consequence of that very intimate relationship which would have existed between Adam and Eve in man's unfallen state'.

3. 2:740 (my emphasis), 674; cf. Vives who asserts that 'every bodye dispiseth' the act of love, without allowing for the possibility of redemption or cherishing reincitement. Cited by JOHN HALKETT, *Milton and the Idea of Matrimony* (Newhaven, 1970), pp. 64–5.

4. *An Answer*, pp. 12–16 (facsimile in W.R. Parker, *Milton's Contemporary Reputation* (Columbus, 1940); see *OED* 'conversation' 3, and Halkett, ch. 3 *passim*, esp. p. 61 and n. 24. In *Colasterion* M replies that, whatever 'conversation' means, it is something only available to the gentry, and not to cast serving-men such as he supposes the Answerer to be (2:742).

5. 2:589; cf. Halkett, p. 84.

6. The Elder Brother avers that the 'lewd and lavish act of sin / Lets in defilement to the inward parts', and the soul thereby 'grows clotted by contagion, / Imbodies, and imbrutes' (ll.465–8); cf. the 'gumms of glutenous heat' (l.917) and EDWARD LE COMTE, *Milton and Sex* (London, 1978) pp. 1–2.

7. I:588–9, and cf. n. 56: M draws a parallel from Herodotus's account of the destruction of the Lydians, undefeated in battle, who were nevertheless made to 'slacken, and fall to loosenes' by the spread of dancing, feasting, and dicing – to which M significantly adds '*Stews*'.

8. pp. 53–8. M assumes that their praise of Boadicea is in fact a secret insult ('as if in Britain women were men, and men women'), and later blames the Normans for bringing in 'Vices which effeminate mens minds' (5:402).

9. 4:i. 309, 312, 476, 518, 625; 3:420–1, 467; cf. 3:195 ('the unmaskuline [*sic*] Rhetorick of any puling Priest or Chaplain'), *SA* 1059–60 ('not sway'd / By female usurpation').

10. 749, 759, 762–4; cf. M's treatment of Solomon, 'that uxorious king, whose heart though large, / Beguiled by fair idolatresses, fell / To idols foul' (*PL*, I:444–6), on whom he proposed to write the tragedy *Salomon Gynaecratumenus* (*Prose*, 8:556). Though W. R. Parker's arguments for the early date of *SA* are often weak, his collection of echoes from the divorce tracts remains impressive (*Biography*, pp. 911–16); the tone and ethos of the Dalila scenes, closely juxtaposed to scenes in which the protagonist mutinies against Divine Providence and wrestles with despair, is not otherwise found in M except in the period of marital difficulty, i.e. from the first edn of *DDD* to the letter to Dati of April 1647 (2:762–3).

11. 819, 932–5; cf. 427, on the 'over potent charms' of Samson's first wife, and Leonora L. Brodwin, 'Milton and the Renaissance Circe', *MS* VI (1974), 21–83, a useful article marred by excessive claims for the importance of its subject.

12. Cf. *SA* 836–9 ('But *Love constrain'd thee*; call it furious rage / To satisfie thy lust: Love seeks to have Love; / My love how couldst thou hope, who tookest the

way / To raise in me inexpiable hate?'), and 1008–9 ('Love quarrels oft in pleasing concord end, / Not wedlock-trechery endangering life').

13. *Prose*, 2:732; See MARY ANN RADZINOWICZ, *Toward Samson Agonistes* (Princeton, 1978), p. 37; cf. Samson's response to Dalila's request to 'approach at least, and touch thy hand': 'Not for thy life, lest fierce remembrance wake / My sudden rage to tear thee joint by joint. / At distance I forgive thee, go with that' (951–4).

14. 2:666–7; M's apocalyptic violence is explored in DAVID A. LOEWENSTEIN, 'Milton and the Drama of History: Historical Vision, Iconoclasm and the Literary Imagination (Cambridge, 1990), pp. 20–4.

15. Cf. KIERKEGAARD, *Works of Love*, tr. Howard and Edna Hong (New York, 1962), pp. 342–3: 'and what is *the ugly*? It is *the neighbour*, whom one SHALL love.'

8 No Meer Amatorious Novel?*

Annabel Patterson

My earliest exercises in Milton studies were governed by the then ruling paradigms of genre study and intellectual history. I had traced Milton's development as a prose polemicist via the metaphors he used, an exercise that would today be carried out using terms like 'the construction of the self'; but in the early 1970s my focus was rhetorical, on how Milton used the aura of classical epic to justify his role in the public arena. Likewise, 'A Last Chance at True Romance' saw *Paradise Regained* through the lens of the Italian romantic epics, Seicento debates about Aristo and Tasso, and Milton's wavering allegiance to that genre. The romance in question was Milton's relation to books and ideas; it was emphatically not a personal relationship.

'No Meer Amatorious Novel?' was written out of very different motives and premises. The choice of topic was accidental and occasional. Invited to give the plenary session address at a conference on 'Seventeenth-Century Prose' at Purdue University, and learning that this was to be staged as an after-dinner speech, that toughest of all academic assignments, my primary concern was how not to be boring. Hence the appearance of that sure-fire topic, sexuality, which in 1987 was still mildly scandalous in relation to Milton. I had also been stung by complaints that *Censorship and Interpretation* took insufficient notice of psychological layers in authorial intentions, and was concerned that feminist criticism seemed then oblivious to the divorce pamphlets. The result was an essay in which genre theory is still residual, but which I found procedurally and theoretically liberating

* Reprinted from *Politics, Poetics, and Hermeneutics in Milton's Prose*, ed. David Loewenstein and James Grantham Turner (Cambridge University Press: Cambridge, 1990).

to write. Compared to James Turner's far more thorough account of the divorce pamphlets in the context of Renaissance thought on marriage and sexuality, it is evidently a *jeu d'esprit*; and, as has been said of masturbation, while that is nothing to be ashamed of, it is nothing to be proud of either.

By-ends

In June 1643, a recently abandoned husband published the first edition of his *Doctrine and Discipline of Divorce*, and about six months later followed the second edition, 'revis'd and much expanded'. The Yale edition of Milton's prose allows us to read these texts superimposed, without defining which text is, as it were, on top. Both title-pages declare that the institution of marriage in England at the time demands revision for 'the good of both sexes', a claim easily refuted by today's readers of both sexes, who quickly discover the passages of masculinist bias that, no matter what happened later in *Paradise Lost*, cannot be explained away.

This essay attempts to locate the *Doctrine and Discipline of Divorce* at the point of intersection between psychobiography and a resurgent genre theory that, in the demise of structuralism, now seems possible. The pamphlet hovers on an undrawn boundary between polemic and narrative, a boundary whose fragility Milton himself discerned and attempted to stabilize by declaring, in a crucial passage to which we shall return, that this was 'no meer amatorious novel' (2.256). In fact, this statement was made in reference not to the pamphlet as a whole, but to the myth of Eros and Anteros that Milton inserted into it as an image of the reciprocal love and need that was central to his redefinition of marriage. Yet in making the defensive comment, Milton showed self-consciousness about the presence of fictional narrative *within* his pamphlet, and used a term (*novel*) whose past and future were both problematic in the emergent poetics of narrative fiction.

For the myth of Eros and Anteros is only one of the interpolated narratives that Milton inserted into the *Doctrine and Discipline of Divorce*, and about the others he was apparently less self-conscious. These include a mini-series of allegories with sexual plots ending with the Eros/ Anteros myth but beginning with the liaison, added to the second edition of the pamphlet, between Custom, who is female, and Error, who is male; and a disguised autobiographical account of Milton's own courtship and the early days of his marriage, told prophetically in the style of the domestic fiction that would shortly replace the fashionable pseudo-historical romances imported from the continent.

These two types of narrative are distinguished both from each other and from the polemical frame by an oblique relationship to truth or the real. The allegories operate by forcing into painful visibility allegory's structural paradox, that it tries to give language incarnational force, to provide imaginary bodies for disembodied abstractions. By their shared sexual emplotment, Milton's allegories in the *Doctrine* reveal the perversity of this enterprise in general, and particularly the unspeakable agenda which required him to resort to allegory when legal or theological vocabularies failed him. In the first two in the series of three, also, the distortions that Milton introduces into familiar symbolic plots anticipate the grotesque family romance between Satan, Sin, and Death in *Paradise Lost*, itself often noted as a problematic shift of generic gears.

The concealed autobiographical novel, by contrast, registers its presence with a naive realism that predicts Defoe or even Richardson in its mundane vocabulary and social setting, but differs from early novelistic technique primarily in reversing the fictional use of personal pronouns. That is to say, where Defoe creates utterly convincing first-person narrators who appear to relate their biographies, Milton conceals his own by the use of the third person. This stratagem is, however, often subverted by the emotional investment that prose itself candidly registers. And there may be a third story told only, as it were, in occasional slips of the lexicon, a lapsarian tale of Milton's delayed and painful sexual coming of age, visible momentarily in metaphors and euphemisms for sexual process and parts of the body, a form simultaneously of linguistic precision and avoidance.

If so, all three types of narrative are, finally, different versions of the same story, the tale of what Milton called his 'owne by-ends.' The phrase occurs in the supplementary address to the Long Parliament that Milton added when he also added his name to the pamphlet, and it stands as one of those disclaimers that proclaim the presence of that which is stated to be absent. 'Who among ye', Milton wrote to the parliamentarians, 'hath not been often traduc't to be the agent of his owne by-ends, under pretext of Reformation' (2.225). This statement certainly encourages us to read Milton in a way that defies the depersonalizing and antianthropological premises of postmodernism, denying us for nearly two decades the commonsense categories of author, *oeuvre* and intention; yet without such categories we cannot even begin to see how interesting is the *Doctrine and Discipline of Divorce*. It is *most* interesting precisely in the relation between intended and unintended meaning, in the textual presence of those 'by-ends' that Milton knew he would be accused (if not traduced) of having allowed into the deep structure of his text.

The naive realism, or novelistic protocols, of the *Doctrine* appear most clearly in Book 1, Chapter 3, where Milton seeks to refute the argument that divorce would be unnecessary if people carefully considered the 'disposition' of their intended mates beforehand. 'But let them know again,' Milton responded to this unheard objection,

> that for all the warinesse can be us'd, it may yet befall a discreet man to be mistak'n in his choice: *and we have plenty of examples*. The soberest and best govern'd men are lest practiz'd in these affairs; and who knows not that the bashfull muteness of a virgin may oft-times hide all the unliveliness and naturall sloth which is really unfit for conversation; nor is there that freedom of accesse granted or presum'd, as may suffice to a perfect discerning till too late: and where any indisposition is suspected, what more usuall then the perswasion of friends, that acquaintance, as it encreases, will amend all: And lastly, it is not strange though many who have spent their youth chastely, are in some things not so quick-sighted, while they hast too eagerly to light the nuptiall torch; nor is it therefore that for a modest error a man should forfeit so great happiness, and no charitable means to release him. Since they who have liv'd most loosely by reasoning of their bold accustoming, prove most successfull in their matches, because their wild affections unsetling at will, have been as so many divorces to teach them experience. When as the sober man honouring the appearance of modestie, and hoping well of every sociall vertue under that veile, may easily chance to meet, if not with a body impenetrable, yet often with a minde to all other due conversation inaccessible, and to all the more estimable and superior purposes of matrimony uselesse and almost liveles.
>
> (2.249–50)

Here Milton, rejecting Fielding's thesis in *Tom Jones* that allowing a young man to sow his wild oats will unite him at last with his true Sophia, introduces a century earlier a far less allegorical story than Fielding's, a story in which the style of naive realism is supposedly explained by the phrase added in 1644 (*'and we have plenty of examples'*) – that is to say, social analysis as the basis for generalization. But the sociological force of 'plenty', along with 'oft-times', 'usuall', 'many', 'often', is undermined by the corrective nature of the argument, which requires the 'sober man' to be perceived as the exception to the carnal rule of the double standard. And where is this sober man to be found, the reader may well ask? The answer, along with a corroborative style and certain exact matches of detail, exists in Milton's early biographies.

The extreme specificity of the contrast between a chaste youth and a sudden haste to light the nuptial torch correlates all too precisely with the story of Milton's sudden marriage in the summer of 1642. 'After Whitsuntide it was, or a little after, that he took a journey into the country; nobody about him certainly knowing the reason, or that it was

any more than a journey of recreation; after a month's stay, home he
returns a married man, that went out a bachelor.' So wrote Milton's
nephew Edward Phillips, who also recorded the temperamental
mismatch between the 'philosophical life' of the husband, and the young
wife who had 'been used to a great house, and much company and
joviality.'[1] There are, of course, the alternatives Milton had explored for
himself in *L'Allegro* and *Il Penseroso*, now given a still more realistic and
social form.

Let us pause for a moment on the question of social form. Another
aspect of coincidence between Milton's supposedly impersonal narrative
of failed courtship and Phillips's admittedly personalized one is the role
that friends play in the marital negotiations. Milton described how 'the
perswasion of friends' worked on the sober young man of small
experience to believe that a suspected 'indisposition' would disappear on
better 'acquaintance'. The phrase reappears in Book 1, Chapter 12, where
he describes those who do not have the 'calling' for marriage, 'but by the
perswasion of friends, or not knowing themselves do often enter into
wedlock' (2:274). Edward Phillips mentions no persuasion in the making
of the original match; but his account is remarkable for its emphasis on
'the strong intercession of friends of both sides' in effecting the
reconciliation. Both texts, therefore, read as a gloss on each other, speak
to the specifically social, economic and sociopolitical interests behind the
marriage, since the poor financial circumstances of the Powells (including
an uncollectable debt to John Milton Sr) and the changing fortunes of the
king's party in the war (which worsened in 1645, suggesting the wisdom
of recovering a republican protector) were undoubtedly stronger motives
on at least one side of the bargain than the emotional argument Milton,
in the *Doctrine*, was attempting to make supreme. It need hardly be said
that these were the conditions in which social historians of marriage have
become increasingly interested, and which have long been posited as the
base of the eighteenth-century domestic novel. It is almost too good to be
true that another of Milton's biographers, perhaps John Phillips, perhaps
Cyriack Skinner, refers to the campaign for divorce as 'the mending of a
decay in the superstructure' (p. 1040), a term that perfectly mandates, if
mandate were necessary, our reading of these stories in terms of their
socioeconomic and political coordinates.

But (to return to the contest between L'Allegro and Il Penseroso in
Milton's story) the *Doctrine and Discipline of Divorce*, itself a severely titled
work, operates solely under the sign of the latter. The would-be divorcé,
invariably referred to as male, is not only sober but melancholy to a fault,
even to aberrancy. Having mischosen his mate, Milton remarked earlier
(Book 1, Chapter 3) that he is far worse off than the single man, for 'here
the continuall sight of his deluded thoughts without cure, must needs be
to him, if especially his complexion incline him to melancholy, a daily

trouble and paine of losse in some degree like that which Reprobates feel' (2:247). And in the same passage Milton emphasizes his individuality, by arguing that he shall 'doe more manly, to be extraordinary and singular in claiming the due right whereof he is frustrated, then to piece up his lost contentment by visiting the Stews, or stepping to his neighbours bed, which is the common shift in this misfortune' (2:247).

One might be tempted to assume, given the actual biography, that the mischosen mate might have been represented as a young and hence permissibly joyous Allegra. Not so. Instead, the question of female character is ambiguated by two alternative hypotheses of feminine unacceptability. One appears in the narrative of unwise courtship, when the 'bashfull mutenes of a virgin' conceals the 'unlivelines and naturall sloth which is really unfit for conversation' (2:249). The other appears much later in the pamphlet (and in its chronological development), when Milton is confronting the argument made by Beza and Paraeus, that the Mosaic dispensation for divorce was awarded for the protection of wives against the cruelty of husbands. 'Palpably uxorious!' exclaimed Milton at this point (Book 2, Chapter 15), in one of the most dramatic utterances of the entire work:

Who can be ignorant that woman was created for man, and not man for woman; and that a husband may be injur'd as insufferably in mariage as a wife. What an injury is it after wedlock not to be belov'd, what to be slighted, what to be contended with in point of house-rule who shall be the head, not for any parity of wisdome, for that were something reasonable, but out of a female pride.

(2:324)

He then inserts a scriptural anecdote from the book of Esther (1:10–22), of 'the cours which the Medes and Persians took by occasion of Vashti, whose meer denial to come at her husbands sending lost her the being Queen any longer.' It is surely no coincidence that the language of the 'divine relater', as Milton here refers to the holy Word, matches that of Edward Phillips, who related how 'Michaelmas being come, and no news of his wife's return,' Milton

sent for her by letter; and receiving no answer, sent several other letters, which were also unanswered; so that at last he dispatched down a foot messenger with a letter, desiring her return. But the messenger came back not only without an answer . . . but . . . reported that he was dismissed with some sort of contempt . . . [which] so incensed our author that he thought it would be dishonorable ever to receive her again.

(p. 1031)

The hidden autobiography, in other words, here carries the story of Milton's marriage from the hasty courtship through early days of contention 'in point of house-rule' and eventually to the repulse that defined the wife as not passively resistant but actively rebellious against her lord and master.

Here, then, both the spoken and the unspoken biography suggest that Milton did not know precisely what he wanted in a wife, docility or liveliness, an ambiguity that his own text records with less candor than that of his nephew, who reported that Milton 'found his chief diversion' while his wife was away and *before* her 'deniall to come at her husbands sending' in visiting Lady Margaret Lee, 'a woman of great wit and ingenuity.' Indeed, whether or not he realized the implications of the admission, Edward Phillips remarks of this phase of the marriage that Milton was 'now as it were a single man again'! Since the characterization of the female as insubordinate was added to the 1644 edition, as was the biblical anecdote of Vashti's refusal, we might speculate that the intense anger that Phillips reported was still seeking an outlet even as Milton was doing his utmost to place his arguments in the respectable and impersonal framework of the thought of the continental reformers.[2]

But there is a more intimate part of the story still, recorded only in the terrain of syntax. In the attack on feminine insubordination, the exclamation 'What an injury is it after wedlock not to be belov'd' seems asymmetrical as to its verb. It should properly read 'What an injury is it after wedlock not to be *obeyed*.' We may understand it, however, as an uncontrollable echo of Milton's scandalous paradox, that the would-be divorcer is actually the best upholder of marriage: 'for to retain still', he wrote:

> and not to be able to love, is to heap up more injury. . . . He therefore who lacking of his due in the most native and humane end of mariage, thinks it better to part then to live sadly and injuriously to that cherfull covnant (for not to be belov'd and yet retain'd, is the greatest injury to a gentle spirit) he I say who therefore seeks to part, is one who highly honours the maried life, and would not stain it.
>
> (2:253)

How could Milton have committed that Freudian slippage from the high-minded 'to retain still and not to be able to love' to the elegiac (and soon to be echoed) 'not to *be* belov'd and yet retain'd'? Who, this syntax asks, is doing the divorcing, and at what moment does it occur? At the failure of love, or at the formal separation? Who injures whom? Does the chiasmus indicate a moment of gender parity in Milton's thinking, or rather the hideous recognition that when he thought he was in control (retaining, but unable to love) he was in fact himself to *be* retained, but not to be beloved?

In a much later passage (Book 2, Chapter 20), Milton reassumed command over this situation, reworking the paradox about injury so as to apply only to the woman:

> The law can only appoint the just and equall conditions of divorce, and is to look how it is an injury to the divorc't, which in truth it can be none, as a meer separation; for if she consent, wherin has the law to right her? or consent not, then is it either just and so deserved, or if unjust, such in all likelihood was the divorcer, and to part from an unjust man is a happiness, and no injury to be lamented. But suppose it be an injury, the Law is not able to amend it, unlesse she think it other then a miserable redress to return back from whence she was expell'd, or but entreated to be gon.
>
> (2:349–50)

So 'not to be retained' has become, simply, 'expell'd', and the story of the wife who refused to return has been exorcised in another, occluded finale, the miserable opportunity imposed by law to 'return back from whence she was expell'd,' the worst punishment that Milton can imagine.

But there is another syntactic symptom of distress in the passage of revealing chiasmus in the eccentric use of personal pronouns. 'He therefore,' wrote Milton, 'who lacking of his due . . . he I say who therefore seeks to part . . . is one who highly honours the maried life.' It is in deference to the late Joan Webber that this part of my argument is subtitled 'The eloquent "he who"', for it was in contemplating how much was accomplished for the study of seventeenth-century prose in *The Eloquent 'I'* that I realized how much more might still be said, not least because Joan Webber's account of Milton's 'I' restricted itself to the pamphlets on church reform. In that context, she was able to argue that Milton's use of the first personal pronoun, along with other syntactical constructions such as passive verbs and ethical datives, indicated a devout striving after impersonality, a wish to express the subordination of his talent to his calling:

> Milton's muting of the 'I' in passages wholly taken up with himself makes his desires seem to rest on God. And often where the 'I' does make itself aggressively felt, an overarching periodic sentence prevents the collision of personal with impersonal simply by encompassing both in a larger order.[3]

This generous reading of Milton's egotistical sublime (ghosts of a fuller version that need to be exorcised) could not, I suggest, have been maintained at this ideal level had Webber turned her meticulous investigation to the divorce pamphlets.[4] For the *Doctrine and Discipline* introduces a new twist to the syntactical device developed in the church reform pamphlets for distinguishing an ideal and disinterested self from a confessedly self-interested author. The ideal 'he who' appears as the heroic agent of reform, 'hee who shall indeavour the amendment of any old neglected grievance in Church or State' (2:224), or 'he who wisely would restrain the reasonable Soul of man within due bounds' (2:227). Both of these are built into the new address to Parliament added in 1644, and contrast with the modest ethical dative: 'For me, as farre as my part leads me, I have already my greatest gain, assurance and inward satisfaction to have done in this nothing unworthy' (2:232). More clearly heroic, participating in the structure of epic and chivalric metaphor with which Milton enlivened his attacks on prelacy, is the 'He therefore who by adventuring shall be so happy as with successe . . . to light the way of such an expedient liberty and truth as this . . . [and] shall deserve to be reck'n'd among the publick benefactors of civill and humane life' (2:239–40). Here, in fact, Milton changed the 'He that' of 1643 to 'He who' in 1644, one of those minuscule alterations that would seem to carry no significance unless perceived as structural.

But alongside these heroic personae exists another, who belongs rather to the world of error and mistaken choice that Milton entered for the first time in the *Doctrine and Discipline*, and for which, paradoxically, the humility of the ethical dative could not serve, because of the need to conceal his 'owne by-ends'. So the new preface introduces also the figure of 'He who marries' and 'intends as little to conspire his own ruine, as he that swears Allegiance' (2:229). He will reappear as the anonymous 'sober man' who featured in the story of unwise courtship, and who surfaces again in the subsequent lament for the failure of love: 'He therefore who lacking of his due . . . thinks it better to part then to live sadly and injuriously . . . (for not to be belov'd and yet retain'd, is the greatest injury to a gentle spirit) he I say who therefore seeks to part, is one who highly honours the maried life, and would not stain it.' Especially in that remarkable construction, 'he I say who', the grammar of self-division is painfully audible

Grinding in the Mill

The three myths or allegorical narratives differ from the 'amatorious novel' we have just been reading by virtue of their uncomfortable blend of high abstraction with an emphatic sexuality, which goes well beyond the incarnational protocols of allegory as a narrative procedure. In Milton's retelling of Plato's myth of the union of Plenty and Poverty (a pagan version of the story of Ruth and Boaz) everything that was happy or high-spirited in the original is erased. In the *Symposium*, Plenty, having overindulged at Aphrodite's birthday party, lies down in the garden of Zeus and falls asleep, whereupon Poverty 'considering her own straitened circumstances, plotted to have him for a husband, and accordingly she lay down at his side and conceived Love.'[5] For Milton, Poverty is recognizable in that loneliness of which Adam complained in the garden, but the myth has gone awry; Plenty vanishes from his text, Penury cannot 'lay it self down by the side of such a meet and acceptable union . . . but remains utterly unmaried . . . and still burnes in the proper meaning of St Paul' (2:252–3). An awkwardness about gender, one might suspect, shows in the conversion of Penury from feminine to neuter, and in the revised genealogy. Instead of the birth of Love, 'Then enters Hate, not that Hate that sins, but that which is onely a naturall dissatisfaction and the turning aside from a mistaken object.' In this version of the myth the sexual engagement (which represents the spiritual or emotional one) either does not occur at all, or, if it does, is so unsatisfactory that it leads to that familiar image of the domestic bedroom, the 'turning aside'.

The myth of Custom and Error with which the 1644 pamphlet begins is also a myth of generation gone askew. Here Custom is the aggressive female ('being but a meer face'), and, like Penury, is seeking a mate who has what she lacks, namely a body. She 'rests not in her unaccomplishment, untill by secret inclination, shee accorporat her selfe with error, who being a blind and Serpentine body without a head, willingly accepts what he wants, and supplies what her incompleatnesse went seeking' (2:223). Lana Cable noted in 1981 the sexual content of this striking opening to the *Doctrine*; but possibly the conventions of academic discourse did not then permit her to say what she meant by the 'obvious . . . implications' of this representation of Error as male.[6] The appropriate gloss, I think, comes from Yeats's late poem, *The Chambermaid's Second Song*, where the blind and serpentine body is identified as 'his rod and its butting head / Limp as a worm, / His spirit that had fled / Blind as a worm.'[7] This myth, too, issues in an allegorical birth, although it is emphatically not an offspring of Custom and Error, but rather a birth they would prevent, crying 'Innovation', 'as if the womb of teeming Truth were to be clos'd up' (2:224). Mysteriously (or perhaps we should say carelessly), a few moments later Truth is no longer the rightful mother, but the child: 'Though this ill hap wait on her nativity, that shee never comes into the world, but like a Bastard, to the ignominy of him that brought her forth: till Time the Midwife rather then the mother of

Truth, have washt and salted the Infant, declar'd her legitimat, and Churcht the father of his young Minerva' (2:225). The editors of the Yale *Prose Works* remark on this 'grotesque' mingling of classical myth with the Anglican service of churching women after childbirth, a relic of the Hebrew purification rites and Old Testament emphases on female uncleanness. But still more unsettling is Milton's distortion of the familial structure of several stories at once, so that Time becomes not Truth's male father, a commonplace of Renaissance thought, but her female midwife; while the role of the father is now usurped by the author of the *Doctrine and Discipline of Divorce*, who both claims the Olympian privilege of paternity *without* the assistance of a woman (the birth of the brainchild *through* the brain) and confesses, by way of the metaphor of churching, to an uneasy physicality that requires some ritual (verbal) exorcism.

Cable also proposed that the 'accorporation' of Custom and Error functions as a grotesque parody of the longed-for union of Eros and Anteros (Book 1, Chapter 6). Perhaps; but what I notice rather is the peculiar misappropriateness of the Eros/Anteros model, literally a tale of passionately incestuous love between brothers, as an image of human *marriage*, whose oddness in this context is only underlined by Milton's disclaimer that 'of matrimoniall love no doubt but that was chiefly meant.' Before attempting to erase this problem by recourse to learned commentary, it might be well to ask whether Milton *needed* to invoke this young all-male image of desire, when he might have just as easily remembered the union of Cupid and 'his eternal Bride' Psyche that concludes the published versions of *Comus*. *That* myth would indeed have stood in pure contrast to the two distorted unions and genealogies that precede it, not least because in that earlier, ideal moment Milton could contemplate the 'blissful birth' of twins, Youth and Joy. Not so young now, he apparently could not bring himself to recall that particular shape of desire, and the myth he chooses belongs rather to the mindset of Adam after the Fall and before reconciliation with Eve:

> O why did God,
> Creator wise, that peopl'd highest Heav'n
> With spirits Masculine, create at last
> This *novelty* on Earth, this fair defect
> Of Nature, and not fill the World at once
> With Men as Angels without Feminine,
> Or find some other way to generate
> Mankind?
>
> (10:888–95; my italics)

Without the 'novelty' of the female, there could be, need be, no 'amatorious novel'. Milton's framing of the Eros/Anteros myth as a

divine fiction sung to him by his 'Author', and his denial that it belongs
in the genre of domestic or romantic fiction, registers both a generic and
a gendered discomfort.

Such a reading can only be reinforced by the language Milton employs
to denote human and heterosexual activity in the *Doctrine and Discipline of
Divorce*. In 1978 Edward Le Comte, in two terse pages, collected some of
these metaphoric phrases, concluded that they registered Milton's
'disgust or scorn', and suggested that if the divorce pamphlets 'reflect a
sexual refusal, they reflect one, or an inclination to one, far more likely to
have come from the husband.'[8] He noted that Milton equates
heterosexual activity not only with animalism – 'a bestial necessity',
'bestial burning', 'animal or beastish meeting', 'a brutish congress' – but
also with physical labor and slavery. Central to this perception is a
sentence Milton added to the 1644 edition: 'that to grind in the mill of an
undelighted and servil copulation, must be the only forc't work of a
Christian mariage, oft times with such a yokefellow, from whom both
love and peace, both nature and Religion mourns to be separated'
(2.258); and Le Comte showed how this image proleptically alludes to the
story of Samson, who in rabbinical tradition was doubly enslaved by the
Philistines, combining toiling at the mill with enforced service as a stud.[9]
The sexual pun derives also from the discourse of common bawdiness.
Le Comte cites the couplet from a 1647 popular rhyme: 'Digby's lady
takes it ill, / That her lord grinds not at her mill.'

But we can now see more clearly how and why the sexual distress in
the *Doctrine and Discipline of Divorce* is entangled with Milton's ideology of
work, that it evinces an intuition of social and economic instability,
expressed in terms of agricultural practice and the politics of landowning,
also found in the early poems.[10] We should group around the grinding in
the mill the following phrases from elsewhere in the pamphlet:
'bondmen of a luckles and helples matrimony' (2.240); 'the work of male
and female' (2.240); 'sowe the furrow of mans nativity with seed of two
incoherent and uncombining dispositions' (2.270); 'an improper and ill-
yoking couple . . . the disparity of severall cattell at the plow' (2.277);
and especially 'God loves not to plow out the heart of our endeavours
with over-hard and sad tasks . . . by making wedlock a supportless yoke
. . . to make men *the day-labourers* of their own afflictions' (2.342; my
italics). This allusion to day-labour connects the pamphlet to the crucial
sonnet on the parable of the talents ('Does God exact day-labor, light
denied?'); but here it reveals more sharply its coordinates in a
socioeconomic analysis that Milton has and has not completed. 'I spake
ev'n now,' he wrote on the question of whether the Mosaic dispensation
could possibly be interpreted as a license or escape-clause given to a
hard-hearted people, 'as if sin were condemn'd in a perpetual *villenage*
never to be free by law, never to be *manumitted*: but pure sin can have no

tenure by law at all, but is rather an eternal outlaw, and in hostility with law past all attonement' (2.288). In the deep structure of Milton's imagination the socioeconomic consciousness is now inseparable from the erotic drama that the pamphlet is staging, *because* Milton has now himself entered the terrain of mistakenness, and is no longer luckily excluded from the curse of labour. Under this curse, which has always connected agricultural labour with genital pain, Milton cannot distinguish the body from the body politic, the master from the slave, the grinder from the ground. He has found himself expected to plow and 'sow the furrow of man's nativity', and worse still, to spend in the process, 'to be made to pay out the best substance of his body, and of his soul too, as some think' (2.271), becoming indistinguishable in this metaphoric exchange from day-labourers, villeins, or even oxen and asses. Milton shares the yoke. Sex is hard work when the heart is not in it; and it would be unkind of his readers to give him the same advice that thousands of mothers gave their daughters: 'Shut your eyes and think of England.'

Yet in a sense he did just that, stylistically. He turned to euphemism. If writing is, as some think, the art of *not* saying what one means, the most profound avoidance, some of Milton's finest writing occurs in the effort to conceal from his readers and probably from himself the precise effect on his psyche of the long-delayed induction into heterosexual experience. Le Comte's formula of 'disgust or scorn' cannot account fully for this language, too lapidary either to allow disgust to register on the reader's sensory scale or to ensure a proper moral detachment. Especially in Chapter 3, where Milton excoriates canon law for its focus on adultery, his language ricochets between what in *Paradise Lost* he would later register as (divine) 'distance and distaste' (IX.9). The admonitory distance is invoked by archaic moral allegories of the body (complete with alliteration), in the 'vessell of voluptuous enjoyment', or the 'fountain' 'from whence must flow the acts of peace and love', or 'the channell of concupiscence' (2.248–9). But the embarrassing carnal knowledge (which is only half-acknowledged) is written in a libidinal narrative that confuses success and failure and is marked by a compulsion to repeat. 'The impediment of carnall performance', the 'stopt or extinguisht veins of sensuality' and the 'disappointing of an impetuous nerve' alternate with 'impatience of a sensuall desire . . . relieved', and the 'prescrib'd satisfaction of an irrationall heat.' Even the surrounding vocabulary is contaminated by the story of tumescence and detumescence; so the canon law prescribes that 'the contract shall stand as firm as ever' however 'flat and melancholious' the emotional relationship may be. Above all, in the notorious 'quintessence of an excrement' Milton rather highlighted than solved the problem of distance and distaste, as abstract thought and philosophical idealism (expressed in a classicizing and pseudoscientific vocabulary) reveal their connections to a venerable tradition of misogynistic disgust. As Freud observed in his case-history of 'Dora', 'the Early Christian Fathers' "inter urinas et faeces nascimur" clings to sexual life and cannot be detached from it in spite of every effort of idealization.'[11]

Each of Milton's allusions to sexual process, then, is a micronarrative, with a different ending, of the search for satisfaction, of the structure of desire, which modern and postmodern criticism, itself responding to Freudian theory, has made synonymous with the novel as a category of thought, as a genre. In Tzvetan Todorov's *The Poetics of Prose* the quintessential novel must articulate the shared paradoxes of desire and narrative, that 'we desire at the same time desire and its object'. When we get what we thought we wanted we no longer want it. The story is over. And he also suggests that one of the novel's essential moods, in the grammatical sense, is the optative, of which the renunciative is a special case.[12] The *Doctrine and Discipline of Divorce* is, I suggest, a special case of the renunciative novel, announcing its genre through the paradox of Milton's statement: 'he I say who therefore seeks to part, is one who highly honours the maried life, and would not stain it' (2.253). If his story remains carnal, for all his attempts to allegorize it, if the individual life breaks through the generalizing and impersonalizing impulse, if the 'by-ends' that criticism is unfairly equipped to notice become visible as criticism itself loses some of its own inhibitions, we need not, I think, today be embarrassed, either for Milton or ourselves.

Notes

1. See John Milton, *Complete Poems and Major Prose*, ed. M.Y. Hughes (New York, 1957), p. 1031. Subsequent citations from early biographers (in the text) will also be from Hughes.

2. See also Book 2, Chapter 18, where Milton redefines fornication as a series of obstinacies derived from Theodosius, which included the 'lying forth of her hous without probable cause' (2:334), and is illustrated by Judges 19:2, where 'the Levites wife is said to have play'd the whoor against him; which Josephus and the Septuagint . . . interpret only of stubbornnes and rebellion against her husband' (2:335). 'And this I shall contribute,' added Milton, 'that had it ben whoordom she would have chosen any other place to run to, *then to her fathers house*' (my italics).

3. *The Eloquent 'I': Style and Self in Seventeenth-Century Prose* (Madison, 1968), p. 197.

4. Webber actually argues that the intrusion of self into Milton's church reform pamphlets constitutes 'the same kind of spiritual autobiography that other Puritans wrote, except that it is translated into literary terms' (p. 217).

5. *Dialogue of Plato*, tr. Benjamin Jowett, 4 vols (Oxford, 1871), Vol. 1, p. 519.

6. 'Coupling Logic and Milton's Doctrine of Divorce', *Milton Studies*, **15** (1981): 147–8.

7. *Collected Poems* (London, 1950), p. 346.

8. *Milton and Sex* (London, 1978), pp. 29–30. This swift-moving and often reckless account of Milton's conscious and unconscious responses to sex and marriage has now been replaced by James G. Turner's more learned and judicious *One Flesh: Paradisal Marriage and Sexual Relations in the Age of Milton* (Oxford, 1987). See the previous essay in this volume.

9. The point originated with Samuel Stolman, ' "To Grind in the Mill . . ." ', *Seventeenth-Century News* **29** (1971): 68–9.

10. See my 'Forced Fingers: Milton's Early Poems and Logical Constraint' in Claude Summers and Ted-Larry Pebworth (eds), *The Muses Common-Weale* (Columbia, 1988), pp. 9–22.

11. *Dora: An Analysis of a Case of Hysteria* (1905), ed. Philip Rieff (New York, 1963). Compare Turner's argument that it was precisely the extent of Milton's idealization of marriage that produced, by its failure to be realized, the disgust. My reading of Milton's sexual vocabulary, however, differs from Turner's emphasis on 'physical particularity' and 'medical precision' (*One Flesh*, p. 198) by attempting to recognize the element of euphemism or self-protective intellectualism that Milton's vocabulary exhibits. All these strategies Milton shares with Freud, whose equally notorious passage in *Dora* about the difficulties of discussing 'such delicate and unpleasant subjects' as 'bodily organs and processes' asserts the distance achievable by 'dry and direct . . . technical names' (p. 65), only to detour into (unintentional) *double-entendre*: 'J'appelle un chat un chat.' (Only Jane Gallop has been bold enough to translate this; see her 'Keys to Dora' in Charles Bernheimer and Claire Kahane (eds), *In Dora's Case* (New York, 1985), p. 209). And it is worth noting that without the prurience by which genitalia were themselves rendered euphemistically in Viennese culture at the turn of the century (as in the famous 'Schmuckkästchen', jewel-case) Freud's repertory of dream-symbols would have been much impoverished.

12. Tr. Richard Howard (Ithaca, 1977), pp. 105–6, 114.

9 The Spirit of *Différance**

WILLIAM MYERS

Milton and Free Will develops an account of how reading can confirm the coherence in principle of a strong version of free will. At its centre is an analysis of Milton's sonnet 'Lawrence of virtuous father virtuous son' which may be summarized as follows. Because, like all language systems, even the most consistent, viz. arithmetic, 'literature obeys the general rule of being unable to supply the rules for its own interpretation', there 'is always a point at which readers are left to their own resources' when they read a text. In a poem like the Lawrence sonnet, however, which is explicitly about discriminating judgement, that point can itself be a part of the meaning, putting 'me into judicious contact with Milton's sense of my potentialities both as a guest and as a reader, and with his dependence on them. But my reaction to that reticence is by no means predictable. I may resent Milton's failure to direct my responses or I may admire the technical skill with which he has avoided just such explicitness. But I can also make Milton's sense of my unpredictability yet another aspect of the poem's meaning, part of what he silently but precisely indicates he is allowing for. Encapsulated in the sonnet, therefore, is a principle of intimacy in separateness, a movingly exact yet open authorial voluntariness Milton's choice, that I should choose for myself is [his] self-effacing gift to me. He invites me into the intimate, domestic world of his desires, hopes and affections, yet, like a good host, he leaves me to myself, and in this very self-effacement, he becomes in the poem fully and movingly himself.' This structure, it is then argued, 'has general application. There is one, and only one, truly discerned but non coercive value which the mind can cognise and respond

---

* Reprinted from William Myers, *Milton and Free Will: An Essay in Criticism and Philosophy* (London, New York, Sydney: Croom Helm, 1987).

to with unqualified freedom, and that is the freedom of another person.'

The main argument in the book is conducted with 'deconstructionist arguments in brackets'. In the following extract those brackets are removed.

The deconstructionist notion of writing, Roland Barthes maintains 'liberates what may be called an anti-theological activity, an activity that is truly revolutionary since to refuse to fix meaning is, in the end, to refuse God and his hypostases – reason, science, law'.[1] Derrida similarly argues that writing reveals a stage or set on which 'the punctual simplicity of the classical subject is not to be found'.[2] Deconstructionism thus threatens to obliterate the phenomenological stage or set on which I have tried to dramatise my main argument about how and in what circumstances a 'strong' version of freedom, the freedom of 'indifference', may be properly attributed to rational beings, since if there was ever a territory in which the classical subject might be deemed to flourish it is surely the works of Milton. The deconstructionist challenge cannot, therefore, be ignored, and it will therefore be necessary to examine briefly, but I hope not inaccurately, some of the less recondite arguments advanced by deconstructionist criticism in recent years.

Deconstructionism derives from post-Saussurean analysis of signs. A rudimentary account of signs would distinguish between the sign itself – the signifier – and that for which it stands – the signified, the latter being always an idea and never an object in reality (the referent). If I say the word 'dog', for example, only my 'meaning' enters the minds of those I am addressing, not a living animal, nor even in most cases anything so definite as a picture. The weakness of such a description of sign-making activity, however, is that, in Derrida's words, it is grounded in 'the principle of non-contradiction' (WD, 217) which he regards as 'the cornerstone of all metaphysics or presence'. This requires that the meaning of a sign should be fixed in a larger system of meaning which is finally coherent and unambiguous, so that when I speak in the company of others we all of us know what is meant, we are present to each other, and the thing meant is present to us all. But words do not have fixed meanings. The word 'dog', for example, does not stand consistently, uniquely and exclusively for one of a species of four-legged animals. It can also be used of a person, as a verb, or (in the case of Winston Churchill) of a mood. We work out what it means in each case from the other signs among which it is placed: 'The dog gnaws a bone'; 'I will dog his footsteps'; 'The black dog is upon me'. This is simply to illustrate Bakhtin's observation that a 'sign can be illuminated only by another sign'.[3]

103

In the traditional view, however, such slippage of meaning is limited. There is supposed to be a core meaning to which the word 'dog' is tethered which limits the play of sense facilitated by other signifiers. A word's meaning is supposed to be determined by its 'root', for example, or by a strong idea to which it has become attached in the course of linguistic history. Again, there is the commonly felt conviction that if the sense of a word is not tied to its own meaning, it is tied to what I mean when I use it, and that it can be made to perform the tricks I wish it to perform in the semiotic circus-ring. One way or another, we traditionally assume that the contexts which make it possible for a word to signify something are under control. Accordingly in our assumptions about language, Derrida suggests, we 'conceive of structure on the basis of a full presence which is beyond play' (WD, 279), and it is this conception which deconstructionism challenges.

Briefly deconstructionism denies that meaning is ever fixed or fixable, and that any attempt to constrain the play of signifiers expresses anxiety or betrays a will to violence. Deconstructionists point out how the openness of language to multiple and contradictory interpretation is particularly obvious in the case of writing because writing is extended in space, its signifiers visibly in waiting, concretely registering the independence of the signifier from the signified. Writing is language with meaning absent, without the presence of an intending mind or a living context to keep it under control. Hence the compulsion to exercise such control by further writing. Scripture provokes the commentator, literature the critic. As Michel Foucault remarks, 'Commentary averts the unpredictable in discourse by giving it its due: it allows us to say something other than the text itself, but on condition that it is the text itself that is spoken and, in a sense, fulfilled.'[4] The commentator or critic, Derrida argues, thus opposes the illogicality of language which he suggests Nietzsche discovered in metaphor.[5] Metaphor, Nietzsche wrote, 'brings about an identification of the nonidentical; it is thus an operation of the imagination'. Derrida's citation of this remark (TS, 83) is followed by an admission that philosophers have always known about the illogicality of language, and have therefore insisted on 'the secondary nature of the sign in relation to the idea' (TS, 84). But Nietzsche, Derrida argues, has shown metaphor to be 'the very structure or condition of possibility of all language and concepts' (TS, 84).

It follows that signifieds are really only the shadows cast by signifiers, not substantial things to which signifiers are attached as so many labels: meanings do not control language but rather language is both constitutive of meanings and indifferent to them. This is because the signifier is ineradicably *different* from what it signifies. It does not even inhabit the same moment, because there is an inevitable delay between the moment a word is heard and the moment when its function is recognised.

This effect is less obvious when language is spoken because speakers and listeners work in the illusion of synchronic interaction: experientially speech generates spontaneous and intimate presence. But writing turns the apparently trivial delays of speech into measurable linear space. It confirms the distance from one end of a sentence to the other, and the time between utterance and understanding. Writing thus puts on record the fact that the sign is never what we like to think it is, that signifier and signified are *different* and that the connections between signifiers by which the signifieds are produced are always subject to delay. Hence Derrida's coinage *différance* – a sign which implies delay and which elides with the orthodox *difference* to suggest the structurelessness of language in logic, time and space.

Différance, however, does not endow the signifier with simple chronological priority over the signified. Derrida attacks the prejudice of 'an Idea or "interior design" as simply anterior to a work',[6] but he also atacks the obverse of this prejudice which subordinates the work to whatever design is discerned in the limitless play of signifiers. This, he suggests, would turn the users of language into Creator-Gods: it would ignore their 'finitude' and 'solitude'. The Old Testament prophet was right, therefore, to be terrified of putting pen to paper and getting things wrong – for writing is always secondary – it reveals what is already there. Hence Derrida's necessarily awkward formulation:

> Meaning must await being written or said in order to inhabit itself. . . .
>   Writing is *inaugural*. . . . It does not know where it is going, no knowledge can keep it from the essential precipitation toward the meaning that it constitutes, and that is, primarily, its future.
>
> (WD, 11)

Meaning, therefore, already is what it has yet to become. Deconstructionism insists on the limitations of language while affirming its limitless freedom; it privileges the signifier but denies it the status of source or origin. It acknowledges no boundaries, no controlling intelligence and will, neither God nor subject nor object. It offers perpetual anxiety – 'we must *decide* whether we will engrave what we hear', Derrida writes, '. . . whether engraving preserves or betrays speech' (WD, 9) – but also affirmation –

> the joyous affirmation of the play of the world and of the innocence of becoming, the affirmation of a world of signs without fault, without

truth, and without origin which . . . determines *the noncentre otherwise than as loss of the centre*.

(WD, 292)

If these arguments have merit my reliance on assumptions about text and reader to illustrate 'the grant of freedom' would seem to be misconceived since for Derrida texts do not exist. He argues that metaphysicians have traditionally assumed that the complete and perfect text of a work was to be found somewhere – in an unpublished manuscript, in the mind of the author, in the mind of God, or perhaps just in principle, and that consciousness could get hold of such a text and learn it completely and definitively. But, he insists, there 'is no text written or present elsewhere which would then be subjected, without being changed in the process, to an operation and a temporalization . . . which would be external to it' (WD, 211). This applies to all texts, actual and conceivable, from his own books to the Book of the Universe, i.e. the comprehensive description of the world hypothesised in possible-world arguments. 'Texts' cannot exist prior to their being read. They arise out of a forgettable past and precipitate themselves into a future which alone can constitute even what they currently are. Texts, therefore, can tell us nothing definitive about their readers, and consequently my entire argument about primary and secondary signification seems unviable. We really are completely without a centre, even the reader-subject discovering noncentre as something other than loss of the centre.

The attentive reader of Milton, however, might question whether this is really so. Thus there is abundant evidence that Milton himself was aware of *différance* (without, of course, knowing the word) and that he understood presence and so the classical subject in its light. In *Paradise Lost*, for example, Raphael is quite explicit about the impossibility of relating

> To human sense the invisible exploits
> Of warring spirits
>
> (5:565–6)

'God, as he really is,' Milton writes in *Christian Doctrine*, 'is far beyond man's imagination, let alone his understanding' (133); the best we can do is 'to form an image . . . in our minds which corresponds to his representation and descriptions of himself in the sacred writings'. What he chooses to give us concerning himself, therefore, are privileged signifiers only. We may 'believe that it is not beneath God to feel what grief he does feel, to be refreshed by what refreshes him, and to fear what he does fear' (135), but that does nothing to bridge the great gulf fixed between all signification and the Divine Referent. God can only appear in discourse as Nietzschean metaphor, as a series of signs with no claim to 'truth', but invested none the less with a legitimate effectiveness in the human imagination sufficient to generate a sense of real and specific obligations in our minds.

This is the view adopted in the poem by Raphael when he undertakes to delineate

> what surmounts the reach
> Of human sense . . .
> By likening spiritual to corporal forms,
> As may express them best
>
> (5:571–4)

Like the author of *Christian Doctrine*, Raphael is an optimist about language, but only after he has taken careful account of the independence of the signifier from the signified. Hence the ambiguity of 'express them best' which may mean that Raphael will make the best of a bad job or that his choice of metaphors will be effective in spite of everything. The latter view is strengthened by Raphael's next words:

> though what if earth
> Be but the shadow of Heaven, and things therein
> Each to other like, more than on earth is thought?
>
> (5:574–6)

The difficulties of narration may, after all, be less than they seem. Thus the one set of significations that we thought we had clearly grasped, namely that 'difference' means difference, can itself be undermined. It can mean astonishing sameness. This does not, of course, reinstate any definite connections between signifier and signified in discourse about God, but it does open up optimistic possibilities within the play of signifiers.

Milton's sense of linguistic play, however, is not confined to his writing about the celestial order. The reckless cosmology of *Paradise Lost* as suggested by the dance of the angels in Book 5 extends the freedom of signs from heaven to earth:

> Mystical dance, which yonder starry sphere
> Of planets, and of fixed in all her wheels
> Resembles nearest, mazes intricate,
> Eccentric, intervolved, yet regular
> Then most, when most irregular they seem,
> And in their motions harmony divine

> So smooths her charming tones, that God's own ear
> Listens delighted
>
> (5:620–7)

The dance is 'mystical' – it signifies a secret – and the sign of this sign is the intricately schematised motion of the planets and fixed stars around the earth: the ingenious equations of the final stages of Ptolemaic astronomy are probably in Milton's mind, but this is a Ptolemaic text in a putatively Copernican age: in reality the stars may not be fixed and the sun may not be a planet. At this point, however, we are so absorbed in the graceful freedom of the signifiers that the transition from doubtful science to pure rhetoric in the personification of Harmony (who is both feminine and divine and therefore a pagan figure) is effected without any sense of strain. So is the transformation of God from the thunderer of his Son's epiphany ten lines earlier to a princely connoisseur of music and choreography in a renaissance court.

But that is not all. This cluster of images has appeared before. In Book I when the great mass of fallen angels are reduced to the size of smallest dwarfs, they are said to be

> like that Pigmean race
> Beyond the *Indian* mount, or faerie elves,
> Whose midnight revels, by a forest side
> Or fountain some belated peasant sees,
> Or dreams he sees, while over-head the moon
> Sits arbitress, and nearer to the earth
> Wheels her pale course, they on their mirth and dance
> Intent, with jocund music charm his ear
>
> (1:780–7)

Here the revels are balefully subject to the inconstant moon, the dancers are not angels but 'elves' – explicitly fictional creatures – and the charmed ear is not God's but that of a drunken rustic. Nevertheless, Hell is here perversely signifying Heaven, though this would hardly be matter of comment if such cross-signification were always as apparently casual and intermittent as this example appears to be. But it is not: it is quite systematic, and we have therefore to accustom ourselves to a text which allows signs even of God himself to slip and slide into theological and moral anarchy.

The most confusing example of this anarchy is probably the intrusion of the two overtly allegorical figures, Sin and Death, into the action of the poem. Their fictionality is flaunted, notably in the allusion to Greek myth in the story of the conception of Sin. It is indicated also in the casual reference to Death as a 'goblin' (2:688), which places him in a fantastic

frame exactly comparable with that of the 'elves' who entertain the
peasant in Book 1. Yet Sin and Death do more than intrude upon the
story; as nearly every commentator has pointed out, they become types,
not only of Adam and Eve, but, with Satan, of the Trinity also. Like the
Son and Eve, Sin comes forth from her progenitor and is embosomed
with him. In Book 2, in words redolent of Heaven and of Eden alike, she
reminds Satan how she had at first seemed 'sign portentous' to the rebel
angels,

> but familiar grown,
> I pleased, and with attractive graces won
> The most averse, thee chiefly, who full oft
> Thy self in me thy perfect image viewing
> Becamest enamoured
>
> (2:760–5)

Here an overt fiction masquerades both as a fact and as a type or sign of
other fact, a signifier, which is explicitly a signifier only, acting the part
of a signified, and in such a way as to suggest the fictionality of every
other person and thing in the poem, up to and including the Father
viewing his own perfect Image in the Son.

Milton, then, perceives and exploits the centrelessness of language in
his treatment of both God and the cosmos, but we have still to examine
whether he does so with the kind of anxiety which a disciple of Barthes
would expect him to exhibit. This will require our analysing his treatment
of the divine attributes, specifically God's omnipresence, immutability
and omniscience as they relate to his conceptions of the divine and the
human.

We know from *Christian Doctrine* that Milton thought that matter was
part of the divine substance from which God's will had been withdrawn.
We have therefore to think of space and matter as existing within
Milton's God, however peripherally, as well as of his God pervading
them. For Milton, then, God is presence and centre. Does this mean that
the idea of God underwrites the illusion of presence and centre in his
writing? The poem apparently says as much. Raphael assures Adam that

> As God in Heaven
> Is centre, yet extends to all, so thou
> Centring receivest from all those orbs; in thee,
> Not in themselves, all their known virtue appears
>
> (9:107–10)

On analysis, however, these words are more complicated than they
seem. The orbs Raphael refers to are the heavenly bodies, and, as we

saw in considering the angelic dance, the reader is expected to know that the earth may not be the centre of the universe after all. Consequently the 'virtue' discovered in those orbs must be a consequence of Adam's conscious assumption of the role of the centre; in his perception of them, and not in their physical relation to the earth, 'all their *known* virtue appears'. Thus Adam's centredness is affirmed, and yet – since the earth is not the true centre after all – he is decentred as well. But so by implication is God, to the extent, at least, that 'As' in the first line quoted means 'In the same way as'. Thus the centre is apparently not tethered to the centre either in Adam's case or in God's.

This notion is developed further when Adam is decentred and faces expulsion from Eden and apparently exile from God's presence. Michael, however, explores the situation more deeply:

> *Adam*, thou knowst Heaven his, and all the earth.
> Not this rock only; his omnipresence fills
> Land, sea, and air, and every kind that lives,
> Fomented by his virtual power and warmed:
> All the earth he gave thee to possess and rule.
> No despicable gift; surmise not then
> His presence to these narrow bounds confined
> Of Paradise or Eden: this had been
> Perhaps thy capital seat, from whence had spread
> All generations, and had hither come
> From all the ends of the earth, to celebrate
> And reverence thee their great progenitor.
> But this preeminence thou hast lost, brought down
> To dwell on even ground now with thy sons:
> Yet doubt not but in valley and in plain
> God is as here, and will be found alike
> Present, and of his presence many a sign
> Still following thee, still compassing thee round
> With goodness and paternal love, his face
> Express, and of his steps the track divine.
>
> (11:335–54)

The centre is thus provisional and unstable. Unfallen Adam would have been patriarchal ruler and Eden the centre of the human world, but with the fall it has lost that pre-eminence, and Adam has lost his own centrality: he must now dwell on 'even ground' with his sons. (Milton is making a strongly republican point here.) In reality, of course, the notion of Eden as centre was an illusion any way, since God's omnipresence has always filled the universe, and even now foments and warms all living things. Consequently in losing his centrality Adam loses nothing since

God, who is the real centre, is not himself centred but spread out everywhere. At the same time Adam becomes, or remains, central, because he is surrounded by signs or traces of God's fomenting and warming power. The divine centre is thus orbital like the stars, even though – or rather precisely because – the stars are not really but only symbolically in orbit around the earth. In insisting on God's omnipresence, therefore, Milton makes all centredness, divine and human, a signifier only, and so subject to the endless displacements of that condition.

But, a deconstructionist might argue, do not Michael's words plainly imply the full presence of God since not even the Fall can erase his Track or trace in creation? 'An unerasable trace,' Derrida argues, '. . . is a full presence . . . a son of God, a sign of parousia' (WD, 230). This is a fundamental objection and it can only be addressed through a consideration of Milton's treatment of God's relation to time and to creation.

We have seen that Milton believed that only tensed actions could be free, yet it is impossible to fix any moment in the poem when God acts *in propria persona*. Even the supreme act which he performs singly and by himself – the generation of the Son – is never present in the narrative, but is referred to through a series of subsequent and symbolic epiphanies. The first of these is particularly mysterious:

> As yet this world was not, and Chaos wild
> Reigned where these Heavens now roll, where earth now rests
> Upon her centre poised, when on a day
> (For time, though in eternity, applied
> To motion, measures all things durable
> By present, past, and future) on such day
> As Heaven's great year brings forth, the empyreal host
> Of angels by imperial summons called,
> Innumerable before the Almighty's throne
> Forthwith from all the ends of Heaven appeared
> Under their hierarchs in orders bright
>
> (5:577–87)

This fascinating sentence begins in uncentred space, or if centred only by anticipation in the fictional sign of a centred earth; it then introduces the notion of a 'day' in chaos, but only to decentre and supplement it, by enclosing it in Time (so as to 'protect' it from Eternity) and by enlarging it structurally with references to present, past and future, and 'Heaven's great year' – an astrological signifier antedating the creation of the heavenly bodies and their mystical, 36,000-year dance. The moment of the begetting is thus concealed by being specified. So is the action itself.

111

The subject of the most important though technically not the main clause of the sentence emerges late – meaning here has emphatically to wait in order to inhabit itself. Nor when it finally appears is that subject God, but only 'the empyreal host'. We are told that the angels are 'called' but not by whom and when they obey they approach not God himself but 'the Almighty's throne'. Finally in the lines following those quoted another main clause appears as from nowhere.

We are then given a mysterious picture, of the Father,

> By whom in bliss embosomed sat the Son,
> Amidst as from a flaming mount, whose top
> Brightness had made invisible
>
> (5:597–9)

The throne has thus become a mountain top so bright as to render the Father invisible and the Son's position uncertain, for either he is sitting *beside* (by) the Father, or he has been embosomed *by* him in bliss and is sitting *amidst* the brightness. And when at last God speaks he announces an action which has already been effected:

> This day I have begot whom I declare
> My only Son
>
> (5:603–4)

Actor and action are programmatically displaced: 'this day', for example, appears to be a period subsequent to the creation of the angels, but Satan and Abdiel will be arguing before the dawning of the next 'day' about whether the newly-begotten Son was instrumental in their own creation, and as Carey and Fowler point out in their note on line 601, the titles with which the Father addresses the heavenly host echo the account in Col. 1:16 of the Son's agency in creating the angels. Thus in his most momentous act, neither the acting God, nor the moment of his efficacy is textually present in Milton's account.

The creation of the world is equally mysterious. Adam sees the problem clearly: 'what cause', he asks Raphael,

> Moved the Creator in his holy rest
> Through all eternity so late to build
> In Chaos
>
> (7:90–3)

(The words 'so late' highlight the problem of locating movements of time in eternity: 'so early' would be just as appropriate.) In the account of the creation, which this question prompts, we are told that the world was made through the agency of the Son 'in a moment' (5:154), but that its making can only be unfolded to human ears in time. God's acts, therefore, 'Immediate . . . more swift/Than time or motion' (7:176–7), cannot be expressed through the deferrals of signification, and consequently God cannot be used to underwrite presence in the poem any more than he can be relied upon to constitute its centre. In the poem, in discourse, he can never be *there*.

The implications of this are deeply paradoxical. God is logically absent from a story in which he is palpably a character with a tendentious speaking part. The paradox can be resolved, however, if we take account of God's immutability and omniscience. Because he is omniscient, nothing is 'appresented' to God. Whereas all the other characters in Milton's later poems are represented as reading each other, more or less successfully. God knows the hearts of his creatures immediately and not through signs. And that is why he is immutable. He has nothing to learn. He is not just present everywhere as the supremely knowing objective observer or reader of the Book of the Universe. He is additionally the knower and experiencer of every event and every circumstance in every moment of every life, and yet he is not himself implicated either in what happens in his creatures or in the actions they perform. Milton perceives his God as the beginning and the end of all things, their centre and their site, but he also perceives him as a necessarily non-functioning presence, a non-functioning centre, a non-functioning author. Indeed his purpose in *Paradise Lost* is to deconstruct any such functioning (or interfering) God which his readers may have in their minds.

He had therefore finally to convince us that 'the Father' in his own poem is a cipher merely, one signifier among many, of the inexpressible reality. Other signifiers of the same reality include the Son, Adam and Satan. Blake was right to see the chief figures in the poem as interchangeable. But it is the Son who is uniquely the sign, the figure of speech, the rhetorical trope of the Father. In him 'all his Father . . ./[is] substantially expressed' (3:139–40); he is the

> divine similitude
> In whose conspicuous countenance, without cloud
> Made visible, the almighty Father shines
> Whom else no creature can behold
>
> (3:384–7)

In the words attributed to the Father, the Son alone is 'My word, my wisdom, and effectual might' (3:170). One has to say 'attributed to the Father', for if the Son himself is the only finally valid sign of the Father in the entire universe, then the words and actions of the figure who is given the name of the Father in the poem can only have the function of illuminating and confirming the signifying function of the figure who is given the name of the Son. They can tell us nothing directly about the Father. Thus while Milton's Father, as God, is superior to the Son as not-God, the *sign* of the Father, both in *Paradise Lost* and in the text of creation, is subordinate to the *sign* of the Son. It follows that the character who so distresses Blake, Godwin, Shelley, Empson, Carey and Hill has least importance on those occasions and in those speeches when he seems most discouragingly to be present.

The Father, then, is not to be found in *Paradise Lost* or the Book of the Universe, not even, at least in his fullness, in the sign of the Son, for while the Son may be a complete realisation of the Father's nature, he appresents only aspects of it – the Father's 'effectual might', for example, and not his latent omnipotence. Even when the Father's 'unclouded Deity' (10:65) blazes forth upon him, he still only expresses 'all his Father manifest' (10:66), and not the Father's unmanifested depths. But the Son, too, is invisible. As the transparent expression of the Father he conceals *himself* from all scrutiny except the Father's. What he is in himself can only be understood indirectly through the system of signs in which he locates himself, specifically in the light of those other bearers of his title, Son of God. These, in the first instance, are the angels (including the fallen angels) but subsequently, since he becomes a man, human beings also. To illuminate the sign of the Son, therefore, and so at one remove, the sign of the Father, we have to turn to the signs of humanity, and in particular to Adam and Eve and the Jesus of *Paradise Regain'd*, each of whom is a reader and re-reader of the self and others. To grasp the sign of humanity, therefore, and through it the sign of the Son in which can be glimpsed the self-revelation of the Father, it is necessary to re-examine the act of *reading* in Milton's poems, by which his characters make sense of themselves, the appresented Other [God], and the contextually presented world.

On the day of her creation, Eve wakes up 'much wondering where/ And what' (4:451–2) she is. From the beginning she is in a world of signs – she can ask questions, even if she lacks sufficient words to make complete sense of her context. Hence the periphrastic awkwardness of her narrative, which represents her gazing at the sky and then recognising in the lake's 'liquid plain' (4:455) the sign of 'another sky' (4:459). But this new sign contains an image as the former does not and so signifies other than at first appears. The image in the lake, however, is not the sign of someone else that it seems at first, but a sign of herself. Moreover, it reflects her incompletely, just as the lake is incomplete as a sign or image of the sky. To find a fuller image of herself (though at the same time one which is disturbingly different) she must meet Adam.

Thus for Eve every sign reveals its own incompleteness, and thereby facilitates further signification, further appresented horizons.

Adam enters the world of signs more assuredly. He speaks as lord of sublunary signification, though he is not the source of his own words since they were in use when the world was being made by the Word. (Signifiers are thus prior to their referents if not to what they signify.) Yet each word that Adam discovers leads him beyond himself to the question of his own origins, and even when his surmise about those origins is confirmed in a dream, together with his authority as constituter of signs, his mind moves unerringly towards the terrain of uncertainty, where what is expressed cannot be named:

> O by what name [he asks], for thou above all these,
> Above mankind, or aught than mankind higher,
> Surpassest far my naming, how may I
> Adore thee . . .?
>
> (8:357–60)

Thus Adam and Eve in their reading of the universe do not discover fixed and defining meanings, but absences and traces. But are they unerasable traces, as Michael's references to 'the track Divine' seem to suggest, and so finally based on a metaphysic of presence? To clarify this problem we need to consider the 'readings' of Jesus in *Paradise Regain'd*.

Like Adam and Eve, Jesus is a reader and a sign of reading, a text subject to interpretation and self-interpretation in time. He develops in and through his readings of Scripture, of the world, of the signs of the times, and of himself. Moreover, like that of Adam and Eve, his reading involves him in a continual reinterpretation of what he has already read. He describes, for example, how he first read himself against other children and found himself more 'Serious to learn and know' (1:203). So he turned to learning, to the Law, and as his knowledge of the latter increased and found confirmation in the Temple, he re-examined himself and found in himself a spirit to perform 'victorious deeds . . . heroic acts' (1:215–16) first for the liberation of Israel, then for that of the world, though his preference was always for persuasion rather than force. However, alerted by his mother to the fact that he was 'no son of mortal man' (1:234) but of 'the eternal King' (1:236), he read the Scriptures yet again and discovered there the evidence of his own messiahship. In consequence he had once more to rethink the future, substituting 'a hard assay even to the death' (1:264) for the victorious and heroic deeds which had earlier attracted him. But he still remained in waiting, a private man, until his baptism confirmed his Sonship of God, and indicated that the time had come for him to proclaim the Authority which he derived from Heaven. Now for the first time his self-reading is to be tested, and in his

conduct during that temptation we can at last decipher the reality of
which all such reading is the sign.

As followers of Jesus, however, we can only read the Jesus-text by the
power of the Spirit; . . . but what does a mind possess when it is
possessed of the Spirit? Not, certainly, unimpeded access to the facts: the
Spirit does not by-pass textuality. Even the Jesus of *Paradise Regain'd* has
no privileges over Satan in this respect. Both are competent readers of
the Jesus-text. At the end of the poem, for example, Satan tells Jesus:

> soon thou shalt have cause
> To wish thou never hadst rejected thus
> Nicely or cautiously my offered aid,
> Which would have set thee in short time with ease
> On David's throne; or throne of all the world,
> Now at full age, fulness of time, thy season,
> When prophesies of thee are best fulfilled.
> Now contrary, if I read aught in Heaven,
> Or Heaven write aught of fate, by what the stars
> Voluminous, or single characters,
> In their conjunction met, give me to spell,
> Sorrows, and labours, opposition, hate,
> Attends thee, scorns, reproaches, injuries,
> Violence and stripes, and lastly cruel death,
> A kingdom they portend thee, but what Kingdom,
> Real or allegoric, I discern not,
> Nor when, eternal sure, as without end,
> Without beginning; for no date prefixed
> Directs me in the starry rubric set.
>
> (4:375–93)

Not a word of this is 'untrue': because the allegoric is also real, and the
real, especially the politically real, is simultaneously a deceit, Satan can
even make good his promises, while in other respects his views are
consistent with and confirmed by the opening speech of Jesus in Book 1.

The two speeches, however, also diverge no less clearly, and a
comparison of some remarks of Satan the morning after he delivers the
speech just quoted and the end of Jesus's opening meditation reveals the
nature of this divergence and therefore what it is in Jesus that the Spirit
of Truth communicates to his followers. Having tormented the sleeping
Jesus with horrific dreams and a storm-tossed night, Satan declares:

> Did I not tell thee, if thou didst reject
> The perfect season offered with my aid

> To win thy destined seat, but wilt prolong
> All to the push of fate, pursue thy way
> Of gaining David's throne no man knows when,
> For both the when and how is no where told
> (4:467–72)

Satan regards not knowing the when and how as intolerable. Accordingly his entire project in *Paradise Regain'd* is to fix the precise 'degree of meaning' attaching to the title Son of God when applied to Jesus. For him, to quote Barthes, 'plural is the Evil';[7] he rebels against the freedom of a shifting title, how it is possible to become what you already are, to be found, as the Father himself expresses it in *Paradise Lost*, 'By merit more than birthright Son of God' (3:309). But Jesus in *Paradise Regain'd* waits for illumination. His speech concludes:

> And now by some strong motion I am led
> Into this wilderness, to what intent
> I learn not yet, perhaps I need not know;
> For what concerns my knowledge God reveals
> (1:290–3)

Aware of his own history as related by his mother, of the promises of Scripture, and of the title conferred on him by the voice from Heaven, Jesus can accept, in Barthes's words, that the 'plural of the Text depends . . . not on the ambiguity of its contents but on . . . the stereographic *plurality* of its weave of signifiers' (159). To fix a meaning, as Satan wishes to, is to consume the sign: instead Jesus accepts his self-reading as 'play, activity, production, practice' (162). Thus the difference between Satan and Jesus is in their responses to *différance*, upon which Satan seeks to impose totalitarian closure, but in which Jesus discerns by faith his Father's will. It would seem then, that in the Christian, the Spirit of Truth is precisely that openness to *différance* manifested by Jesus in *Paradise Regain'd*.

But what does such openness involve? In the first place a responsible awareness of oneself as the site of the problem and the challenge. This is made clear in Milton's account of the reading of Scripture. In *Of Civil Power* he writes:

we of these ages, having no other divine rule or authoritie from without us warrantable to one another as a common ground but the holy scripture, and no other within us but the illumination of the Holy Spirit so interpreting that scripture as unwarrantable only to our selves and to such whose consciences we can so persuade, can have no ground in matters of religion but only the scriptures. And these being

> not possible to be understood without divine illumination, which no
> man can know at all times to be in himself, much less to be at any time
> for certain in any other, it follows clearly, that no man or body of men
> . . . can be the infallible judges or determiners in matters of religion to
> any other men's consciences but their own.
>
> (7:242–3)

Here we have a notably powerful affirmation of a world of signs in which
the noncentre is determined otherwise than as loss of centre. Truth is
Scripture only; the light required to read it by is both uncertain and
deeply personal; we can only grasp what is said contingently and for
ourselves alone. The act of doing so, however, is no desperate expedient,
but a profoundly self-constituting human act.

Nevertheless, openness to *différance* also involves a deconstruction of
the self, amounting to *total* self-effacement. At the beginning of *Paradise
Regain'd*, Jesus accepts the prospect of 'many a hard assay even to the
death' (1:264); he subsequently forgoes every opportunity for epiphany
offered in the course of the poem; and by its end he has still not specified
his own nature to himself – Scripture, his mother's narrative and the title
given to him by the voice from heaven remain an irreducibly plural text
requiring unlimited collaboration. He accepts, in effect, that he can never
be fully in the presence of himself, that he continues to await
supplementation. He thus collaborates in his own decomposition. But he
is not effacing himself before nothing, as a modern deconstructionist
critic like Vincent Leitch effaces himself before *différance*. For Leitch, the
'qualities of play and detour characteristic of différance keep it from
appearing as origin, as being-present . . . as master-concept or word.
Neither process nor product, différance is nothing'.[8] But for Jesus
différance is everything. He is after all the sign of the Father.
Consequently his self-effacement, his identification of himself with
différance, not only reveals the hidden essence which the glory of
messiahship concealed in *Paradise Lost*, but also the will of the Father
expressed by, and therefore concealed within, the sign of the Son.
Différance in *Paradise Regain'd* is thus the glass in which Jesus sees that of
which he is the image. In identifying himself with his own plurality as a
text, he encounters not a mere reflection of himself such as Eve found in
the waters of the Lake, but an image which is truer for being, as Adam
later was for Eve, another person. He effaces himself before a reality
greater than himself – his Father; but the Father, as the one of whom
Jesus is the sign, must therefore be himself in a state of free and
unconditional self-effacement before his Son. The ultimate reality in
Milton's final poems, the most available sign of which is the Spirit of
Truth working in the mind and heart of the Christian reader, is God's
grant of freedom to the Son, and thence to all other acting persons in

creation, his primordial and unconditional commitment, proclaimed in *Paradise Lost*, to

> the high decree
> Unchangeable, eternal, which ordained
> Their freedom
>
> (3:126–8)

Milton's God, therefore, is not absent from creation merely as an expedient for making matter, nor even by virtue of there being no logical point of entry for a transcendental signifier into the cosmic text, but by choice, in the mystery of a total self-abnegation which effects total self-realisation. He does not encounter the alterity of his creatures phenomenologically; rather, he separates himself from them and endows them with a sovereignty exactly comparable with his own self-expressing and self-effacing heart.

Notes

1. ROLAND BARTHES, 'The Death of the Author', *Image Music Text*, tr. Stephen Heath (Glasgow: Fontana/Collins, 1977), p. 147.

2. JACQUES DERRIDA, *Writing and Difference*, tr. Alan Bass (London: Routledge & Kegan Paul, 1978), p. 227. Hereafter cited in the text as WD.

3. V.H. VOLOSINOV, *Marxism and the Philosophy of Language*, tr. Ladislaw Matejka and I.R. Titunik (London and New York: Seminar Paper, 1973), p. 36. (This work is now generally attributed to Mikhail Bakhtin.)

4. Quoted in M. SHERIDAN, *Michel Foucault: The Will (to) Truth* (London and New York: Tavistock Publications, 1980), p. 125.

5. JACQUES DERRIDA, 'The Supplement of Copula', *Textual Strategies and Perspectives in Post-Structuralist Criticism*, ed. J.V. Harrari (London: Macmillan, 1980). Hereafter cited in the text as TS.

6. JACQUES DERRIDA, *Of Grammatology*, tr. Gayatri Chakravorty Spivak (Baltimore and London: The Johns Hopkins University Press, 1976), p. 11.

7. ROLAND BARTHES, 'From Work to Text', *Image Music Text*, p. 160.

8. VINCENT B. LEITCH, *Deconstructive Criticism: An Advanced Introduction* (London: Hutchinson, 1983), p. 43.

10 The Politics of *Paradise Lost**

MARY ANN RADZINOWICZ

In 'The Politics of *Paradise Lost*' I fly the colours of a school of Miltonists who share a common desire to locate the poet in the rich complexities of his own historical moment. Such a school might be said to have been founded by David Masson, variedly exemplified by William Haller, Ernest Barker and Christopher Hill, and represented currently by Joan Bennett, Keith Stavely and Michael Wilding. My own attitudes towards the subject seem to me most like those of Haller crossed with Stavely and Wilding. A monument of the concerns of this school as well as an indispensable tool for individual scholars of its persuasion would be the Yale edition of Milton's complete prose works. Indeed, I think that one of the most interesting developments in current literary theory as applied to John Milton has been the use of the poet's prose works in the interpretation of his *oeuvre*. My book *Toward Samson Agonistes: The Growth of Milton's Mind*, an attempt at tracing the trajectory made by the interrelationships of almost all the works of Milton's brain read chronologically, would have been incomparably more difficult without the Yale prose.

It is Milton's contribution to the political history of his age, in contradistinction, say, to the social or religious, however, that particularly concerns me in this essay, as often elsewhere. Milton's work has never lacked for political readers. My work resembles that of those who comment on the history of Milton's ideology, or on Milton's changes of stance in the developing relationship between his times and his politics. Ernest Sirluck was an early inspiration. I agree with Steven Zwicker and Kevin Sharpe in finding it interesting that the

* Reprinted from *Politics of Discourse: The Literature and History of Seventeenth-Century England*, ed. Kevin Sharpe and Steven N. Zwicker (Berkeley: Los Angeles, London: University of California Press, 1987).

moralizing politics of *Paradise Lost* was anachronistic when it appeared in 1667 in the Restoration and yet an inspiration to revolutionary change only eleven years later at the time of the Glorious Revolution. The strategies I've used in this essay to get at Milton's paideutic politics are those I tend to favour, the biographical and intertextual.

One received opinion concerning *Paradise Lost* tells us that when Milton's political hopes for his nation were dealt the fatal blow of the Restoration, he withdrew into regions of the mind where he could find other-worldly solace and mingled no more with politics. Of this view Coleridge gave the romantic account:

> In [Milton's] mind itself there were purity and piety absolute; an imagination to which neither the past nor the present were interesting, except as far as they called forth and enlivened the great ideal in which and for which he lived; a keen love of truth, which, after many weary pursuits, found a harbour in a sublime listening to the still voice in his own spirit, and as keen a love of his country, which, after a disappointment still more depressive, expanded and soared into a love of man as a probationer of immortality. . . . He was, as every truly great poet has ever been, a good man, but finding it impossible to realize his own aspirations, either in religion, or in politics, or society, he gave up his heart to the living spirit and light within him, and avenged himself on the world by enriching it with this record of his own transcendent ideal.[1]

Offered with varying degrees of approbation depending on the critic, that picture of the epic poet abandoning politics for religion, to endow the world with a sublime rather than a politically or historically critical vision, remains current. It is the view made official or marmorealized for this generation in *A Milton Encyclopedia*, for example, in which Michael Fixler writes, 'The Restoration guaranteed a political amnesty to all but the worst offenders against the Stuarts, and Milton was one of those who narrowly escaped proscription. Thereafter he was prudently silent, except for an allusion to tyrants in *Paradise Lost* that caused a small flutter.'[2]

A contrary position argues that *Paradise Lost* participates in Milton's persistent concern with politics but reveals the unrepentant radical wrestling hard to bring his libertarian views into accord with his theology. This stand also received its standard formulation by a romantic, William Blake. Blake located the ideological content of the epic in the struggle between Satan and God, a struggle he said was internalized and unresolved in the poet: '[Milton] wrote in fetters when he wrote of Angels of God, and at liberty when of Devils & Hell because he was . . . of the Devils party without knowing it.'³ Its continuing currency can be seen in Jackie DiSalvo's examination of Milton's 'revolutionary contradictions.' By her reading, Milton, 'spokesman for a new elite as well as the scourge of an old one,' deposits in Satan's 'democratic, antipatriarchal, irreligious views' his own pre-Restoration republicanism. The resulting 'contradictory allegiances of his poem and . . . repressive implications of his ideology' reveal the 'double-edged' nature of the poem.⁴

If one might characterize the first position as *Paradise Lost* read without reference to history, the second position reads *Paradise Lost* by historical hindsight or second sight, to find encrypted in Milton's poem political positions predictive of our own. It is not so much that Milton is seen to be a source of some aspects of the thought of these times; rather, it is that he is their prophetic prototype. For Herman Rapaport, for example, Milton becomes the forerunner of the brutalized, dehumanized modern state.⁵

Both these judgments – of politics abandoned and of politics encrypted – draw force from undoubted features of the poem. Its subject is biblical – the Fall of Man – and like the Bible's, its declared object is the justification of God's ways. Both justify God by blaming man's choices for his fall and by registering the salvation of believers. That being so, it can seem either that Milton's eye is on the end of time and he does not care about interim human arrangements or that his faith in the people is too diminished to support politics. Second, its normative language is at once ethical, religious, and political and is just as much the property of devils and fallen men as of angels or inspired men. Hence it can seem either that Milton represents his own earlier positions taken over by bad creatures for bad ends, or repudiated by weak men tempted, or even that he conceals his own political hopes in the good rebellion of the Fallen Angel or the just power of the angelic few.

This essay will offer a different picture of the poem than either the picture of political disengagement or of political encryption. I will argue that in line with Milton's humanistic understanding of the nature and function of heroic poetry, *Paradise Lost* has a public role to play in the poet's own day. Milton responds to the expectation of a 'fit audience' for epic poetry that it will 'imbreed and cherish in a great people the seeds of virtue, and public civility.'⁶ His poem is paideutic. In fitting himself for the writing of heroic poetry, he cautioned himself 'not [to presume] to sing high praises of heroic men, or famous cities, unless he have in himself the experience and the practice of all which is praiseworthy.'⁷ Accordingly he made himself both teacher and public servant before subsuming those vocations in the calling of heroic poet. *Paradise Lost* constitutes a course in political education, and political education serves in Milton's epic purposes that a political program might play in another kind of work. Accordingly the essay will examine the problems of subject and language – taking up Milton's conception of biblical authority, his radicalization of the story of the Fall, and his ways of using fallen language – as these matters become the very themes in the poem's political education, the problems set by the poet-political teacher in the way a Socratic educator sets problems, the occasions for debate, and instances for correction.[8]

Paradise Lost, then, is directed on the political level 'to make the people fittest to chuse, and the chosen fittest to govern.'[9] Consequently I will deal with Milton's political ideas as an overt subject in the poem. The overt political thought itself presents a sufficient challenge for interpretation without resort to remoter levels of signification, where dwells the politics of criticism rather than the politics of discourse. The political concepts addressed in *Paradise Lost* are the three dominant ideas of continuous concern to Milton: freedom, order, and degree; their interrelationship; their appropriate protection; and their development through changing institutions in the course of history. Milton's method is not that of the propagandist for this or that institution or program; his method is that of the teacher. The text he sets before his readers is a biblical text, and with the political implications of choosing such a text we may begin.

The politics of the biblical subject

Several times as a young writer of prose Milton set himself to prove that a political or legal arrangement – divorce, for example, or the Presbyterian form of church government – which he desired in the 1640s had been especially recommended or urged in Scripture centuries earlier. That is not the method of argument in political matters the heroic poet adopted in *Paradise Lost*. He does not search Scripture seeking precedents, freely interpreting the text in order to find them. He reads Scripture seeking its rational interpretation. Satisfied that he has rightly judged the significance of this or that occasion, his interpretation does not become the precedent to which current affairs are made conformable; rather, the free use of reason in an act of interpretation becomes the precedent, the mode by which current affairs are judged.

One paradigmatic example may illustrate Milton's political way with the Bible. His procedure is to offer a course in political education through biblical texts set to be interpreted. The persistently corrective effect of reading Scripture is the lesson he now provides, in contradistinction to that youthful practice of arguing that his own positions are supported by decisive precedents. In the prose work closest in time to *Paradise Lost, The Readie and Easie Way*, written in the consciousness of the defeat of the Good Old Cause, Milton holds that 'to make the people fittest to chuse, and the chosen fittest to govern' is

> to mend our corrupt and faulty *education*, to teach the people faith not without virtue, temperance, modesty, sobriety, parsimony, justice; not to admire wealth or honour; to hate turbulence and ambition; *to place everyone his private welfare and happiness in the public peace, liberty and safety*.

The first and last points enjoin his readers not to rest in the insight they already have and not to identify the public welfare with their own private moral well-being. It was not for that exclusive purity of conscience that Milton thought God covenanted with mankind. As teaching the triad of political ideas of freedom, order, and degree is half the point in Milton's Bible course, the other half is teaching the politics of historical covenant and progressive revelation.

The paradigm of Milton's Bible-based political education is Solomon's advice, 'Go to the ant.' In *The Readie and Easie Way to Establish a Free Commonwealth* (second edition) Milton writes,

> And what madness is it, for them who might manage nobly their own affairs themselves, sluggishly and weakly to devolve all on a single person; and more like boys under age than men, to commit all to his patronage and disposal, who neither can perform what he undertakes, and yet for undertaking it, though royally paid, will not be their servant, but their lord? How unmanly must it needs be, to count such a one the breath of our nostrils, to hang all our felicity on him, all our safety, our well-being, for which if we were aught else but sluggards or babies, we need depend on none but God and our own counsels, our own active virtue and industry; *Go to the Ant, thou sluggard, saith Solomon; consider her ways, and be wise; which having no prince, ruler, or lord, provides her meat in the summer, and gathers her good in the harvest*, which evidently shows us, that they who think the nation undone without a king, though they look grave or haughty, have not so much true spirit and understanding in them as a pismire; neither are these diligent creatures hence concluded to live in lawless anarchy, or that commended, but are set the examples to imprudent and ungoverned men, of frugal and self-governing democracy or commonwealth; safer and more thriving in the joint providence and counsel of many industrious equals, than under the single domination of one imperious lord.[10]

The test from Proverbs is interpreted as supporting Milton's desired commonwealth by an argument from nature, not from scriptural law or revelation. Solomon becomes a good moral naturalist in Milton's hands, not one of God's secretaries.

When the same instance occurs in *Paradise Lost*, the ant enters unaccompanied by Solomon, having just been created with all its political evidence before Solomon's reign:

> . . . First crept
> The parsimonious emmet, provident
> Of future, in small room large heart enclosed,
> Pattern of just equality perhaps
> Hereafter, joined in her popular tribes
> Of commonalty.
>
> (7:484–9)

Here the ant predicts both the natural argument and Solomon's way of making it. In both cases made through the 'Minims of Nature,' the argument from Scripture (Solomon) is really an argument from nature (the ant); in the second case history (the 'Hereafter') shows men gaining illumination. God covenants with mankind to protract history so that such increases in understanding may take place.

So it is with all Milton's political instances involving scriptural scenarios in *Paradise Lost*. In them Scripture is history and not authority; no interpretation is coercive; no public policy comes with God's fiat behind it to overrule freedom. Furthermore, as in matters of faith the Bible provides progressive revelation, so in matters of civil policy, if rightly read, it records illuminating changes. Even the negative instances of Hell are rendered cautionary by their unreasoned quality and not merely as the vile precedents of evildoers. Sometimes, after all, the fallen angels do well in civil matters:

> O shame to men! Devil with Devil damned
> Firm concord holds, men only disagree
> Of creatures rational, though under hope
> Of heavenly Grace; and God proclaiming peace,
> Yet live in hatred, enmity, and strife
> Among themselves, and levy cruel wars,
> Wasting the Earth, each other to destroy:
> As if (which might induce us to accord)
> Man had not hellish foes enow besides,
> That day and night for his destruction wait.
>
> (2:496–505)

John Milton

As the paradigm of the ants predicted, all the biblical kingdoms of
Heaven, Hell, and earth are shown in *Paradise Lost* as scenes in a
historical or realistic fiction. They permit lessons to be taught about
liberty, order, and degree. They are not given as scriptural precedents,
offering a divine model, cautioning against a diabolical model, or
correcting a human model. When God is shown as King of Heaven in the
epic, Milton's principal biblical sources are Ezekiel and Daniel,[11] but his
most prominent source is Arthurian romance – Spenser, not Scripture.
What Milton utterly repudiated as unfit for 'higher argument' ('tinsel
trappings,' 'gorgeous knights') he briefly uses to suggest God's glory; but
God's heavenly enthronement offers no model for a human state. One
scene may stand for all Milton's depictions of kingship in Heaven, that in
book 5, in which Raphael opens the education of Adam by describing
God's appointment of the Son. On a flaming 'holy hill' sit God and the
Son: The 'empyreal host / Of angels' are 'by imperial summons called'
together. They arrive in 'orders bright' organized under ensigns,
standards, and gonfalons that 'Stream in the air, and for distinction serve
/ Of hierarchies, of orders, and degrees' (5:588–91), and they wheel in
concentric circles around God's throne. He addresses them proclaiming
His Son His heir – or, rather, His kingly vicegerent, since inheritance
cannot be at issue where monarch and subject are all immortal. The
words of institution Milton writes for God stress the initiation of a
peculiar political state:

> This day I have begot whom I declare
> My only Son, and on this holy hill
> Him have anointed, whom ye now behold
> At my right hand; your Head I him appoint;
> And by my Self have sworn to him shall bow
> All knees in Heaven, and shall confess him Lord:
> Under his great Vice-gerent reign abide
> United as one individual soul
> For ever happy
>
> (5:603–11)

Here on the heels of a feudal picture of Heaven, Milton installs a
vicegerent Son. He rejects the Son's hereditary right for a much more
political reason than the theological question of the Father's unique
unbegottenness, however. He rejects it in order to instate the Son as Son
on the grounds of merit; and, as we shall see, he insists on vicegerency
rather than kingly inheritance in order to wash out the political inference
that kingship on earth mysteriously resembles or is sanctioned by
kingship in Heaven. The Son's merit was the grounds God recognized in
book 3 when the offer to die for mankind was made:

126

[Thou] hast been found
By merit more than birthright Son of God,
Found worthiest to be so by being good,
Far more than great or high.

(3:308–11)

The appointment in terms of merit creates a fraternity or a united community that God's imperial decree publishes. The angels are 'for ever happy' to be led and united by the best created being, whom the angel Abdiel calls 'one of our numbers.' It is impossible to argue that this concept of merited 'sonship' is a necessary part of the subordinationism so familiar to theology, or that its grounds in God's desire to augment the quantum of freedom and fraternity in the universe is a necessary aspect of that perfectly unheretical doctrine, let alone that either proposition is particularly biblical. Milton enthrones God in a scene from a medieval romance made quasi-biblical. He enthrones the Son in a meritocracy of which the natural political result is a loosening of God's empire and a strengthening of ties among creatures. And finally, although he attributes this arrangement to God's calculated relinquishment of power, not to His tightening of it, the arrangement is held to be valuable for its reasonableness (it promotes unity and happiness), not for its divine binding.

Milton's meritocracy endorses hierarchy or degree. That has given it a bad name with those who have not noticed the class structure in their own political arrangements and have gone on to ask questions about the roots of the class structure. What is distinctive about Milton's hierarchy, however – its individualistic, voluntaristic, and meritocratic basis – is equally what makes his concept of covenant distinctively nonbiblical or, as Milton would prefer no doubt, Gospel rather than Old Testament. Covenant in the Old Testament is entirely an external arrangement made by God according to His will, unmerited by human beings, unproposed by the human will, and tribal as often as individual. Milton's sense of gospel covenant or Christian liberty is a different matter. With respect to religious institutions, it produces a fraternity of voluntary Protestants, all equally priests: 'Obviously,' he writes, 'if religious matters were not under our control, or to some extent within our power and choice, God could not enter into a covenant with us, and we could not keep it, let alone swear to keep it.'[12] Christian liberty also produces the possibility of sustained political evolution throughout history, the element in which progressive, independent, and free civil contracts are made. Of human covenants, or social and political contracts, Milton is sure that they must be entered into voluntarily, that they bind only as they reasonably fulfil the conditions for which they were made, and that they tend to failures related to man's fall, although the protraction of human history was intended in the divine covenant for their perfecting.

Satan, of course, as we shall see, is one of the sharpest critics of God's first devolution of power in appointing the Son vicegerent. Through the diabolical interpretation of Heaven's civility, Milton makes a number of points about the language of politics in his own day. But what of Satan's own political example? Whatever Satan has to say of God's tyranny and however beautifully Milton conducts that argument to secure political paideia, Satan's actual example is of a frozen meritocracy or tyranny. Like an Alexander or a Tamburlaine, a hero of power, Lucifer leads his own troops into battle. Once seated in Hell on his 'Throne of Royal State' made by Mammon more magnificent than 'Babilon, / . . . or great Alcairo,' he too is 'by merit raised / to [his] bad eminence.' His reign is condemned for its exploitive imperialism (as bad as anything the Turks can parallel) and its rapacity (likened to that of the ubiquitous spice merchants in an irony condemning both). Milton's biblical authority for Satan's bad kingship is Revelation 2.13: 'I know where . . . Satan's throne is,' but his sultanizing of Satan's tyrannic kingship as well as his echo of Spenser's presentation of Lucifer in the court scene indicates the contemporary associations with Romish pomp, illegal capital formation, and unconstitutional usurpation Milton wishes to promote.[13] (With respect for fiscal morality, from the Lady's hopes in *Comus* for just distribution, through the advice to Fairfax on the subject of sequestration that 'public faith [be] cleared from the shameful brand / Of public fraud,' to Milton's scornful rejection of the economic argument for monarchy in *The Readie and Easie Way* – 'lest tradesmen should mutiny for want of trade' – the poet has shown himself to be uneasy about business amorality. He takes the same jaundiced view of exploitiveness in *Paradise Lost* and lodges a criticized commercialism in Mammon's procedures.) As we shall see, Milton entrusts to Abdiel the general political reasoning against Lucifer's claim to uphold freedom in heroic defiance of God's tyranny.

The first presentation of purely earthly kingship in *Paradise Lost* is a sort of divine pleasantry involving Adam's suzerainty over the animal kingdom. When the animals pass before Adam to receive their names, Milton's model is a coronation ceremony:

> . . . each bird and beast behold
> After their kinds; I bring them to receive
> From thee their names, and pay thee fealty
> With low subjection;
>
> (8:342–5)

God pretends to see in the animals' inferiority to Adam grounds for their subjection to man and man's pleasure in lording it over them: 'They . . . reason not contemptibly; with these / Find pastime, and bear rule; thy realm is large.' Milton uses the occasion, however, to demonstrate the incommensurability of God and man, not of beasts and man, and to do so in a way that once and for all negates any claim that man does well to imitate God's ways, political or other, for he cannot. Adam explains:

> Thou in the secrecy although alone,
> Best with thyself accompanied, seekest not
> Social communication, yet so pleased
> Canst raise thy Creature to what height thou wilt
> Of union or communion, deified;
> I by conversing cannot these erect.
>
> (8:427–32)

What Adam can do to increase 'social communication' is to multiply his own kind through 'wedded love . . . / Founded in reason, loyal, just and pure, relations dear.' The scene ends with God's approval of Adam's wish for a mate. Even here the political emphasis is on the establishment of wise institutions after a session of educative reasoning.

Historical kingship, as recorded in the Bible, Milton treats in the last two books of *Paradise Lost*, commencing with Nimrod's tyranny that wickedly ends the pure, brotherly, simple historical commonwealth of Noah's stock 'dwelling / Long time in peace by families and tribes' in 'fair equality, fraternal state.' Adam is shocked by Nimrod's usurpation of authority. He expostulates,

> O execrable son so to aspire
> Above his brethren, to himself assuming
> Authority usurped, from God not given;
> He gave us only over beast, fish, fowl
> Dominion absolute; that right we hold
> By his donation; but man over men
> He made not lord; such title to himself
> Reserving, human left from human free.
>
> (12:64–71)

Milton's interpretation of Nimrod as a figure of the tyrant follows traditional Christian exegesis. Hughes cites Josephus, St Gregory, Dante, and Sir John Fortescue, who treat Nimrod as 'foiled empire builder'; Fowler adds St Jerome and St Basil.[14] But to detest tyranny and to argue republicanism are not the same. And Adam's republicanism is Milton's addition. Clearly human beings left free from other human beings acquire monarch or lord only unwisely.

Michael specifically bends scriptural material toward the presentation of historical lessons of a significantly meritocratic and republican cast. When he praises Adam's condemnation of Nimrod, he makes the point that the burden of upholding liberty falls on man and that political liberty is a matter of individual responsibility. Then he adds,

> Yet sometimes nations will decline so low
> From virtue, which is reason, that no wrong,
> But Justice, and some fatal curse annexed
> Deprives them of their outward liberty
> Their inward lost . . .
>
> (12:97–101)

Those words commence another stage of God's covenant. Although they fall on the ear with bleakness, sharply critical of Milton's own day and predictive of other eras of mindless polity, they do not result in a disengagement from politics or a flight into simple private paradises.

The language of politics and the radical myth of the Fall

Paradise Lost depicts the course of political evolution, then, and not the values of the Puritan Revolution, as Milton argues in favour of the principles of liberty, order, and degree. To read the politics of the poem demands that we interpret a language common to religion and politics that in Milton's day was appropriated by sectarian and secularist, by conservative and radical. In the controversial prose written nearest in time to *Paradise Lost* and when the collapse of the commonwealth was certain or nearly so, Milton drew on a single vocabulary for matters of both politics and religion to write 'against two of the most prevailing usurpers over mankind, superstition and tyranny' to effect 'the liberation of all human life from slavery.'[15] He made no linguistic distinction between the spheres of spirit and state. Thus in *A Treatise of Civil Power in Ecclesiastical Causes*, he opens a phrase with the words 'a free, elective and rational . . .' to complete it with the word 'worship'; in *The Readie and Easie Way* not worship but government attracts the same words, 'free,' 'voluntary,' and 'rational.'[16] In that tract he tells us he is speaking still 'the language of that which is not called amiss the good old Cause.'[17] It is not the case that in writing prose in that language Milton used plain perspicuous terms that differentiated between civil and religious matters, whereas in writing poetry he did not. It is the case, however, that he was well aware that the same terms can signify opposed positions, whatever the medium used. In the end Milton took advantage of poetry's linguistic self-consciousness in proffering his post-Restoration politics in that medium.

That the language of the 'good old Cause' can be common property of men of opposed persuasions Milton knew and often said. He referred to that linguistic ambiguity both when he wrote with a scholarly skepticism in *De doctrina Christiana* – 'if there be anything like a universal meaning for language' – and when he delivered in Sonnet XI, 'I did but prompt the age to quit their clogs,' a punning, ironic rebuke to the 'detractors of certain treatises,' the divorce tracts, and *Areopagitica*. There he turned against his Presbyterian opponents the very phrase they used to attack him, that his divorce proposal was a 'mere authorizing of licence,' by identifying their 'bawl for freedom' with their demand for the licensing of books: 'Licence they mean when they cry liberty.'[18] He made a like point about linguistic appropriation through Nimrod, the political tyrant in *Paradise Lost*,

> [Who] from rebellion shall derive his name,
> Though of rebellion others he accuse.
> (12:36–7);

a like point about the sloganeering of language in *Samson Agonistes* when he referred to

> . . . that sore battle when so many died
> Without reprieve adjudged to death
> For want of well pronouncing Shibboleth.
> (287–9)

and a like point about ambiguity through the Devil's advocacy when Satan claims in *Paradise Regained* that the title 'The Son of God' 'bears no single sense' (4:516). In *Paradise Lost*, partly because language is ambiguous and important normative words are so susceptible to appropriations, Milton invoked the heavenly Muse Urania, 'by that name / if rightly thou art called, . . . / The meaning, not the name I call' (7:1–2, 5).

To *Paradise Lost* conceived as political text, Milton brought two strategies to stabilize and dramatize his meaning. First he embodied in the poem a radicalization of the story of the Fall; whatever key terms might slip or suffer outright theft the tale itself would record to reinforce his meaning. As we shall see, he radicalized the scriptural story by rationally interpreting several features found in Genesis. He lodged freedom to choose not only in prelapsarian but also in fallen man as the law of his being; he defined Adam's and our humanity as consisting of reason and choice; he identified trial and changed choices as the source of purification for the fallen. Second, he made his course of political education actually turn on the correction of false usages; increasing linguistic sophistication would protect his readers from the misinformation he thought made right choice so difficult. Milton had earlier offered a similarly political account of the fall of Adam and Eve in *Areopagitica* by arguing the hereditability of Adam's freedom for Adam's sons, to demonstrate that the Fall proves the law of liberty to be the very law of God's universe, whatever, at this or that historical juncture, men may take to be their law. In *Paradise Lost* by making Satan's rebellion an antecedent myth of the Fall, repeated in postlapsarian falls (specifically Nimrod's), Milton further radicalizes the story. He extends the Fall into a sequence of falls that, far from necessitating man's fate, reaffirms religious and political liberty. Satan's rebellion is political as well as spiritual, no mere subplot but part of a repeated pattern, a design in which failure itself enforces the doctrine of free choice. So too Nimrod's fall instances the repeated pattern. Every fall involves the misuse of language, resolved only with its correction. And finally, as fall and renewed freedom in religion create the condition for progressive revelation, so by the interconnectedness of political and religious language that same pattern endorses continuous change and development in politics.

Perhaps the simplest way to indicate how the Genesis story was radicalized by the Puritans in general and by Milton in *Areopagitica* in particular is to contrast it with the myth of another garden state implying human choice and perfectibility: the myth of Utopia, a myth to which Milton was clearly attracted when he wrote *The Readie and Easie Way*. Both myths carry the emblem of cognate icons: Eden, a tree wrapped about by the serpent reaching for the apple; Utopia, Hermes's winged or twig-tipped staff enwrapped by two serpents. Each icon – the symbol of man's fall and the image of his scientific power – stands for a vision of man and of change. The Genesis story had its parallel in the *Corpus Hermeticum* translated by Ficino in 1471 and disseminated in sixteen editions before 1500. (That work taught that man was made in the image of God and given dominion over the creatures, had divine creativity within himself as brother to the creating Demiurge, took on mortal body by his own choice in an act involving no fall, in his bodily human form retained his creativity, and could therefore as man reacquire his knowledge of nature to use it for good. He could, that is, make scientific utopias.) Respecting change and permanence, the Paradise myth offers a narrative demonstration that things were not always the way they are now; they have been changed by the Fall from their first estate. If changed from what they were, they may be changed again. As Robert Burton put it, 'Ye have been otherwise, you may and shall be again.'[19] The first change was a horror, a trans*gression* or stepping over the boundary of Eden, of nature and its law. The narrative suggests, however, that change as transgression may become change as trans*cendence*, a change back up and into the circle of God's stability. That version of the Fall is a thoroughly conservative myth: 'Turn back, o man, forsake thy foolish ways.' To radicalize it is to argue that Adam's freedom as well as his punishment are inherited by all his sons: man set on his feet once more by grace and led by his God has only to find in America or make in England a new sacred place and there reform what has been ill-done. If the utopian myth seems more radical in that it does not dub change 'transgression,' it was not so construed in Milton's country and day. The impulse to make utopias was regularly construed in the English Renaissance as suggesting paternalistic and ritualized social arrangements for stability and permanency. Bacon's *New Atlantis* is a typical case. It is not that utopias cannot render radical political states, for of course they often have. But in Milton's day utopia seldom was, whereas the Genesis myth not only could be, but repeatedly was, made to argue social and political reform.

Clearly either myth can make change tolerable and impermanence temporary. The *Readie and Easie Way*, Milton's version of utopia, clearly argues, notwithstanding its courageous republicanism, for a 'perpetual Senate' so that the nation 'firmly constituted to perpetuity' may live 'forever in a firm and free commonwealth.'[20] While repeatedly drawing biblical analogies to the sinful servitude the people will choose if they restore the Stuart monarchy, Milton does not refer to the Fall at all. But *The Readie and Easie Way* is scarcely a revolutionary document; revolution once over, there will be no more revolution. Certainly Milton never repudiated a free commonwealth as a political ideal for his nation, but among all political corrections in *Paradise Lost* is one self-correction, a correction of the very concept of a permanent and changeless political utopia and an acknowledgement that political wisdom is founded through time and experience by stages of choice. Here is how Milton has Michael describe to Adam the lawgiver Moses leading the Chosen People out of bondage into the 'wild Desert':

> *Moses* once more his potent rod extends
> Over the sea; the sea his rod obeys;
> On their embattled ranks the waves return,
> And overwhelm their war: the race elect
> Safe towards Canaan from the shore advance
> Through the wild desert, not the readiest way,
> Lest entering on the Canaanite alarmed
> War terrify them inexpert, and fear
> Return them back to Egypt, choosing rather

> Inglorious life with servitude; for life
> To noble and ignoble is more sweet
> Untrained in arms, where rashness leads not on.
> This also shall they gain by their delay
> In the wide wilderness, there they shall found
> Their government, and their great senate choose
> Through the twelve tribes, to rule by laws ordained.
>
> (12:211–26)

Here Milton directly recalls the attempt of his own 'Readie . . . way' to forestall the rush of the English people back to monarchy in the Restoration, a move he had there likened to the Chosen People's 'choosing them a captain back for Egypt.'[21] He concedes that the choice of something '*not* the readiest way' led to the 'gain' of that very government he so wished for his own people, the 'great senate . . . to rule by laws ordained,' and by implication he suggests that the patience he regards as the highest kind of fortitude has great political value.

Milton does, however, refer in *The Readie and Easie Way* to Nimrod and his analogue, the tower-builder in Luke, to speculate on how the restoration of monarchy will be received in the rest of the modern political world:

> [W]hat will they at best say of us and of the whole English name, but scoffingly as of that foolish builder, mentioned by our Saviour, who began to build a tower, and was not able to finish it. Where is this goodly tower of a commonwealth, which the English boasted they would build to overshadow kings, and be another Rome in the west? The foundation indeed they laid gallantly; but fell into a worse confusion, not of tongues but of factions, than those at the tower of Babel; and have left no memorial of their work behind them remaining, but the common laughter of Europe.[22]

Through the reference to Nimrod Milton draws a double historical parallel between Scripture and his own times, not in proof that God requires the English to preserve their commonwealth but that any reasonable man can see how bad statecraft is like bad architecture and the foolish builders of either are worthy of being mocked.

Although *The Readie and Easie Way* is unrevolutionary in conserving the commonwealth by planning for its frozen permanence, Milton nevertheless makes clear his conviction that kingship implies idolatry, that monarchy implies an apostasy from the rule of free reason, and that his detestations 'tyranny and superstition' are Siamese twins. The autocrat is shown there 'to pageant himself up and down in progress among the perpetual bowings and cringings of an abject people, on either side deifying and adoring him for nothing done that can deserve it.'[23] Religion and politics face the same danger: idolatry. Idolatry is enslavement whether its agent be potentate or prelate. Idolatry of ruler is tyranny; of priest, superstition.

As I have suggested, Milton renders the Fall useful for political education (1) by lodging freedom in both prelapsarian and fallen man as the law of his being, (2) by identifying choice through reason as constitutive of humanity, and (3) by converting trial, struggle, or change itself into the source of purification. Given the figure of Adam in rational choice as the model of the properly human, both religious and political implications for individual free choice naturally follow. Only uncoerced faith is true religion, so that 'if [a man] believe things only because his pastor says so, or the assembly so determines . . . though his belief be true, yet the very truth he holds becomes his heresy.'[24] Autocracy in church or state idolatrously diverts to a human being, honour rightly God's alone.

Milton further radicalizes that radicalized myth of the Fall in *Paradise Lost* by charting a sequence of falls, commencing with the rebellion of Satan and his angelic peers. In the course of that fall Lucifer, debating with Milton's spokesman Abdiel, shows clearly that he has read Milton's prose tracts. He opens his oration, which will urge rebellion against God's tyranny:

> Thrones, Dominations, Princedoms, Virtues, Powers
> If these magnific titles yet remain
> Not merely titular, since by decree
> Another now hath to himself ingrossed
> All power, and us eclipsed under the name
> Of king anointed . . .
>
> (5:722–7)

His contempt for *decree* seems only a slight misapplication of *The Reason of Church Government*: 'In the publishing of human laws . . . to set them barely forth to the people without reason or preface like a physical prescript, or only with threatening, as it were a lordly command, in the judgement of Plato was thought to be done neither generously nor wisely.' His contempt for the *name* of kingship is no misreading at all of *Eikonoklastes*: 'the gaudy name of Majesty . . . a name than which there needs no more among the blockish vulgar, to make it wise, admired, and excellent, nay to set it next the Bible, though otherwise containing little else but the common grounds of tyranny and popery.'[25]

His scorn of the authority merely of 'old repute . . . or custom' usurps Milton's very language in the antiprelatical tracts.[26] In the conclave in Hell the language of Mammon, who calls Heaven a 'state of splendid

vassalage,' of Satan, who speaks of the 'Tyranny of Heaven,' of
Beelzebub, who names God 'our Conqueror . . . Of force . . . Almighty,'
echoing Satan's 'whom Thunder hath made greater' – all that language is
preempted from Milton's own words 'In liberty's defense,' where the
English people are praised variously for resisting vassalage, tyranny, and
insolent conquest.[27]

Like Satan, Milton repeatedly made the point that 'Degrees / Jar not
with liberty' (6:792–3). He would appoint the noblest, worthiest, and
most prudent to determine state affairs in his commonwealth, their
degree to conform to their merit: 'For nature gives the wisest dominion
over those less wise, not a wicked man dominion over the good or a fool
over wise. Whoever takes away their dominion from such as those
behaves altogether in conformity with nature.'[28] His model of an ideal
state is a class structure with unfixed status for every individual and
plenty of room to rise 'improved by tract of time.' Milton's own words
likewise endorse Lucifer's outrage at monarchy over such as live by right
as king's equals: 'a people which has the choice never gives up title to its
own power fully and absolutely to its king, and by nature it cannot; the
grant is only for the sake of the welfare and freedom of the people, and
when the king has failed to secure those the people is taken to have
made no grant. A tyrant is he who regarding neither law nor the
common good, reigns only for himself and his faction.'[29]

Notwithstanding Milton's apparent endorsement of Lucifer in these
echoes, the answer Lucifer receives from Abdiel wrests the language of
revolution back from him and reattaches it to a properly political
narrative of the Fall. A similar correction occurs in Milton's account of
Nimrod's rebellion and fall (12:6–79). That fall is another in the sequence
of falls, which sequentiality makes political lessons out of the stages of
the myth. The episode incorporates Adam's shocked censure of
'authority usurped, from God not given,' and Adam's understanding is
the argument for his sons to read Milton's poem as, among other things,
an education for voters. Nimrod emerges after the sons of Noah, 'this
second source of men,' have dwelt 'long time in peace by families and
tribes under paternal rule'. Then arose Nimrod, 'of proud ambitious
heart . . . not content / With fair equality, fraternal state,' who shattered
the concord of men on earth and brought about a condition very like
Hobbes's 'state of nature,' not Milton's rational state of nature. Nimrod
will 'arrogate dominion undeserved / Over his brethren, and quite
dispossess / Concord and law of Nature from the earth.' Then in his
'ambition to tyrannize' he and his crew build the tower of Babel 'to get
themselves a name, lest far dispersed / in foreign lands their memory be
lost, / Regardless whether good or evil fame.' Like Hobbes again,
Nimrod, who derives his name from 'rebellion' (from Hebrew *marad*),
'Though of rebellion others he accuse', believes that he can make names

mean what he wills them to mean: if he stands on a high tower, he is high; if men call him great, he is great. The kind of rebuke he gets from God exactly answers his assault on 'rational liberty'; God 'sets upon their tongues a various spirit to rase / Quite out their native language.' The Hobbesian linguistic takeover where terms have meaning only relative to their users results in plurality of tongues. The plurality of tongues thus marks the rupture of coherent truth as it emerges from the Creator and the fracturing of every man's fraternal access to it. (It might be noted in passing that both the tower and Hobbes's *Leviathan* display the marks not only of absolutism and linguistic relativity but also of utopianism, by their claims to fixedness and perpetuity.)

Adam's judgment is Milton's; Nimrod committed both tyranny and aspostasy:

> . . . Man over men
> He made not Lord; such title to himself
> Reserving, human left from human free.
> But the usurper his encroachment proud
> Stays not on man; to God his tower intends
> Seige and defiance.
>
> (12:69–74)

Yet as usual Michael extends Adam's reaction in his comment, and Milton converts one more fall into a pattern of radical political paideia. The fall of language into confusion affects men's ability to live in political fraternity. Inner liberty, the reasonable capacity to learn and communicate truth, is the essential precondition for political liberty. Only free men can be brothers; self-enslaved men either struggle for dominion or slackly yield to it:

> . . . Yet know withall,
> Since thy original lapse, true liberty
> Is lost, which always with right reason dwells
> Twinned, and from her hath no dividual being:
> (12:82–5)

Michael then draws for Adam an internal model of the external political model he has shown him:

> Reason in man obscured, or not obeyed,
> Immediately inordinate desires

> And upstart passions catch the government
> From reason, and to servitude reduce
> Man till then free.
>
> (12:86–90)

The deprivation of outer freedom is the inevitable result of the surrender of inner freedom: 'Tyranny must be / Though to the tyrant thereby no excuse.' Justice 'deprives men of their outward liberty, Their inward lost'; and Michael concludes in tragic vein, 'Thus will the latter, as the former world / Still tend from bad to worse.'

As the fall of Satan is used to imply a collective ideal of organic change in opposition to his claim that liberty is nothing but the space in which the self competes for self-aggrandizement, so the fall of Nimrod and its consequences in linguistic relativity are used to imply a contrary ideal to his political vision of the imperial tribe of powerful conquerors led by the mightiest of all. What succeeds is a man capable of self-sacrifice and a nation of his lineage 'in whom *all* nations shall be blessed.' Hence Michael's narrative concludes not with the heroic struggle Adam expects between the usurper tyrant Satan and the greater man but with a 'cure' of men to be achieved 'Not by destroying Satan, but his works / In [Adam] and in [his] seed.' The final lesson of the Fall pattern or sequence is a Christian revolutionary lesson, not a fixed program for political or religious action.

If we read the Fall as a sequential pattern, the poem offers scope for heroic virtue by disclaiming the triumph of one sufficient heroic virtue. The pattern enacts a series of radical correctives, affirming each time a movement to renewed choices in stages of enlightenment. Every fall is accompanied by the proposal of one coercive fixed meaning and concludes with the falsity of the claim made clear in the illumination of alternative meaning. Satan poses as liberator, but a contrary vision of organic change as liberation emerges in the free collective fulfilment suggested by Abdiel. Adam's fall, however, shows man inheriting liberty as well as fallenness and so 'once more on even ground against his mortal foe.' Nimrod's fall is Michael's chance to preach the radical politics of self-conquest as the means to eliminate tyranny and show the absurd falsity of the heroics of linguistic and political usurpation. The expulsion scene goes so far as to correct the very word 'fall' into the 'great deliverance . . . to come . . . on all mankind.' The openness of the epic's conclusion, with the world all before Adam and Eve, offers to Milton's own time the resumption of the challenge to read correctly the easily abused linguistic sign. Adam is not promised utopia, shown fixity, or taught monocausality, for Milton has successfully resisted the

temptation himself to appropriate 'the language of that which is not
called amiss the good old Cause' for a utopian program.

Notes

1. SAMUEL TAYLOR COLERIDGE, Lecture X, *Literary Remains* (London, 1836),
   quoted from James Thorpe (ed.), *Milton Criticism: Selections from Four Centuries*
   (London: Routledge & Kegan Paul, 1951), p. 97.

2. 'Politics, Milton's' by Michael Fixler in Vol. 6 of *A Milton Encyclopedia*, gen. ed.
   William B. Hunter, Jr (Lewisburg, PA: Bucknell University Press, 1979).
   For perhaps the most extreme statement of this position, see Hugh M.
   Richmond, *The Christian Revolutionary: John Milton* (Berkeley, Los Angeles and
   London: University of California Press, 1974), *passim*. Richmond argues that
   political defeat leading to Milton's abandonment of idealist Platonic political
   thought was the very precondition for the creation of the great poem.
   Similarly, in *Milton the Puritan* (London: Macmillan, 1977), A.L. Rowse writes,
   'The Restoration was the best thing that could have happened to Milton. It
   forced him to drop dealing with the ephemera of politics, back upon his own
   true genius, the life of the imagination and its expression in poetry' (p. 215).
   Finally, one might note that although Charles R. Geisst – in the most recent
   study of *The Political Thought of John Milton* (Cambridge: Cambridge University
   Press, 1984) – finds that Adam's fall was a fall into political experience (p. 46),
   he does not specify what in that fallen location Adam or Milton or the reader
   would find political experience to be.
   Jackie DiSalvo notes that 'in quest of [a] political Milton one has had to turn
   mainly to historical studies focused primarily upon his prose, by Arthur
   Barker, Edgell Rickword, William Haller, Don Wolfe, Zera Fink, A.S.P.
   Woodhouse, George Sensabaugh, and Florence Sandler'. See *War of Titans:
   Blake's Critique of Milton and the Politics of Religion* (Pittsburgh: University of
   Pittsburgh Press, 1983), p. 9.

3. 'The Marriage of Heaven and Hell' in *The Poetry and Prose of William Blake*, ed.
   David V. Erdman, rev. edn (New York: Doubleday, 1970). Christopher Hill
   adds, 'the young Wordsworth recalled Milton the libertarian, Shelley recalled
   Milton the defender of regicide'. See 'A Bourgeois Revolution?' in *Three British
   Revolutions, 1641, 1688, 1775*, ed. J.G.A. Pocock (Princeton: Princeton
   University Press, 1980), p. 133.

4. DISALVO, *War of Titans*, pp. 15, 10, 12, 42. She points to support for her
   analysis in Malcolm Ross, *Milton's Royalism: A Study of the Conflict of Symbol and
   Idea in the Poems* (Ithaca, NY: Cornell University Press, 1943), pp. 75–119;
   CHRISTOPHER HILL, *Milton and the English Revolution* (New York: Viking, 1978);
   and EDGELL RICKWORD, 'Milton, the Revolutionary Intellectual' in *The English
   Revolution*, ed. Christopher Hill (London: Lawrence & Wishart, 1940).

5. HERMAN RAPAPORT, *Milton and the Post Modern* (Lincoln: University of
   Nebraska Press, 1983). Rapaport conceives his task in examining 'Milton and
   the State' to be 'to counter the Anglo-American reception of Milton as a great
   humanist in the democratic tradition' (p. 171). He notes, 'I stress, not Milton's
   resistance, but his complicity with the most repellent aspects of fascist, or
   totalitarian action' (p. 172). He speaks of Milton's 'mind harboring a darker
   fascination with dictatorial takeover, with what amounts to another absolutism

much bleaker and calculating than the foppery of Charles I and the grand schemes of the Anglicans under Archbishop Laud' (p. 176).

6. *The Reason of Church Government*, 1:816.

7. *An Apology against a Pamphlet call'd A Modest Confutation of the Animadversions upon the Remonstrant against Smectymnuus*, 1:890.

8. I am very far from proposing that one read the course of political education performed in *Paradise Lost* as a kind of 'Surprized by Ideology', by analogy to the way in which Stanley Fish handles ethical and other ideas in *Surprized by Sin: The Reader in 'Paradise Lost'* (New York: St Martin's Press, 1967). Milton did not, by my reading, calculate a magnificent plot to entrap his readers into such misinterpretations and corrections as would lead him to salvation. His political paideia is overt and historical; it results in progressive enlightenment as to the very slowness and difficulty involved in human arrangements within fallen history. Where Henry James is Fish's tutelary genius, Socrates is Milton's.

9. *The Readie and Easie Way to Establish a Free Commonwealth*, 2nd edn, 7:443.

10. 7:427. The addition to the first edition of the material 'neither . . . Lord' interprets Proverbs 6:6–8 as supporting from nature Milton's argument for a commonwealth.

11. See MICHAEL LIEB, *Poetics of the Holy* (Chapel Hill: University of North Carolina Press, 1981), pp. 121–7, on the influence of Ezekiel, and ALASTAIR FOWLER, *The Poems of John Milton* (London: Longman 1968), p. 713, on the influence of Daniel on Milton's portrayal of God as king. See Ross, *Milton's Royalism*, p. 105, for a clear picture of Milton's Spenserian characterization of Heaven.

12. *Christian Doctrine*, 6:389.

13. See CLAES SCHAAR, *The Full Voic'd Quire Below: Vertical Context Systems in 'Paradise Lost'* (Lund: Gleerup, 1982), pp. 217–6, for a discussion of all the literary strands brought together in the scenes of Satan's enthronement. See MERRITT Y. HUGHES, 'Satan and the "Myth" of the Tyrant' in *Ten Perspectives on Milton* (New Haven: Yale University Press, 1965), pp. 169–71, for an analysis of the aspects of the tyrant Milton emphasizes.

14. MERRITT Y. HUGHES (ed.), *John Milton: Complete Poems and Major Prose* (New York: Odyssey Press, 1957), pp. 454–5; and Hughes, 'Satan and the "Myth" of the Tyrant', *passim*. ALASTAIR FOWLER (ed.), *Paradise Lost* in *The Poems of John Milton* (London: Longman, 1968), pp. 1028–32.

15. *The Readie and Easie Way . . .*, 2d edn, 7:421.

16. *A Treatise of Civil Power*, 7:262. The corresponding words in *The Readie and Easie Way* are used again and again severally.

17. 7:462.

18. The pun is argued for and explained in E.A.J. Honigmann (ed.), *Milton's Sonnets* (New York: St Martin's Press, 1966), pp. 32–3.

19. ROBERT BURTON, *The Anatomy of Melancholy*, ed. Holbrook Jackson (London: J. M. Dent & Sons, 1931), III:415.

20. 7:409, 421, 444.

21. 7:462.

22. 7:422–3

23. 7:426. See also, 'Whereas a king must be adored like a demigod, with a dissolute and haughty court about him . . .' (7:425).

24. 2:543.

25. *The Reason of Church Government*, 1:746. See also *Eikonoklastes*, 3:338–9.

26. *Animadversions* . . ., 1:70, 'that long use and custom . . . hath been nothing else but . . . superstitious devotion'; *Reason of Church Government*, 'not of custom and awe, which most men do' (1:746).

27. See, *inter alia*, *A Defense of the People of England*, 4,i:338, 'this king was a tyrant'; '[who would] ravage the whole realm with fire and sword, since he is so little subject to the laws as to be permitted what he wills' (347); 'He had long planned to turn the government of England into a tyranny, but he thought he could not carry out his plans unless he had first done away with the best part of the citizens' military strength' (529).

28. *A Defense of the People of England*, 4,i:425–6.

29. *A Defense of the People of England*, 4,i:467, 521.

11 When Eve Reads Milton: Undoing the Canonical Economy*

Christine Froula

How do the modes of authority constructed in and through literary texts inform the authority of the literary canon? More specifically, what role does gender play in our conceptions of authority and of literary value? Taking *Paradise Lost* as a canonical text *par excellence*, 'When Eve Reads Milton' brings the poem into dialogue with feminist theory to explore the interrelations of gender and authority both in Milton's depictions of Adam and Eve and in his representations of his own poetic authority. Arguing that Milton's poem reveals the repression of maternal authority as the genesis both of Genesis and of *Paradise Lost*, Froula points to the need to augment a pedagogy that approaches 'Great Books' as sacred texts, and the canon as (in Harry Levin's words) 'our most valued patrimony, our collective memory', with one that, while recognizing literary value, also calls into question the unexamined hierarchies invoked by the Arnoldian ideal, 'the acquainting ourselves with the best that has been thought and said in the world'. Through strategies of rereading that expose the deeper structures of authority and through reading canonical texts alongside texts of a different stamp, teachers of canonical literature might, Froula suggests, pursue a kind of cultural psychoanalysis, transforming 'bogeys' that hide invisible power into investments both visible and alterable.

The appearance of 'When Even Reads Milton' in 1983 elicited a critical response from Edward Pechter and a reply by the author (1984). Since then, it has been widely cited in debates about the literary canon and, more generally, in work on women and social authority.

Let a woman learn in silence with all submissiveness. I permit no woman to teach or to have authority over men; she is to keep silent.

1 Tim. 2:11–12

---

* Reprinted from *Critical Inquiry* **10** (1983).

In *Jacob's Room*, with her nose pressed against a Cambridge window, Virginia Woolf's narrator describes the don within holding forth in speech that is at once coin and communion wafer to an audience of admiring undergraduates:

> Sopwith went on talking. . . . The soul itself slipped through the lips in thin silver disks which dissolve in young men's minds like silver . . . manliness. He loved it. Indeed to Sopwith a man could say anything, until perhaps he'd grown old, or gone under, gone deep, when the silver disks would tinkle hollow, and the inscription read a little too simple, and the old stamp look too pure, and the impress always the same – a Greek boy's head. But he would respect still. A woman, divining the priest, would, involuntarily, despise.[1]

In the sixty years since Woolf wrote this passage, women in significant numbers have broken the barriers which excluded Woolf herself from 'Oxbridge', and now inhabit some of the rooms formerly occupied by Jacob and his dons. I begin with it, however, not to measure women's progress from cultural exclusion but because in contrasting the places and stances of 'man' and 'woman' in the cultural economy, Woolf opens a more complicated question concerning the effects of women's *in*clusion: How are the dynamics of canonists selecting, readers interpreting, teachers teaching, and students learning affected by what is beginning to be a critical mass of women in the academy? Woolf's image is useful to a feminist critique of the literary canon because, rather than focusing on a canonical work, it abstracts what we might call the canonical mode of authority embodied in the don's speech and presents different responses of 'man' and 'woman' to this authority. The don, as 'priest', mediates between his sacred books and his flock. A man, partaking of the 'silver disks', respects; a woman, for whom the male-impressed currency is both inaccessible and foreign, involuntarily despises priestly authority. That woman can 'divine' for herself challenges such authority, implying independence of the don's exclusive mediation. Further, even if we suppose her to have acceded to the don's role as cultural mediator, both her historical exclusion and her independent view suggest that she must play that part in a different way, reforming the traditional model of cultural authority in fidelity to her own experience.

But how might Woolf's 'woman' transform the priestly model that has been instrumental in her own cultural oppression? To ask this question is to conceive cultural authority not merely as a commodity which women seek to possess equally with men but as power which has a political dimension realized in particular stances toward literary texts and literary history, toward language and stories, students and curricula. As the traditional literary canon exists in problematic relation to women, so do the modes of literary authority enshrined in those texts, upon which the social authority that institutes the canon and draws our models of literary history patterns itself. Sixty years after Woolf wrote, it is not only – nor even all – women who are alienated from the modes of authority invoked by cultural canons and priests; for present purposes, therefore, I will borrow Woolf's representation of 'man' as one who 'respect[s] still' the don's mystified cultural authority and 'woman' as one who, 'divining the priest', raises questions about the sources, motives, and interests of this authority. This definition identifies 'woman' not by sex but by a complex relation to the cultural authority which has traditionally silenced and excluded her. She resists the attitude of blind submission which that authority threatens to imprint upon her; further, her resistance takes form not as envy of the 'priest' and desire to possess his authority herself but as a debunking of the 'priestly' deployment of cultural authority and a refusal to adopt that stance herself. Women, under this local rule, can be 'men', as men can be 'women'.[2]

Following the ground-breaking studies of Simone de Beauvoir, Mary Ellmann, and Kate Millett, many feminists have explored the politics of reading the patriarchal canon, which, as Elaine Showalter points out, holds up to the female no less than to the male reader the ideal of thinking 'like a man'.[3] Judith Fetterley, for example, has shown how the study of the traditional American literary canon presses the female reader to identify with the male point of view – the position of power – against herself.[4] In the last fifteen years, women professors of literature have begun to redress the male bias, both by including women authors in the curriculum – in established courses which their very presence exposes as having been previously, and invisibly, preoccupied with 'men's studies', as well as in courses focused on women writers – and by employing the critical and pedagogical strategies of the 'resisting reader' exemplified by de Beauvoir, Millett, Fetterley, and many others.

The effect of this work has been not simply to balance male bias with female (or marginal) bias – the 'opening' of the canon – but to disrupt the canonical economy as such, the dynamics of cultural authority.[5] Feminists have moved from advocating representation of voices formerly silenced or 'marginalized' by the established curriculum to recognizing that such representation implies and effects a profound transformation of the very terms *authority* and *value* – cultural and aesthetic or literary – that underwrite the traditional idea of the canon.[6] As Fetterley puts it: 'To expose and question that complex of ideas and mythologies about women and men which exist in our society and are confirmed in our literature is to make the system of power embodied in the literature open not only to discussion but . . . to change.'[7] Since the opening of the literary canon has been in some degree accomplished, we can now begin to analyze the impact of formerly silenced voices on the political economy of the literary canon, on the 'system of power' that controls which texts are taught and how they are taught. How are 'women' writers and teachers, formerly excluded from positions of cultural authority, affecting the economy of literature? I will take up two aspects of this large question: first, the radical challenge that feminist perspectives pose to the concept of a canon as such – not merely to the history and politics of canon-formation but to the *idea* (and ideal) of 'the canon' – and, second, the critique of traditional modes of literary authority that emerges from reading 'canonical' and 'marginal' texts side by side.

The Politics of Orthodoxy: Canonists vs Gnostics

I begin by extrapolating from Elaine Pagels' book, *The Gnostic Gospels*, to the power dynamics of literary authority, first, as claimed by texts and, second, as 'respected' or 'despised' by readers, teachers, and students. Pagels' study of the second-century gnostic writings discovered at Nag Hammadi in 1945 illuminates the politics implied in the canonist's stance by showing how the rediscovery of the gnostic texts – successfully suppressed by the church fathers in the struggle to establish a unified Church – dispels the widespread myth that all Christians shared the same doctrine in the apostles' time. She shows that early Christianity appears to have been 'far more diverse than nearly anyone expected before the Nag Hammadi discoveries' and that the establishment of the 'one, holy, catholic, and apostolic Church' required the suppression not merely of dissenting voices but of an antithetical conception of spiritual authority embodied in certain gnostic writings.[8]

There are, of course, many important differences between the deployment of cultural authority in the social context of second-century Christianity and that of twentieth-century academia. The editors of the *Norton Anthology*, for example, do not actively seek to suppress those voices which they exclude, nor are their principles for inclusion so narrowly defined as were the church fathers'. But the literary academy and its institutions developed from those of the Church and continue to wield a derivative, secular version of its social and cultural authority. Since Matthew Arnold, the institution of literature has been described in terms which liken its authority to that of religion, not only by outsiders – Woolf's woman 'divining the priest' – but by insiders who continue to employ the stances and language of religious authority; see, for instance, J. Hillis Miller's credo in a recent issue of the *ADE Bulletin*: 'I believe in the established canon of English and American literature and in the validity of the concept of privileged texts. I think it is more important to read Spenser, Shakespeare, or Milton than to read Borges in translation, or even, to say the truth, to read Virginia Woolf.'[9] Such rhetoric suggests that the religious resonances in literary texts are not entirely figurative, a point brought out strikingly by revisionary religious figures in feminist texts. In her recent essay '"The Blank Page" and the Issues of Female Creativity', Susan Gubar cites as some of the 'many parables in an ongoing revisionary female theology' Florence Nightingale's tentative prophecy that 'the next Christ will perhaps be a female Christ', H.D.'s blessed Lady carrying a 'Bible of blank pages', and Gertrude Stein's celebration of *The Mother of Us All*.[10] The *revisionary* female theology promoted in *literary* writing by women implicitly counters the patriarchal theology which is *already* inscribed in literature. The prophesied female Christ, blank Bible, and female Creator revise images familiar in the literary tradition, and, in contrast to earlier appropriations of religious imagery by Metaphysical, Pre-Raphaelite, and other poets, make visible the patriarchal preoccupations of literary 'theology'. These voices, like the gnostic voices recovered at Nag Hammadi, are only now being heard in chorus; and Pagels' study of 'the gnostic feminism' (as the *New York Review of Books* labeled it) helps to illuminate some aspects of a cultural authority predicated on the suppression or domination of other voices.

Reconsidering patristic writings in light of the contemporary gnostic writings, Pagels argues that claims for exclusive authority made by the self-styled orthodoxy of the early Christian Church depended upon a mystification of history: the church fathers, in order to establish privileged texts, claimed that Jesus himself had invested the spiritual authority of the Church in certain individuals, who in turn passed this power on to their chosen successors. Their claim to a privileged spiritual authority rested upon the interpretation of the Resurrection as a historical event witnessed by the eleven remaining disciples. By this interpretation, all 'true' spiritual authority derives from the apostles' witnessing of the literally resurrected Christ – an unrepeatable experience. Remarking the political genius of this doctrine, Pagels outlines its consequences, showing how the restriction of authority to this small band and their chosen successors divided the community into those who had power and those who didn't, privileged authorities and those whom such claims to privilege would dispossess of authority. The interpretation of the Resurrection as a historical event placed its advocates in a position of unchallengeable political dominance: 'It legitimized a hierarchy of persons through whose authority all others must approach God' (*GG*, p. 27).

By contrast, the gnostics, interpreting the Resurrection in symbolic terms, resisted the mediating spiritual authority that the 'orthodox' sought to institute in the Church. Pagels illustrates this conflict between the orthodox and gnostic positions by analyzing a passage from the

gnostic 'Gospel of Mary' in which Mary Magdalene comforts the disciples
as they mourn after Jesus' death. Mary tells them: '"Do not weep, and
do not grieve, and do not doubt; for his grace will be with you
completely, and will protect you."' Peter then invites Mary, Pagels
writes, '"to tell us the words of the Savior which you remember." But to
Peter's surprise, Mary does not tell anecdotes from the past; instead, she
explains that she has just seen the Lord in a vision received through the
mind, and she goes on to tell what he revealed to her.' Andrew and
Peter ridicule Mary's claim that the Lord appeared in her vision, but Levi
defends her: '"Peter . . . if the Savior made her worthy, who are you to
reject her?" Peter, apparently representing the orthodox position, looks
to past events, suspicious of those who "see the Lord" in visions:
Mary, representing the gnostic, claims to experience his continuing
presence' (*GG*, p. 13).[11]

The gnostic position, then, held that those who had received *gnosis*,
that is, self-knowledge as knowledge of divinity,

> had gone beyond the church's teaching and had transcended the
> authority of its hierarchy. . . . They argued that only one's own
> experience offers the ultimate criterion of truth, taking precedence over
> all secondhand testimony and all tradition – even gnostic tradition!
> They celebrated every form of creative invention as evidence that a
> person has become spiritually alive. On this theory, the structure of
> authority can never be fixed into an institutional framework: it must
> remain spontaneous, charismatic, and open.
>
> (*GG*, p. 25)

Pagels' study of 'the politics of monotheism' illuminates the fact that the
Church's aspirations to 'catholicism', or universality, rendered the
gnostic and orthodox interpretations of the Resurrection not merely
different, nor even antithetical, but mutually exclusive. The coincidence
of spiritual and political authority in the Church's self-styled orthodoxy
(or 'right opinion') made 'heretics' of gnostics, defining as politically
dangerous those who did not subscribe to the church fathers' mystified
historical authority. By contrast, prior to any consideration of the 'truth'
of their writings, the gnostics neither claimed for themselves nor
honored the historically based, absolute authority that the church fathers
claimed. It was not, then, a question merely of competing canons, of
differing doctrines or guidelines propounded by groups vying for
cultural dominance, but of two mutually contradictory stances toward
spiritual authority: one defined in such a way as to subsume political
power and the other defined in such a way as to preclude the mediation
of spiritual authority and, thus, the concept of a transcendentally
grounded political authority.

Pagels concludes that the gnostic gospels reopen for our time the central issue of the early Christian controversies – 'What is the source of religious authority? . . . What is the relation between the authority of one's own experience and that claimed for the Scriptures, the ritual, and the clergy?' (*GG*, p. 151) – for that issue was formerly settled by fiat, by the violence of political suppression as the cult of orthodoxy, aspiring to *culture*, sought and gained dominance over other cults. In literary culture, the concept of the canon preserves in secularized form some important aspects of the politics of cultural domination which Pagels elucidates in the early Christian Church. As the rediscovery of the repressed gnostic texts casts a new light on the conquests of orthodoxy and the idealization of 'one faith' at the cost of many voices, so the entry of marginal texts into the modern literary curriculum not only 'opens up' the canon but opens to question the idea of a canon. To explore more fully the workings of canonical authority in a literary context, I will turn now to a passage in *Paradise Lost* – the canonical text par excellence of English literature – which represents the conversion of Eve to orthodoxy. My interest in this passage is not in the dimensions of Milton's views on women as such but in the lines of force already inscribed in the Genesis story that Milton's retelling makes visible.[12]

The Invention of Eve and Adam

Eve's story of her first waking in book 4 of *Paradise Lost* is an archetypal scene of canonical instruction. Nowhere are the designs of orthodoxy more vividly displayed than in this passage in which Eve herself utters the words which consign her authority to Adam, and through him to Milton's God, and thence to Milton's poem, and through the poem to the ancient patriarchal tradition.[13] Eve opens her narrative with an apostrophe to Adam –

> O thou for whom
> And from whom I was formed flesh of thy flesh,
> And without whom am to no end, my guide
> And head
>
> (4:440–3)

– which shows that she has already absorbed the wisdom of her teachers, for she echoes Adam's naming of her (see 8:494–7) adapted from Genesis 2:23. She repeats this gesture of self-subordination at the end of her own reminiscences. In the space between, however, Eve remembers an origin innocent of patriarchal indoctrination, one whose resonances the covering trope of narcissism does not entirely suffice to control. Recalling her first waking 'Under a shade on flowers', Eve remembers that she heard a 'murmuring sound / Of waters issued from a cave', which led her to a 'green bank' where she lay down to 'look into the clear / Smooth lake, that seemed another sky' (4:451–9). But it is not, of course, only 'another sky' that Eve sees reflected in the pool; she also sees what she does not yet understand to be her own image:

> A shape within the watery gleam appeared
> Bending to look on me, I started back,
> It started back, but pleased I soon returned,
> Pleased it returned as soon with answering looks
> Of sympathy and love; there I had fixed
> Mine eyes till now, and pined with vain desire,
> Had not a voice thus warned me, What thou seest,
> What there thou seest fair creature is thyself,
> With thee it came and goes; but follow me,
> And I will bring thee where no shadow stays
> Thy coming, and thy soft embraces, he
> Whose image thou art, him thou shalt enjoy
> Inseparably thine, to him shalt bear
> Multitudes like thyself, and thence be called
> Mother of human race
>
> (4:461–75)

This scenario imputes to the newborn Eve as her first desire a 'vain' narcissism, against which her gently accomplished conversion to the wiser purposes of Adam and God seems a fortunate rise. But the master plot in which the untutored Eve plays the role of doomed narcissist only partially obscures the actual terms of her conversion, which require that she abandon not merely her image in the pool but her very self – a self subtly discounted by the explaining 'voice', which *equates* it with the insubstantial image in the pool: 'What there thou seest . . . is thyself.' The reflection is not *of* Eve: according to the voice, it *is* Eve. As the voice interprets her for herself, Eve is not a self, a subject, at all; she is rather a substanceless image, a mere 'shadow' without object until the voice unites her to Adam – 'he / Whose image thou art' – much as Wendy stitches Peter Pan to his shadow.

Having reproduced the voice's call, Eve continues in her own voice with a rhetorical question that gestures toward repressed alternatives:

> what could I do
> But follow straight, invisibly thus led?
> Till I espied thee, fair indeed and tall,

Under a platan, yet methought less fair,
Less winning soft, less amiably mild,
Than that smooth watery image; back I turned,
Thou following cri'd'st aloud, Return fair Eve,
Whom fliest thou? whom thou fliest, of him thou art,
His flesh, his bone; to give thee being I lent
Out of my side to thee, nearest my heart
Substantial life, to have thee by my side
Henceforth an individual solace dear;
Part of my soul I seek thee, and thee claim
My other half: with that thy gentle hand
Seized mine, I yielded, and from that time see
How beauty is excelled by manly grace
And wisdom, which alone is truly fair.

(4:475–91)

As the benefits or 'graces' of conversion promised by the voice – sexual pleasure and 'Multitudes like thyself' – begin to materialize in Adam, the still autonomous Eve repeals the bargain, for the advertised original does not equal in interest the self she has been called upon to renounce. As she turns away to follow her own desire, Adam himself takes over from the voice the burden of educating Eve to her secondariness, recounting the 'history' of her derivation from his rib. This tale informs Eve of an ontological debt she has unwittingly incurred to the generous lender of her 'Substantial life' – not that she might exist to, for, and from herself but rather that he might 'have thee by my side / . . . an individual [inseparable] solace dear'. Eve is 'Part' of Adam's whole, his 'other half', to which he lays 'claim' by an oxymoronic gentle seizure; her debt to him, as he represents it, is such that she can repay it only by ceding to him her very self.

Eve's relation to Adam as mirror and shadow is the paradigmatic relation which canonical authority institutes between itself and its believers in converting them from the authority of their own experience to a 'higher' authority. It also illustrates the way in which patriarchal culture at large imprints itself upon the minds of women and men. Eve's indoctrination into her own 'identity' is complete at the point at which her imagination is so successfully colonized by patriarchal authority that she literally becomes its voice. As her narrative shows, she has internalized the voices and values of her mentors: her speech reproduces the words of the 'voice' and of Adam and concludes with an assurance that she has indeed been successfully taught to 'see' for herself the superiority of Adam's virtues to her own, limited as far as she knows to the 'beauty' briefly glimpsed in the pool. In this way she becomes a 'Part' not only of Adam but of the cultural economy which inscribes itself in her speech – or, more accurately, which takes over her speech: Eve does not speak patriarchal discourse; it speaks her.[14] The outer limits of her speech are given by the possibilities of this discourse. So long as she does not go beyond those limits her 'credit' in the patriarchal system is ensured. It is not simply, then, that Eve accepts Milton's cultural currency at 'face value'. Rather, as the nativity story in which she traces her transformation from newborn innocent – tabula rasa – to patriarchal woman suggests, she *is* its face value. It is her image that appears on its bills of credit, the image of the idealized and objectified woman whose belief in her role underwrites patriarchal power.

The cultural economy erected upon Eve's credence exists on condition that Eve can 'read' the world in only one way, by making herself the mirror of the patriarchal authority of Adam, Milton's God, Milton himself, and Western culture that the voice tells her she is. Indeed, the poem's master plot is designed precisely to discourage any 'Eve' from reading this authority in any other way. As Diana Hume George points out, it is not primarily narcissism to which the beautiful talking serpent tempts Eve but *knowledge*: to cease respecting the authority fetish of an invisible power and to see the world for herself.[15] That *Paradise Lost*, the story of the Fall, is a violent parable of *gnosis* punished attests to the threat that Eve's desire for experience rather than mediated knowledge poses to an authority which defines and proves itself chiefly in the successful prohibition of all other authorities.

To question the 'face value' of Milton's cultural currency from within the poem, as Milton's Eve does, is to be blasted by the cultural and poetic authority that controls its plot and representation. But a gnostic 'Eve', reading outside the bounds of that authority and not crediting the imagery that Milton would make a universal currency, disrupts that economy by a regard which makes visible what can work only so long as it remains hidden – the power moving Eve's conversion, that is, the power of Milton's God. In Eve's nativity scene, this power is imaged in the disembodied 'voice'; and it is precisely the *invisibility* of this voice and of the 'history' – originating in Adam's dream (see 8:287–484) – by which Adam attributes to Eve her secondary status that strikingly links this imagery to the church fathers' mystified history of the Resurrection, that invisible past invoked to justify their claims to privileged spiritual authority. The invisible voice that guides Eve away from the visible image of herself in the world to him whose image she is allegorizes what is literally the *secret* not only of spiritual and literary authority in Milton's poem but of cultural authority as such. The mystified authority of Christian doctrine underwrites the voice's injunctions, as it does the church fathers' claims to 'right opinion'. In both literatures, invisibility is a *definitive* attribute of authority: the power of the voice and of the church fathers, like that of the Wizard of Oz, resides in and depends upon invisibility.[16]

The dynamics of visibility and invisibility in Eve's and Adam's nativities uncover the hidden operations of power in Milton's text, which elaborately exfoliates the cultural text it draws upon. Their autobiographical narratives reveal a powerful subtext, at once literary and cultural, that works to associate Eve with visibility and Adam with invisibility from their first moments. As Maureen Quilligan observes, the relation of Eve's nativity imagery to Adam's replicates the relation between Eve and Adam themselves; for when Adam woke, 'Straight toward Heaven my wondering eyes I turned, / And gazed a while the ample sky', requesting it and the 'enlightened earth' to 'Tell, if ye saw, how came I thus, how here?' (8:257–8, 274, 277). 'Where Adam looks up at the true sky and then springs up, immediately to intuit his maker,' Quilligan writes, 'Eve bends down to look into "another sky" – a secondary, mediated, reflective sky: a mirror, in more ways than one, of her own being'.[17]

Adam's leaping upright to apostrophize a transcendent sky while Eve, recumbent, gazes into a 'sky' that is to Adam's as her knowledge is to his – not the thing itself but a watery reflection – indeed supports the ontological hierarchy so crucial to Milton's purposes in *Paradise Lost*. But these images also intimate – or betray – the deep structure of that hierarchy: a defense against the apparent ascendancy of *Eve's* power. Eve's first act is to move toward the maternally murmuring pool that returns an image of herself in the visible world. Her 'father' is out of sight and out of mind, but the reflecting face of the maternal waters gives back an image of her visible self. Adam, by contrast, is a motherless child. He sees with joy the 'Hill, dale, and shady woods, and sunny plains, / And liquid lapse of murmuring streams', but he does not identify with earthly bodies – not even his own (8:262–3). Adam 'perus[es]' himself 'limb by limb' (8:267), but like Emerson concludes that his body is 'Not-Him'. The sight of it only inspires him with questions that presuppose not the maternal life source from which bodies come but a father:

> Tell, if ye saw, how came I thus, how here?
> Not of myself; by some great maker then,
> In goodness and in power preeminent;
> Tell me, how may I know him, how adore,
> From whom I have that thus I move and live
> (8:277–81)

Adam projects a specifically male Creator, subordinating body and earth – all that Adam can see – to an invisible father.

While it might seem that in these two scenes Milton is simply setting up intimations of Adam's intrinsic spiritual superiority to Eve, Adam's nativity offers another reading of his orientation toward transcendence. Adam's turn to 'higher' things can also be read as alienation from his body and the visible world, an alienation which his God and the establishment of a hierarchical relation to Eve are designed to heal. Apostrophizing a sky and earth which give back no self-image, Adam finds none until he succeeds in turning Eve into his reflection: 'Whom fliest thou? whom thou fliest, of him thou art.' In this relation, Eve's visible, earth-identified being is subordinated to Adam's intangible spiritual being. Thus Eve can tell Adam that it is she who enjoys 'So far the happier lot, enjoying thee / Preeminent by so much odds, while thou / Like consort to thyself canst nowhere find' (4:446–8) and that he has taught her to 'see / how beauty is excelled by manly grace / And wisdom, which alone is truly fair' (4:489–91). The visible 'beauty' of Eve's image bows to the invisible fairness of 'manly grace / And wisdom' in a contest which appears to originate in Adam's need to make the visible world reflect himself.

Adam's need to possess Eve is usually understood as complemented by her need for his guidance, but Milton's text suggests a more subtle and more compelling source for this need: Adam's sense of inadequacy in face of what he sees as Eve's perfection. The apparent self-sufficiency glimpsed in her nativity account ('back I turned', interestingly misrepresented by Adam in book 8, lines 500–10) is amplified by Adam in talking with Raphael. When he first saw Eve, Adam recalls, 'what seemed fair in all the world, seemed now / Mean, or in her summed up, in her contained' (8:472–3), and he cannot reconcile her apparent perfection with God's assurance of his own superiority. He worries about whether:

> Nature failed in me, and left some part
> Not proof enough such object to sustain,
> Or from my side subducting, took perhaps
> More than enough; . . .
>
>   [for] when I approach
> Her loveliness, so absolute she seems
> And in herself complete, so well to know
> Her own, that what she wills to do or say,
> Seems wisest, virtuousest, discreetest, best;
> All higher knowledge in her presence falls
> Degraded, Wisdom in discourse with her
> Loses discountenanced, and like folly shows;
> Authority and Reason on her wait,

> As one intended first, not after made
> Occasionally; and to consummate all,
> Greatness of mind and nobleness their seat
> Build in her loveliest, and create an awe
> About her, as a guardian angel placed.
> (8:534–59)

What is interesting about Adam's representation of his own sense of inadequacy with respect to Eve is that it focuses on the body – specifically, *on the rib* which, he fancies, God took from his body to make Eve. That Adam's anxiety should take this particular form suggests that the 'completeness' he fears in Eve and lacks in himself attaches to the function Adam associates with his rib: the power to create a human being. Adam's dream of Eve's creation from his rib fulfills his wish for an organ that performs the life-creating function of Eve's womb. The initial difference between Adam and Eve, then, is not Adam's inner superiority but simply sexual difference; Adam's fantasy of Eve's subordinate creation dramatizes an archetypal womb envy as constitutive of male identity.[18]

Considered in this light, the God that Adam projects in his nativity appears designed to institute a hierarchy to compensate for the disparity he feels between himself and Eve. It is not that Adam is an imperfect image of his God, rather, his God is a *perfected* image of Adam: an all-powerful *male* Creator who soothes Adam's fears of female power by Himself claiming credit for the original creation of the world and, further, by bestowing upon Adam 'Dominion' over the fruits of this creation through authorizing him to name the animals *and Eve*. The naming ritual enables Adam to translate his fantasy of power from the realm of desire to history and the world, instituting male dominance over language, nature, and woman. The perfection Adam attributes to the God who authorizes his 'Dominion' counters the power he perceives in Eve. As Eve seems to him 'absolute . . . / And in herself complete' so must his God possess these qualities in order to compete with her. Milton's curious elaboration of Genesis 2:18 makes a point of God's perfection in contrast to Adam's imperfection without Eve: God baits Adam after he requests a companion, saying in effect, 'I'm alone; don't you think I'm happy?' and Adam replies, 'Thou in thyself art perfect, and in thee / Is no deficience found; not so is man' (8:415–16). Adam's 'perfect' God enables him to contend with the self-sufficiency he sees and fears in Eve, precisely by authorizing Adam's possession of her. Through the dream of the rib Adam both enacts a parody of birth and gains possession of the womb by claiming credit for woman herself. In this way he himself becomes as 'perfect' as he can, appropriating in indirect and symbolic but consequential ways the creative power and self-sufficiency he attributes to Eve and to his God.

The shadow of the repressed mother, then, falls as tangibly over Adam's nativity scene as it does upon Eve's. Necessitated by Adam's awe of Eve's life-giving body and his wish to incorporate her power in himself, this repression mutely signals that patriarchal power is not simply one attribute among others of Adam's God but its primary motive and constituent. As the nativity scene represents Him, Adam's God is a personification of patriarchal power, created in the image of and in competition with the maternal power that Adam perceives in Eve. The overt hierarchy of God over Adam and Adam over Eve which is the text's 'argument' is underlain (and undermined) by a more ancient *perceived* hierarchy of Eve over Adam, still apparent in the 'ghostlier demarcations' of Adam's transumptive myth. In the power dynamics of Adam's nativity scene, the self-sufficient Eve and the compensatory God that Adam projects out of his fear are the true rivals, as Christ's jealous rebuke to Adam after the Fall confirms:

> Was she thy God, that her thou didst obey
> Before his voice, or was she made thy guide,
> Superior, or but equal, that to her
> Thou didst resign thy manhood, and the place
> Wherein God set thee above her
>
> (10:145–9)

The nativities of Adam and Eve in Milton's poem bear out the archetypal association of maleness with invisibility and of femaleness with visibility that some theorists argue is given in male and female relations to childbirth and, through childbirth, to the world and the future. In *Moses and Monotheism*, Freud celebrates civilization as the triumph of invisibility over visibility. Freud links what he labels 'the progress in spirituality' in Western culture to three tropes of invisibility: the triumph of Moses' unrepresentable God over idols, 'which means the compulsion to worship an invisible God'; the evolution of symbolic language, through which abstract thinking assumed priority over 'lower psychical activity which concerned itself with the immediate perceptions of the sense organs'; and 'the turning from the mother to the father', from matriarchy to patriarchy, which, says Freud, 'signifies above all a victory of spirituality over the senses . . . since maternity is proved by the senses whereas paternity is a surmise'.[19] Following Dorothy Dinnerstein, Jonathan Culler shifts the priorities of Freud's reading of human history. The establishment of patriarchal power, he suggests, is not merely an instance, along with the preference for an invisible God, of the triumph of spirituality; rather, 'when we consider that the invisible, omnipotent

God is God the Father, not to say God of the Patriarchs, we may well
wonder whether, on the contrary, the promotion of the invisible over the
visible . . . is not a consequence or effect of the establishment of paternal
authority'.[20] Dinnerstein and other feminists go further, interpreting
hierarchical dualism not as a 'consequence or effect' but as the *means* of
establishing paternal authority, a *compensatory* effort on the part of the
male to control a natural world to which he is bound in relatively remote
and mediated ways.[21] Freud himself runs significantly aground on the
question of what motivates the hierarchy of the invisible over the visible:
'The world of the senses becomes gradually mastered by spirituality, and
. . . man feels proud and uplifted by each such step in progress. One
does not know, however, why this should be so' (*MM*, p. 151). In fact, a
few pages earlier, he argues that the *invisibility* of Moses' divine patriarch
aroused in the minds of believers 'a much more grandiose idea of their
God' and that this august invisible god endowed believers themselves
with grandeur by association: 'Whoever believed in this God took part in
his greatness, so to speak, might feel uplifted himself' (*MM*, p. 143). So
Adam's first colloquy with his God raises him above the earth to
literalized heights, the mount of Paradise: 'Adam, rise / . . . / . . . he took
me raised, [and] led me up / A woody mountain; whose high top' makes
Earth seem 'scarce pleasant' (8:296–306). Adam's God enables him to
transcend earthly being and in so doing to gain a power he hungers for,
as his 'sudden appetite / To pluck and eat' the fruits of paradise implies
(8:308–9).

Returning now to Eve's nativity narrative, we can see that her story
allegorizes Freud's analysis of the 'triumph' of invisibility. The God that
Adam sees is invisible to her; she, too, progresses from a 'lowly'
absorption in images of the senses to more grandiose 'conceptions'; and
she turns away from the maternal waters in which she finds her reflected
image to identify with a patriarchy whose power is specifically *not*
visible, prevailing even though it is to all *appearances* 'less fair, / Less
winning soft, less amiably mild, / Than that smooth watery image' of
herself in the world. The fable of Eve's conversion from her own visible
being in the world to invisible patriarchal authority traces a conversion
from being in and for herself to serving a 'higher' power – from the
authority of her own experience to the hidden authority symbolized in
the prohibited Tree of Knowledge.

Yet this power is not transcendent; it must be authorized in Eve's belief
– a belief enlisted through the invisible voice's claim that it *already* exists
and, further, through its equally strategic representation of Eve as a mere
'shadow' or image that has and can have no value except for what
patriarchal authority attaches to her. Eve's value is created by the
patriarchy whose discourse she becomes. Her narrative proves the
'triumph' of her education or colonization; she has received the

imprimatur of the realm, has *become* its text, image, and token of value. Assuring her own power within the terms it offers her, she also assures its literal power: her discourse makes its invisible power visible *as herself*. Her passive role in the patriarchal cultural economy – 'what could I do, / But follow straight invisibly thus led?' – resembles that of the paper on which monetary value is inscribed.[22] The imprinting of patriarchal authority upon Eve, like the printing of paper money, transforms intrinsically worthless material into pure value. Any object chosen to be the medium of trade must, of course, be worth less than its exchange value; otherwise, it is soon de-idealized, reverting from an image of value to an object of value.[23] Similarly, in order for her to serve as the idealized currency of patriarchal culture, Eve's intrinsic value must be denied; her self, her subjectivity, must be *de*valued to resemble the worthless paper on which the inscription designating money, or credit, is stamped. Eve's subjectivity, her being-for-herself, is the 'paper' upon which patriarchal authority imprints its own valuation, thereby 'uplifting' her allegedly worthless being ('shadow', reflection, 'image') to pure value.

Gubar observes that numerous images of women in texts by male authors suggest that 'the female body has been feared for its power to articulate itself'.[24] Milton's Eve brings the threat of woman's self-articulation into focus: it is the danger posed by her speaking from her body, from an experience that exists outside patriarchal authority, as did the untutored, self-reflective consciousness Milton represents as narcissistic. Such speech threatens the very basis of the cultural currency. As woman begins to speak a discourse no longer defined and limited by the patriarchal inscription, Eve's voice recovers its intrinsic value. Just as paper would no longer be available to serve as a medium of exchange were its use-value to exceed its exchange-value, so it no longer profits Eve to hand over the 'blank pages' of her subjectivity to the patriarchal imprint. At this point, the patriarchal currency fails: to overturn a cliché, it is no longer worth the paper it's printed on.

What the failure of its currency means for the patriarchal economy is not that we no longer read its texts but that we read them in a different way, using interpretive strategies that mark a shift from a sacred to a secular interpretive model, from an economy of invisible transactions to one of *visible* exchange. Concluding *A Room of One's Own*, Woolf refers to *Paradise Lost* as 'Milton's bogey'.[25] From a gnostic vantage point, *Paradise Lost* loses its power as a 'bogey' or scarecrow and becomes, instead, a cultural artifact situated in history, its power analyzable as that of an ancient and deeply ingrained pattern in Western thought, reinvented to serve the interests of modern society and realized in language of unsurpassed subtlety and *explicable* sublimity. Read in such a way that the invisible becomes visible; the transcendent, historical; the sacred icon, a cultural image; the 'bogey', old clothes upon a stick, Milton's poem becomes as powerful an instrument for the undoing of the cultural economy inscribed in it as it was for its institution – more powerful, indeed, than less 'pure' forms of patriarchal currency.

The critique of patriarchal/canonical authority assumes that literary authority is a mode of social authority and that literary value is inseparable from ideology. The 'Eves' no longer crediting their image in Milton's poem value his literary achievement no less than do such proponents of canon-making ideologies as Harold Bloom; but the poem no longer shuts out the view. Precisely because of the ways in which our own history is implicated in the poem, we continue to hear the other voices which Milton's literary and cultural history making dominates and which, presenting different models of literary/social authority, disrupt the canonical economy of Milton's text as the gnostic voices disrupted the economy of Christian orthodoxy.

We may wonder how far the Miltonic sublime derives from linguistic virtuosity and how far from thematic resonances that literary history proves all but invisible to mortal sight. Milton's nativity scenes, I have argued, reveal that the repression of the mother is the genesis of Genesis. Moreover, Milton at once mirrors and exposes the repression that shapes his epic story in the construction of his Muse, which is to say, of his own poetic authority. Opening *Paradise Lost*, Milton invokes what seems at first a perfectly conventional 'Heavenly Muse' – identified by Merritt Y. Hughes with the Urania of book 7 and the Celestial Patroness of book 9 – to tell his epic story (1:6). At line 7, this protean figure metamorphoses into Moses' Muse, the Muse of Genesis, through whose inspiration Moses 'first taught the chosen Seed, / In the beginning how the Heavens and Earth / Rose out of Chaos' (1:8–10). At line 17, the Muse undergoes another, more startling, translation, from *witness* of Creation to *Creator*:

> And chiefly thou, O Spirit, that dost prefer
> Before all Temples th'upright heart and pure.
> Instruct me, for Thou know'st: thou from the first
> Wast present, and with mighty wings outspread
> Dovelike sat'st brooding on the vast abyss
> And mad'st it pregnant
>
> (1:17–22)

It is finally this imagined author of Creation that Milton asks to tell, through him, the story of the Creation.

Milton's startling invocation of the creator as Muse marks the difference between Homer's polytheistic culture and the monotheistic authority of Judeo-Christian tradition, even as it reveals what is at stake in Milton's revisionary move: the identification of his poetic authority with nothing less than divine revelation as his culture conceives it – that is, with the sublimated social authority of his own culture. Milton moves beyond his merely conventional epic Muse to invoke his God directly, thereby representing his poetic authority as mediating between divine authority and the 'nation' for whom he meant his poem to be 'example'. Much as the doctrine of the Resurrection as historical event supports the church fathers' claims to authority, Milton's Muse underwrites his claims to a poetic authority indistinguishable from revelation, a power grounded in priority of witness to human history – in *having been there*, where his hearers were not. By constructing his Muse as his God, Milton creates a mutually confirming relation between his poetic authority and divine authority as Judeo-Christian culture represents it: as his God confirms his poem, his poem confirms his God, first, highest, and indeed only witness to the Creation it describes.

Milton's creator-Muse, then, is at once a model for and a projection of his own ambitious poetic authority. As Milton's Muse, this 'Spirit' dramatizes its function as Logos, the Word that calls all things into being: its authority for the creation of song is inseparable from its authority for the Creation itself. As such, it is a figure for the cultural authority to which Milton aspires as creator and poet, the absolute authority for history that only one who is both creator and namer can claim. Like Moses' invisible God, like the invisible voice that calls Eve away, like the God who leads Adam to the mount of Paradise, Milton's creator-Muse 'uplifts' him from the human to the sublime, from blindness to vision, from the limitations of the visible to invisible power. It meets Milton's prayer:

> what in me is dark
> Illumine; what is low, raise and support;
> That, to the height of this great argument
> I may assert Eternal Providence,
> And justify the ways of God to men.
>
> (1:22–6)

As Milton transforms his Muse into his god, an attendant change occurs: the apparently conventional, presumably female 'Heavenly Muse' is transsexualized even as it is elevated. That this is no accident of iconographic tradition is clear from Milton's embellishment of Genesis 1:2: 'The earth was without form and void, and darkness was upon the face of the deep; and the Spirit of God was moving over the face of the waters.' Milton's apostrophe, '[thou who] with mighty wings outspread / Dovelike sat'st brooding on the vast abyss / And mad'st it pregnant', transforms his Muse not just into a creator-god but into that powerful, self-sufficient *male* Creator so crucial to Adam in his relations with Eve. Milton's image heightens the procreative 'hovering' or 'brooding' of the Hebrew text but in such a way as to annihilate its female aspect: the maternal – and *mater*ial – life-giving waters of Genesis 1:2 become, in Milton, darkness and silence, an 'abyss', even as the male impregnator, 'Spirit' and divine voice, becomes the author of both the Creation and the creation story which Milton tells.[26]

Milton's voiding of maternal creativity in his epic invocation once more brings all the elements of Freud's 'progress in spirituality' into play. The male Logos called upon to articulate the cosmos against an abyss of female silence overcomes the anxieties generated by the tensions between visible maternity and invisible paternity by appropriating female power to itself in a parody of parthenogenesis. Milton's image of creation is archetypally patriarchal, figuring an absolutely original and self-sufficient paternal act, prior to and unthreatened by all others, from which issues the visible world. Depicting the genesis of the world as the genesis of patriarchal authority, Milton recapitulates that genesis and that authority in his own. His emphatic suppression of the female in his transformation of Genesis is integral to his authority in patriarchal culture, preenacting the silencing of Eve and the Fall which follows upon her violation of the orthodox prohibition of knowledge.

Yet Milton himself reckons the cost of such authority as the repression of another kind of knowledge, that *human* knowledge the absence of which Woolf remarks when she says that Milton gives her 'no help in judging life; I scarcely feel that Milton lived or knew men and women'.[27] In the invocation to book 3, Milton writes of his literal blindness in terms which do not represent the invisible power of the sublime as a simple triumph over the visible, or spiritual power as satisfactory compensation for loss of the visible world:

> Thus with the year
> Seasons return; but not to me returns
> Day, or the sweet approach of even or morn,
> Or sight of vernal bloom, or summer's rose,
> Or flocks, or herds, or human face divine;
> But cloud instead, and ever-during dark
> Surrounds me, from the cheerful ways of men
> Cut off, and for the book of knowledge fair
> Presented with a Universal blank
> Of Nature's works, to me expunged and rased,
> And wisdom at one entrance quite shut out.
> So much the rather thou, Celestial light
> Shine inward . . .

that I may see and tell
Of things invisible to mortal sight.

(3:40–55)

These invocations, which play out in small the sexual dynamics of
Paradise Lost, suggest that the story of the epic enterprise, the victory of
invisibility, and the compensations of 'Celestial Light' have not yet been
fully told. If the epic tradition has in a very real sense been built upon
female silence, then the patriarchal authority Milton establishes in
Paradise Lost is no mere precondition for his story; it *is* that story.

Notes

1. VIRGINIA WOOLF, *Jacob's Room* (1922; New York, 1978), pp. 40–1.

2. Since the male–female relationship is the archetypal hierarchy in Western
   culture, 'woman' has become a fashionable image for analysts of cultural
   politics, notably in deconstructive theory and practice. The dangers of this
   appropriation to the interests of actual women have been discussed by Nancy
   K. Miller in 'The Text's Heroine: A Feminist Critic and Her Fictions', *Diacritics*
   12 (Summer 1982): 48–53. She argues for combining a post-humanistic theory
   which throws centre, periphery and subject into question with a critical
   practice that does not lose sight of the *literally* marginal and precarious position
   female authors and teachers now hold in the academy. While it is manifestly
   not true that the 'canonical' and 'gnostic' stance toward authority that I explore
   in this essay belong in any simple way to actual men and women, respectively,
   history – and literary history – render these alignments no more heuristic than
   descriptive.

3. ELAINE SHOWALTER, 'Women and the Literary Curriculum', *College English* **32**
   (May 1971): 855.

4. See JUDITH FETTERLEY, *The Resisting Reader: A Feminist Approach to American
   Fiction* (Bloomington, Ind., 1978).

5. This 'opening' was propounded from Third World, feminist, and Marxist
   points of view in the collection of essays that appeared in the wake of the
   1960s questioning of authority *The Politics of Literature: Dissenting Essays on the
   Teaching of Literature*, ed. Louis Kampf and Paul Lauter (New York, 1972), and
   later in *English Literature: Opening Up the Canon*, ed. Leslie A. Fiedler and
   Houston A. Baker, Jr, Selected Papers from the English Institute, 1979, n.s. 4
   (Baltimore, 1981).
   In order to situate the issues of my argument, it is useful to recall here Ernst
   Robert Curtius' description of the intellectual economy that he considered to
   have replaced the concept of the canon in the twentieth century. Citing Valéry
   Larbaud, he distinguishes between 'la carte politique et la carte intellectuelle
   du monde'. The anachronistic French model of national canons competing for
   the colonization of intellectual territories has ceded, he says, to literary
   cosmopolitanism, 'a politics of mind which has left behind all pretensions to
   hegemony, and is concerned only with facilitating and accelerating the
   exchange of intellectual merchandise' (*European Literature and the Latin Middle
   Ages*, tr. Willard R. Trask [1948; Princeton, NJ, 1973], pp. 271, 272). In Curtius'

account, which posits the transformation of cultural imperialism into a world market in which intellectual 'goods' are freely exchanged, not only the concept of a closed canon but the canonizing stance itself becomes obsolescent along with the hegemonic and universal (or 'catholic') pretensions of parochial cultures – Judeo-Christian, national, or European. The evangelical projects of ethnocentric beliefs are presumed dead or defunct, and belief in the supremacy of a single cultural authority gives way to diverse and mutually translatable cultural 'currencies'. These admit of equation and free exchange in a global economy governed not by transcendent and hegemonic conceptions of value but by *translatability* – of sensibility as well as language. Curtius' idealized image of a free-market cultural economy usefully distinguishes the cultural issues of the twentieth century from those of earlier periods, but his wishful depoliticization of this economy can be understood only in the context of nationalist politics in the first half of the century. In fact, the 'intellectual free market' has the defects of its economic analogue, and both are, in any case, virtually male monopolies.

6. See, for example, FLORENCE HOWE, 'Those We Still Don't Read', *College English* **43** (January 1981): 16.

7. FETTERLEY, *The Resisting Reader*, p. xx.

8. ELAINE PAGELS, *The Gnostic Gospels* (New York 1979), p. xxii; all further references to this work, abbreviated *GG*, will be included parenthetically in the text. Critics who object that Pagels gives scant attention to the diversity of voices within Christian orthodoxy err in supposing her discussion to concern unity and diversity as such rather than the politics implicit in orthodox and gnostic stances toward spiritual authority. The gnostic position as she describes it leads logically not to political anarchy but rather to a demystification of the political sphere.

9. J. HILLIS MILLER, 'The Function of Rhetorical Study at the Present Time', *The State of the Discipline, 1970s–1980s, ADE Bulletin* **62** (September–November 1979): 12; cited by Sandra Gilbert, 'What Do Feminist Critics Want? or, A Postcard from the Volcano', *ADE Bulletin* **66** (Winter 1980): 20. Miller acknowledges the 'strongly preservative or conservative' character of his pronouncement (p. 12).

10. SUSAN GUBAR, '"The Blank Page" and the Issues of Female Creativity', *Writing and Sexual Difference, Critical Inquiry* **8** (Winter 1981): 261, 262.

11. For the complete text, see 'The Gospel of Mary' in *The Nag Hammadi Library in English*, ed. James N. Robinson, tr. Members of the Coptic Gnostic Library Project of the Institute for Antiquity and Christianity (New York, 1977), pp. 471–4.

12. John Milton's sexual politics has become an issue of increasing importance in Milton criticism in the last decade; among many illuminating studies are Marcia Landy, 'Kinship and the Role of Women in *Paradise Lost*', *Milton Studies* **4** (1972): 3–18, and '"A Free and Open Encounter": Milton and the Modern Reader', *Milton Studies* **9** (1976): 3–36; Barbara K. Lewalski, 'Milton on Women – Yet Once More', *Milton Studies* **6** (1974): 3–20; Diane McColley, '"Daughter of God and Man": The Subordination of Milton's Eve' in *Familiar Colloquy: Essays Presented to Arthur Edward Barker*, ed. Patricia Bruckmann (Ottawa, 1978), pp. 196–208; Joan Malory Webber, 'The Politics of Poetry: Feminism and *Paradise Lost*', *Milton Studies* **14** (1980): 3–24; Northrop Frye, 'The Revelation to Eve' in *'Paradise Lost': A Tercentenary Tribute*, ed. Balachandra Rajan (Toronto, 1969), pp. 18–47; and Marilyn R. Farwell, 'Eve, the Separation Scene, and the Renaissance Idea of Androgyny', *Milton Studies* **16** (1982): 3–20.

13. Milton draws his account of the creation of Adam and Eve mainly from that by the J[ahwist] scribe (Gen. 2:4–3:20, ninth–tenth century BC), rather than from the P[riestly] scribe's account (Gen. 1:26–7, fifth–sixth century BC). In the P scribe's text, female and male are co-originary. But, for a discussion of the exaggeration of patriarchal values in the J scribe's Hebrew text by the translators of the English texts, see CASEY MILLER and KATE SWIFT, *Words and Women: New Language in New Times* (New York, 1978), pp. 15–16, citing Phyllis Trible's 'Depatriarchalizing in Biblical Interpretation', *Journal of the American Academy of Religion* **41** (March 1973): 35–42.

14. The limits of Eve's discourse in her nativity story illustrate the interest of the concept of authority as reframed by Michel Foucault: ' "What are the modes of existence of this discourse?" "Where does it come from; how is it circulated; who controls it?" ' ('What is an Author?', *Language, Counter-Memory, Practice: Selected Essays and Interviews*, ed. Donald F. Bouchard, tr. Bouchard and Sherry Simon [Ithaca, NY, 1977], p. 138).

15. See DIANA HUME GEORGE, 'Stumbling on Melons: Sexual Dialectics and Discrimination in English Departments' in *English Literature: Opening Up the Canon*, pp. 120–6.

16. Foucault theorizes that invisibility is inherent in and necessary to the workings of power: 'Power is tolerable only on condition that it mask a substantial part of itself. Its success is proportional to its ability to hide its own mechanisms. . . . For it, secrecy is not in the nature of an abuse; it is indispensable to its operation' (*The History of Sexuality: Volume I, an Introduction*, tr. Robert Hurley [New York, 1980], p. 86).

17. MAUREEN QUILLIGAN, *Milton's Spenser: The Politics of Reading* (Ithaca, NY, 1983), pp. 227–8. Quilligan pursues a different line of argument, reevaluating Eve's centrality in the poem read as integrally concerned with instituting 'a new kind of family structure concurrent with the "rises" of protestantism and of capitalism with its free market ideologies' (p. 177).

18. Milton develops with subtlety and precision the motive of womb envy already strikingly apparent in the J scribe's creation story (Gen. 2:4–3:20). The motive of compensation in Adam's appropriation of the power of naming – language – is illuminated by his naming the woman Eve (*Hawwah*), derived from the Hebrew root *havah* ('to live'). Other details contribute to this interpretation of the rib fantasy, not least Eve's impressive birth announcement in Genesis 4:1: ' "I have acquired a man with the help of Yahweh." ' Such a reading suggests that the cultural conditions that conduce to the malaise of penis envy are 'erected' on a prior malaise of womb envy; and, indeed, so patriarchal a historian as Amaury de Riencourt writes that our 'original' creation story 'was taken wholesale' from a *more* original Sumerian mythology centred not on patriarchal namers but on female fertility gods (*Sex and Power in History* [New York, 1974], p. 37; see also pp. 36–8). On this last point, see Wolfgang Lederer, 'Envy and Loathing–The Patriarchal Revolt', *The Fear of Women* (New York, 1968), pp. 153–68. See also Virginia R. Mollenkott, 'Some Implications of Milton's Androgynous Muse', *Bucknell Review* **24** (Spring 1978): 27–36.

19. SIGMUND FREUD, *Moses and Monotheism*, tr. Katherine Jones (New York, 1967), pp. 142, 144, 145–6; all further references to this work, abbreviated *MM*, will be included parenthetically in the text.

20. JONATHAN CULLER, *On Deconstruction: Theory and Criticism after Structuralism* (Ithaca, NY, 1982), p. 59; see also pp. 58–60.

21. The most extensive exploration of this theme, linking the structures of individual psychology in Western society to those of its cultural institution, is

Dorothy Dinnerstein, *The Mermaid and the Minotaur: Sexual Arrangements and Human Malaise* (New York, 1976).

22. Feminist theories have drawn upon Marxist anthropologists' analyses of women as objects of exchange in kinship systems to analyse women as the 'goods' through which patriarchal power passes; see, for example, Gayle Rubin, 'The Traffic in Women: Notes on the "Political Economy" of Sex', *Toward an Anthropology of Women*, ed. Rayna R. Reiter (New York, 1975), pp. 157–210, and Luce Irigaray, 'Des Marchandises entre elles' [When the goods get together], *Ce Sexe qui n'en est pas un* [This sex which isn't one] (Paris, 1977), pp. 189–93, tr. Claudia Reeder in *New French Feminisms: An Anthology*, ed. Elaine Marks and Isabelle de Courtivron (New York, 1981), pp. 107–10. I am conceiving the issue of cultural authority in terms of credit rather than barter or coins in order to analyse the workings of patriarchal authority, but my argument has some parallels to Irigaray's discussion of the disruption of the patriarchal sexual economy effected by women's removing themselves from this market.

23. Ideally, the medium of trade should be intrinsically worthless; Gresham's law that 'bad' money (coins of baser metals) drives out 'good' money (gold or silver coins) points to the advantage of the almost 'pure' credit embodied in paper money. Gold and silver coins are money conceived as portable stores of value rather than as credit.

24. GUBAR, '"The Blank Page" and the Issues of Female Creativity', p. 246.

25. WOOLF, *A Room of One's Own* (1928; New York, 1957), p. 118. Woolf says that women will write 'if we . . . see human beings . . . and the sky, too, and the trees or whatever it may be in themselves; if we look past Milton's bogey, for no human being should shut out the view' (p. 118). Gilbert takes up the image in 'Milton's Bogey: Patriarchal Poetry and Women Readers', Gilbert and Gubar, *The Madwoman in the Attic: The Woman Writer and the Nineteenth-Century Literary Imagination* (New Haven, Conn., 1979), pp. 187–212. Gilbert identifies women writers with Eve and Satan, all 'resisting readers', but, I think, does not fully rescue their gnostic readings from the patriarchal framework within which they are damned.

26. For a related reading of Milton's Muse, see Mollenkott, who views it as androgynous and as 'beautifully symboliz[ing] the womb envy that is so deeply repressed in the human male' but does not acknowledge its appropriation of female procreativity (p. 32). See also Farwell, n. 12 above.

27. VIRGINIA WOOLF, *A Writer's Diary*, ed. Leonard Woolf (New York, 1954), p. 5.

12 Fallen Differences, Phallogocentric Discourses: Losing *Paradise Lost* to History[*]

MARY NYQUIST

What does it mean to situate a text historically? What sort of claims can literary-critical discourse make when the relations between text and context are kept open? Is it possible to 'correct' a reading without validating positivistic assumptions? Or without contributing to the recuperative aims of the academic study of canonical authors? What is at stake in a misogynist (mis)reading, specifically one that has a venerable and complex history? These questions are particularly pressing when it comes to Milton, who in recent years has been constructed as pro-feminist, as patron saint of the companionate marriage, or, at the very least, as consciously in charge of the contradictory meanings of his literary texts. By reflecting on the issues raised by my own critical discourse in this essay, I try to counter this apologetic, author-centred institutional investment. At the same time (as the unabridged version of the essay shows more clearly), I hold open the possibility that such self-consciousness, with its attendant tolerance for conflicting meanings, is compatible with a responsiveness to the text's participation in the economic and social formations of its time.

I

Milton may be what Virginia Woolf said he was, the first of the masculinists, but he is certainly not the last. And in the case of the simile that is this essay's point of departure, Milton's misogyny would seem actually to be exceeded by that of his ostensibly more enlightened twentieth-century commentators. The simile, to be found in lines

---

[*] Reprinted from *Post-Structuralism and the Question of History*, ed. Derek Attridge *et al*. (Cambridge: Cambridge University Press, 1987).

1059–63 of Book 9 of *Paradise Lost*, elaborates Eve and Adam's awakening after their first fallen love-making:

> So rose the Danite strong,
> Herculean Samson, from the harlot-lap
> Of Philistean Dalilah, and waked
> Shorn of his strength, they destitute and bare
> Of all their virtue.

With only one or two not very clearly developed exceptions, modern critics and editors alike are determined to find in this simile an analogy between Samson's betrayal by Dalilah and Adam's by Eve, in spite of the fact that on the level of syntax alone it is perfectly clear that both Adam and Eve are being compared with Samson. The *anagnorisis* that Milton here dramatises is a literary enactment of Genesis iii.7, 'And the eyes of them both were opened, and they knew that they were naked';[1] and biblical commentators on this verse have always used the plural pronoun in discussing this stage of the Fall. Yet even Northrop Frye, our century's most influential theorist of the relations between the Bible and literature, can claim that the simile associates Samson with the fallen Adam.[2] In what follows, I shall both enact and analyse a variety of readings – all ideologically charged – of this simile and its textual context. In doing so I'll be entering current debates about the relations of post-structuralism, feminism and Marxism by raising, among others, the following issues: the institutional and hermeneutical status to be given this misogynistic reading (whether, for example, it is appropriate simply to refer to it as a misreading); the theoretical and ideological implications of an attempt to correct it by an appeal to history and to an historically inflected notion of authorial self-consciousness; and, finally, the possibility of regarding the text both as historical product of the critical acts that mediate its reception and as the product of determinate social forces at work in the historical moment of its inception.

I would like to start by asking how the misconstruing of this simile is to be accounted for. As has long been noted, the lines immediately preceding the simile are somewhat problematical, textually.[3] But since editors and commentators who do not point to these textual matters perpetuate the misreading, there is obviously more at work here than faulty or misleading pointing. It's hard to avoid the suspicion that one thing behind this misreading is the figure of Milton the injured husband, who here as elsewhere – most memorably in *Samson Agonistes* – uses a poetic occasion of his own devising to pay off old scores and give voice to his own misogynistic feelings. Indeed, one wonders whether the very existence of *Samson Agonistes* as a text signed and authored by Milton does not provide the necessary cultural condition for the production of the Samson simile's misreading. Commentators on Milton have long been accustomed to comparing Adam and Samson as heroes whose relations with the paternal order are ruptured when they submit to their wives. And both heroes have been assumed to stand in an expressive relationship with the biographical Milton; or, to be more precise, with the Milton whose presence in both *Paradise Lost* and *Samson Agonistes* has ever since the eighteenth century been made to communicate his own unhappy marital experiences. That the model of authorship this frequently assumes is not in any straightforward or simple sense expressive can be seen in Thomas Newton's annotative remarks on the antifeminist diatribe delivered by the chorus in *Samson Agonistes*. Newton (who does not, incidentally, misconstrue the Samson simile) states that the reflections of the chorus 'are the more severe, as they are not spoken by Samson, who might be supposed to utter them out of pique and resentment, but are deliver'd by the Chorus as serious and important truths. But by all accounts Milton himself had suffer'd some uneasiness through the temper and behaviour of two of his wives; and no wonder therefore that upon so tempting an occasion as this he indulges his spleen a little, depreciates the qualifications of the women, and asserts the superiority of the men, and to give these sentiments the greater weight puts them into the mouth of the Chorus.'[4] Besides relying on a view of the chorus that today's scholars would no longer accept, this piece of biographical criticism draws on two interestingly different views of authorship. Like the fictional Adam in *Paradise Lost* and Samson in *Samson Agonistes*, Milton is here presented by Newton as succumbing himself, irrationally and as a result of private emotion (feeling interpreted from a masculinist perspective as justified), to a 'tempting' occasion involving women. But as author of occasion as well as of text, Milton is also regarded as the conscious and ideologically motivated manipulator of his readers' responses – as an author who indulges his spleen, but who cannily manages to do so with a calculated view to the authority of his fictionally displaced utterances.

As the very form of Newton's remark – the editorial annotation – indicates, the figure of Milton the injured husband is both a biographical and institutional construct, a construct that contributes in its own way to our culture's reifying of the author of *Paradise Lost*. More than two centuries later, it may be virtually impossible to disentangle the figure of the powerful and influential author, Milton, from the figure of the harsh and authoritative patriarch, the patriarch being just as determined not to forgive and forget as Milton the author is determined not to die – Roland Barthes's announcement of 'The Death of the Author' notwithstanding. In his essay 'What is an Author?' Michel Foucault analyses what he calls the 'author-function', the way in which the circulation and functioning of certain discourses within a society are governed by the figure of the author. His analysis produces, among other things, the following aphoristic remark: 'The author is the principle of thrift in the proliferation of meaning.'[5] Although this principle is only implicitly at work in comments on our simile such as Fowler's annotative 'See Judges xvi for the story of Samson's betrayal by Dalilah', it is clearly operative in the more crudely explicit reading given it by John Knott, who states that in this simile 'Milton confirmed Eve's abrupt descent from graceful innocence to guilt by comparing her with Dalilah', which he develops by saying: 'And as any reader of *Samson Agonistes* knows, Milton's insult is worse than calling Eve "whore", since it implies that her treachery is directed against God as well as Adam.'[6] Besides positing the figure of the author as patriarch, whose stern voice (actually the critic's) is heard insulting and berating Eve, this too-zealous reading definitely illustrates the principle of thrift at work, for it establishes a neat and unproblematical homology between epic simile and closet drama, a homology that assumes Milton is in both works engaged in *representing* a betrayal.

One could argue that by referring the Samson simile in *Paradise Lost* back to the Samson-identified author, author of *Samson Agonistes*, modern commentators obscure the heterogeneous uses to which Milton puts the Samson story by privileging the personal and domestic. After all, the story is alluded to in a number of political tracts; and in *The Reason of Church Government*, where it receives an allegorical elaboration, Milton has the prelates (male to a man) playing Dalilah to the King's Samson.

II

If the modern reading of the Samson simile is to be regarded, unequivocally, as a *mis*reading, however, it must be set against a reading which is correct not only in the narrow sense of being responsive to the allusive import of the plural 'they' but also by virtue of being conceptually coherent. Such a reading I should now like to attempt, yet before doing so want to stress that its coherence (as well, perhaps, as any authority it might possess) derives in part from an appeal to historical documents, in particular to Protestant commentaries on Genesis. Two historically specific features of Milton's Reformed interpretation of the Genesis story are relevant to the Samson simile's interpretation. The first is a consequence of Renaissance humanism and Protestantism's tendency to dissociate evil from Eve or woman. As Roberta Hamilton and others have argued, this dissociation should be regarded as part and parcel of the development of a specifically bourgeois view of marriage.[7] But it also

informs the Reformers' reading of the Genesis exchange between the
serpent and Eve, which for the first time in its exegetical history is
regarded as an exchange positioning Eve as a responsible, theologically
informed speaking subject. The second feature, which is of more direct
relevance to the Samson simile, concerns the view of the Fall developed
by Protestant exegetes, who regard it as a linear and sequential dramatic
process, with the result that what is taken to be the active and
progressive experience of transgression precedes the moment of
conscious discovery.[8]

Especially as formulated by Augustine, the Christian doctrines of the
Fall and of Original Sin have always insisted that the loss of innocence,
immortality and other original goods occurred as a result of the penalty
imposed by the paternal deity for the act of transgression; but they also
want to suggest that the penalty is not so much vengefully exacted as it is
implicit in the very act of disobedience or of wilful human agency itself.
While this theologico-juridical schema is formulated in an outrageously
dry, propositional discourse at many points in *Paradise Lost*, in the
Samson simile's immediate context it is articulated with an action that is
vividly represented. Although the representation takes place in the
medium of narrative, it becomes clear that many of its salient features are
generically dramatic when the speeches by Adam that precede and
follow the passage I cite in full here are taken into account:

> So said he, and forbore not glance or toy
> Of amorous intent, well understood
> Of Eve, whose eye darted contagious fire.
> Her hand he seized, and to a shady bank
> Thick overhead with verdant roof embowered
> He led her nothing loath; Flowers were the couch,
> Pansies, and violets, and asphodel,
> And hyacinth, Earth's freshest softest lap.
> There they their fill of love and love's disport
> Took largely, of their mutual guilt the seal,
> The solace of their sin, till dewy sleep
> Oppressed them, wearied with their amorous play.
> Soon as the force of that fallacious fruit,
> That with exhilarating vapour bland
> About their spirits had played, and inmost powers
> Made err, was now exhaled, and grosser sleep
> Bred of unkindly fumes, with conscious dreams
> Encumbered, now had left them, up they rose
> As from unrest, and each the other viewing,
> Soon found their eyes how opened, and their minds
> How darkened; innocence, that as a veil

> Had shadowed them from knowing ill, was gone,
> Just confidence, and native righteousness,
> And honour from about them, naked left
> To guilty shame: he covered, but his robe
> Uncovered more. So rose the Danite strong
> Of Philistean Dalilah, and waked
> Shorn of his strength, they destitute and bare
> Of all their virtue: silent, and in face
> Confounded long they sat, as strucken mute,
> Till Adam, though not less than Eve abashed,
> At length gave utterance to these words constrained.
> (9:1034–66)

The theologico-juridical schema makes its presence felt in this passage when the Genesis opening of the eyes is explicated by an emphasis on a mental loss or nakedness that marshals in a whole troop of abstract virtues: innocence, confidence, righteousness, honour, shame. Yet the emphasis falls also, dramatically, on the actors' discovery that the change has already, unbeknownst to them, occurred; that against expectation, innocence and her virtuous partners have simply disappeared.

The simile actually serves to explicate the intimate and discursively motivated temporal relationship between *Paradise Lost*'s central *peripeteia* and *anagnorisis*. It establishes an analogy between Samson arising from the 'harlot-*lap* / Of Philistean Dalilah' to discover that he is 'Shorn of his strength', and Eve and Adam arising from 'Earth's freshest softest *lap*' (9:1041) – no-one in the history of Milton criticism seems to have noticed the carefully plotted parallelism here – to discover that they are 'destitute and bare / Of all their virtue'. Informing the simile's concern with a retrospective discovery of loss is Protestantism's theology of the Word, a theology so logocentric as to be able to align Samson, who has unknowingly been shorn of his strength as a result of breaking his Nazarite vow, with Adam and Eve, who have unknowingly lost their original innocence as a result of denying the Father's Word. Within the logocentric framework established by the epic's dominant discourse, the discovery or *anagnorisis* is ultimately supposed to be of greater importance than the reversal. The discovery of loss is more important than the loss – of strength in Samson's case or of sexual innocence in that of Eve and Adam – itself, since the discovery is supposed to make possible a conscious recognition of the ideal value of that which is no longer possessed. In short, the simile suggests Eve and Adam awaken into what the epic takes to be human history by discovering that history has already, in a lap(se) of time, been made.

Against this reading, the modern misreading's pairing of Samson and

Adam seems fixated on an atemporal form of proportional analogy. But while this interpretative thriftiness is certainly modern and bourgeois, it also probably draws on features of an archaic and self-universalising patriarchal symbolic order, according to which the representation of lack or loss can only but affirm the hierarchically ordered polarity of the sexes. As my reading would suggest, the signifier 'Shorn of his strength' is associated metaphorically with the signifier 'destitute and bare / Of all their virtue'. Both mark the existential basis of change ('Shorn of his strength' suggesting precisely the way Samson's unshorn hair functions as a metonymy for his strength, itself a metonymy for his spiritual integrity, and 'destitute and bare' suggesting the way Eve and Adam's unselfconscious nakedness functions as a metaphor for innocence); and both signifiers, joined by 'waked', appear to have been generated by a prior action. But read as modern commentators misread this simile, the signifier 'Shorn of his strength' would appear unconsciously to efface itself by collapsing into its presumed signified, Samson's experience of sexual depletion, the detumescence or, symbolically, the castration, Dalilah is guilty of bringing about. And since Eve cannot be represented as sharing *that* experience, the entire simile is without more ado taken to compare its two male subjects. It is of course only – to use Derrida's coinage – in a phallogocentric discourse governed by an economy of the same, where the phallus as privileged signifier dictates that differences be produced only and always as difference from the same, that is, from the unitary male subject who is able always to represent his own oneness, that such a slippage – from a Samson who lacks to a post-coital 'they' not capable of including Eve – can take place.

It might at this point be thought that this critical unconscious is largely a fiction fabricated to fulfil the needs of a feminist theory of the text's consumption. But the phallocentric determinants of the Samson simile's misreading are revealed in a surprisingly literal manner by J. M. Evans in his edition of Books 9 and 10 of *Paradise Lost* for the *Cambridge Milton for Schools and Colleges* series. In his commentary on Book 9, Evans refers to the *anagnorisis* by saying 'Adam's eyes are opened', omitting reference to either Eve or the Genesis 'they'.[9] His introduction to the volume concludes with a chart on which are mapped the differences between 'pre-Fall', 'Fall', and 'post-Fall' states, the final entry of which opposes 'erect penis' on the unfallen states to 'flaccid' on the fallen. Claude Lévi-Strauss is mentioned in the words prefacing the chart.[10] Later, in the concluding 'Topics for Book 9', a specific myth reported in *The Raw and the Cooked* is cited, a myth linking sexual intercourse, reproduction and death. The myth tells the tale of a first man who, created in a state of perpetual tumescence, was taught by the first woman how to soften his penis in copulation; when the demiurge saw the limp penis, he cursed the man, consigning him to the reproductive cycle and therefore to death.[11] While Evans nowhere explicitly develops a coherent misogynistic misreading of the Samson simile, the textual apparatus he provides clearly more than enables such a reading. By the time a student of the Cambridge Milton series gets to Book 11 of *Paradise Lost*, where Michael says to Adam that 'Man's woe' begins from 'Man's effeminate slackness', a fairly graphic understanding of that slackness will have been shaped.

The misreading also completely obscures the novelty or historical specificity of *Paradise Lost*'s situating of the *anagnorisis* on the other side of an act of love-making. The Genesis opening of the eyes has of course traditionally been associated with an awakening of conscience. I suggest that in *Paradise Lost* this awakening is mediated by Eve and Adam's visual recognition in one another of the lineaments of gratified desire. The sexualised body – rather specifically, and significantly, the face – therefore plays a role in producing a new form of subjectivity. Yet this new and fallen subjectivity would seem to have as the condition of its possibility a sexual experience inaccessible to consciousness. In the first volume of his *History of Sexuality*, Foucault discusses what he calls 'the principle of a latency intrinsic to sexuality' as one of the principles ensuring the modern deployment of sexuality. This principle is concerned, he argues, not as in earlier periods with what the subject her- or himself wishes to hide, but with what seems by definition hidden from the subject.[12] That *Paradise Lost* portrays the emergence of something very like this principle at the moment of the epic's pivotal scene of recognition suggests that the scene might be registering – or, more accurately, given the history of its reception, perhaps unconsciously acknowledging – its own role in the production of a new form of subjectivity. Since this historically new subjectivity deploys sexuality in a way that intensifies the affective bonds of the heterosexual couple, the Samson simile – if read correctly – can itself be regarded as a literary marker of historical change.

Further extrinsic support for the Protestant reading I am proposing here can be found in *The Westminster Confessions of Faith*, which in a unique departure from an androcentric tradition uses the plural pronoun so consistently in the opening sections of its chapter on the Fall that it indicates the generic 'Man' of its heading is to be equated with 'our first parents' rather than with Adam, humankind's patriarchal representative.[13] Milton's heading for his chapter on the Fall in *De Doctrina* also stresses the potentially non-hierarchical oneness of Adam and Eve: 'Of the Fall of Our First Parents, and of Sin'.[14] But to continue marshalling support in this way is to continue forging a somewhat troublesome because positivistic link between an historicised and a 'correct' reading.

III

It is also, at the same time, to ignore what eighteenth-century commentators on *Paradise Lost* considered the most noteworthy feature of Milton's representation of the Fall's aftermath; of the fallen lovemaking of Adam and Eve, and the waking from it which evokes the Samson simile.

Writing in the *Spectator* in 1712, Addison was the first to draw attention to the intertextual relation between the scene of Adam and Eve's love-making and the scene in Book 14 of the *Iliad* in which Hera, adorned with the enchanting zone of Aphrodite, comes upon Zeus, who greets her by proposing they make love and by declaring that he has never before so intensely desired any goddess or woman, including Hera herself. Adam's 'converse' with Eve after he has eaten of the forbidden fruit – in lines immediately preceding the lengthy passage quoted above – is said by Addison to be an 'exact Copy' of Zeus's passionate declaration to Hera:[15]

> But come, so well refreshed, now let us play,
> As meet is, after such delicious fare;
> For never did thy beauty since the day
> I saw thee first and wedded thee, adorned
> With all perfections, so inflame my sense
> With ardour to enjoy thee, fairer now
> Than ever, bounty of this virtuous tree.
> (9:1027–33)

Although a similar invitation to love-making is uttered by Paris in Book 3 of the *Iliad*, the scene in Book 14 in which Zeus responds sexually to Hera's artificially heightened attractiveness is clearly the principal source of Milton's 'copying', which in this instance takes the form of what we would now call an overt allusion. That the allusion is unquestionably overt is established by Milton's imitation of other features of Homer's scene, such as the way the lovers' verbal exchanges come to an end when Zeus takes Hera in his arms and they make love on a peak of mount Ida which, as Addison notes, produces underneath them a bed of flowers they fall asleep on when sexually satisfied.

It is not only Zeus's invitation and the love-making itself that Milton imitates, however. As Thomas Newton points out in his 1749 edition of *Paradise Lost*, in an annotation modern editors pass on to their readers,

Adam's post-discovery speech 'O Eve, in evil hour' is based on the passage in Book 15 of the *Iliad* in which Zeus lashes out verbally at Hera upon awakening from a post-coital slumber to discover that he has, through her, lost control of the battle. As has already been mentioned, Newton construes the Samson story correctly: 'As Samson waked shorn of his strength, they waked destitute and bare of all their virtue.'[16] Yet the awakening he is really interested in is Adam's post-coital verbal awakening to an outrage that resembles Jupiter's. The intertextual reading Newton produces tells the story of the progress in the two patriarchs of an emasculating or effeminate desire: 'As this whole transaction between Adam and Eve is manifestly copied from the episode of Jupiter and Juno on mount Ida, has many of the same circumstances, and often the very words translated, so it concludes exactly after the same manner in a quarrel. Adam awakes much in the same humour as Jupiter, and their cases are somewhat parallel; they are both overcome by their fondness for their wives, and are sensible of their error too late, and then their love turns to resentment, and they grow angry with their wives; when they should rather have been angry with themselves for their weakness in hearkening to them.'[17] By suggesting an ironic dimension, Newton here modifies Pope's openly misogynistic comments in his edition of this book of the *Iliad*, where he states that both Adam and Zeus, whose 'Circumstance is very parallel', awaken 'full of that Resentment natural to a Superior, who is imposed upon by one of less Worth and Sense than himself, and imposed upon in the worst manner by Shews of Tenderness and Love'.[18] Newton's reading is less stridently masculinist, for he implies that far from being the legitimate expression of patriarchal self-righteousness, the anger verbalised by Zeus and Adam merely indicates, ironically, the defensive self-deception that results when patriarchal superiority becomes unsettled. Where the emphasis of Pope's discussion falls on the evil consequences of female duplicity, Newton's stresses the instability of male superiority. But in spite of this, by concentrating, like Pope, on the similarities or parallels between Adam and Zeus, Newton contributes to a masculinist reading of the passage in *Paradise Lost* we are here considering. Granted, Newton generously remarks that the positions of the two patriarchs are 'somewhat' rather than 'very' (Pope's choice) parallel. Yet even a qualified parallelism seems the product of a decidedly phallogocentric structure of thought. For it tends to obliterate the difference between the scene of sexual seduction which Hera consciously designs, with an intent to deceive Zeus, and the scene of Adam's transgression against the Father's Word, a scene in which *Paradise Lost* has Eve participate only ambiguously since she is herself deceived. The critics' parallelism also erases the narrative or temporal difference between Book 9's two scenes of temptation against the Word and the scene of the fallen Eve and

Adam's love-making on 'Earth's freshest softest lap'. That even Newton's modest parallelism ends up conflating verbal or intellectual temptation and sexual seduction can be seen in his statement that both Jupiter and Adam 'should rather have been angry with themselves for their weakness in hearkening to them', a statement which unmistakably, even if unintentionally, echoes the patriarchal Lord's judgement of Adam; the phrase echoed appears both in Genesis iii:17, 'Because thou hast hearkened unto the voice of thy wife', and in *Paradise Lost*, 10:198.

But is this difference-denying parallelism generated solely by masculinist commentators or is it implied by *Paradise Lost*'s overt allusion to the *Iliad*? It is of course impossible to imagine on what grounds such a question might be given a definitive answer. One could argue, against the neo-classical commentators cited above, that the allusion functions ironically and that it intends to mark the *difference* between Zeus's anger at his seductress Hera and Adam's, which is 'fallen' or inherently and therefore illegitimately self-exculpating. Yet *Paradise Lost* makes any rigorous pursuit of this line of thought rather difficult, since the narrator has already, officially, remarked that Adam was 'not deceived, / But fondly overcome with female charm' (9:998–9). If in referring to the parallel weakness of Zeus and Adam in 'hearkening' to their wives Newton echoes both Genesis and Milton's epic, in stating that 'they are both overcome by their fondness for their wives' he echoes these very lines from *Paradise Lost*. Newton's echo therefore draws attention to the way the narrator's interpretative intervention itself conflates spiritual fall and sexual seduction, thereby sanctioning a reading of the overt allusion to the *Iliad* which concentrates on the parallels between Zeus and Adam.

Instead of illustrating, unequivocally, Adam and Eve's mutual recognition of a mutual change, the simile now appears significantly and inescapably expressive of the deeply sexist attitudes that its context, with its exclusively patriarchal spokesmen (Book 9's narrator, Adam, Zeus, and then Addison, Pope, Newton), makes explicit. If Hera is to Zeus what Eve is to Adam, then the Samson simile suggests, in spite of itself, that Eve has the same relation to Adam as her temptress daughter, Dalilah, has to Samson. The sexes become related just as our phallocentric cultural tradition would lead us to expect they would be: the (either 'somewhat' or 'very') righteously aggrieved Zeus, Adam and Samson are aligned against the beguiling and deceitful Hera, Eve and Dalilah.

But what are we to make of the contradictory possibilities for meaning our discussion has so far opened up? The question is tricky precisely because the contradictions have not before been exposed. What are we to make of the way the Samson simile's allusive context undermines its ostensible meaning? We could, if we wished to use New Critical terms, talk about the 'tension' between the 'correct' reading of the Samson simile and its error-inducing context. Invoking the figure of the author, and the psychological determinants the use of this figure sanctions, we could then refer this tension back to Milton's own ambivalence about the relations about the sexes. But we could also, much more appropriately, see in this remarkable instance of intertextuality the signs of an historically, not psychologically, determined ambivalence. In this case, the text would testify to the success with which a dominant patriarchal ideology, here represented by the overt allusion to the *Iliad*, is able to contain and defuse egalitarian sentiments, the limited expression of which might be encouraged, historically, by an emerging bourgeois family structure. To put this another way, the allusive context exposes what will increasingly become the merely formal status of the equality of the sexes in bourgeois society, an equality here elaborated in the Samson simile. The simile therefore uses the theologico-juridical schema to acknowledge that both Adam and Eve are, technically, guilty; it defers to Genesis, signifying, according to the letter of the text, that the eyes of them both have been opened. But it does so in a context that indicates clearly that this does not really matter; that what *really* counts is what has happened to Adam, father of mankind, Man. Indeed, the simile could be said to work in the way the title of Milton's first divorce tract does, *The Doctrine and Discipline of Divorce; Restored to the Good of Both Sexes, From the Bondage of Canon Law . . . to the True Meaning of Scripture. . . .* The title promises, boldly, an enlightenment that its androcentric values tend repeatedly to withhold. That in *Paradise Lost* it is a patriarchal figure, Samson, to whom both Adam and Eve are compared is thus of crucial importance, ideologically; the syntactical priority of Samson to the 'they' for whom he is a figure suggests that 'Samson' functions in the slippery and misleading way the generic masculine still continues to do in our culture.[19] *Paradise Lost* would thus seem to generate the counterpart in poetic discourse of the sexist linguistic practice which codes the word 'man' equivocally to mean generic humankind at the same time that, in context, it most often means exclusively the representative or exemplary male being. If we focus on the context that the allusion to the *Iliad* seems to provide, we find the ostensibly generic 'man', as it were, being cancelled by the masculine pronoun 'he', which thereby undoes the equality *Paradise Lost* appeared, in the briefly enlightened simile, to endorse.

IV

So far, I have followed eighteenth-century commentators in regarding Book 9's allusive use of the *Iliad*'s scene of immortal love-making in a way that suggests *Paradise Lost* simply re-represents specific feaures of Homer's representation. I have also limited the discussion to the imitation of basically dramatic features, such as Zeus's invitation to make love and his angry awakening, undeceived. But as Pope points out, in observations modern editors transmit, Milton also makes use of the passage in Book 14 of the *Iliad* in which the earth is presented as responding sympathetically to the sexual embrace of the two gods:

> So speaking, the son of Kronos caught his wife in his arms. There /
> underneath them the divine earth broke into young, fresh
> grass, and into dewy clover, crocus and hyacinth
> so thick and soft it held the hard ground deep away from
> them. /
> There they lay down together and drew about them a golden
> wonderful cloud, and from it the glimmering dew descended.[20]

In his notes on this passage Pope points to two places in *Paradise Lost* where it has been imitated. Citing lines 510–17 of Adam's narrative in Book 8, Pope remarks: 'The Creation is made to give the same Tokens of Joy at the Performance of the nuptial Rites of our first Parents, as she does here at the Congress of Jupiter and Juno.'[21] Adam there says:

> To the nuptial bower
> I led her blushing like the morn, all Heaven
> And happy constellations on that hour
> Shed their selectest influence; the Earth
> Gave signs of gratulation, and each hill;
> Joyous the birds; fresh gales and gentle airs
> Whispered it to the woods, and from their wings
> Flung rose, flung odours from the spicy shrub.

Closely related, though not so vividly linked to the moment of sexual intercourse – which, significantly, does not actually get represented – is the following passage from the narrator's description of the 'blissful bower' in Book 4:

> each beauteous flower,
> Iris all hues, roses and jessamin
> Reared high their flourished heads between, and wrought
> Mosaic, underfoot the violet,
> Crocus, and hyacinth with rich inlay

> Broidered the ground, more coloured than with stone
> Of costliest emblem . . .
>
> (4:697–703)

Of these lines Pope says that they 'are manifestly from the same Original'; and that 'the very Turn of *Homer*'s Verses is observed, and the Cadence, and almost the Words, finely translated'.[22] Finally, turning to the invitation and the love-making reproduced in Book 9, but without commenting at all on Milton's use of natural vegetation there, Pope shifts into an openly evaluative, not to say quintessentially moralistic, vein: 'But it is with wonderful Judgment and Decency he has used that exceptionable Passage of the Dalliance, Ardour, and Enjoyment: That which seems in Homer an impious Fiction, becomes a moral Lesson in Milton; since he makes that lascivious Rage of the Passions the immediate Effect of the Sin of our first Parents after the Fall.'[23]

Here the notion of imitation clearly implies transformation and appropriation. But it is possible that Homer's scene of immortal love-making has been transformed more radically than Pope's comfortable moralising of Milton's supposed moralisation of Homer supposes. Although Pope elsewhere in his annotations refers to Plato, in commenting on the story of Hera and Zeus he does not; nor, for that matter, does any more recent critic, so far as I know. Yet it would certainly not be merely fanciful to suggest that the most influential and moralistic of commentators on Homer has mediated Milton's own appropriations. In Plato's critique of imitation in Book III of the *Republic*, Socrates, as is well known, takes Homer to task for representing the gods falsely, in ways unworthy of them and potentially dangerous to his audience. Among the numerous passages from Homer that Socrates singles out for censure is the sexual scene in Book 14 of the *Iliad*, of which he asks, is it really appropriate for young people to hear 'how Zeus lightly forgot all the designs which he devised, awake while the other gods and men slept, because of the excitement of his passions, and was so overcome by the sight of Hera that he is not even willing to go to their chamber, but wants to lie with her there on the ground and says that he is possessed by a fiercer desire than when they first consorted with one another'.[24] What Plato is referring to here is that specific moment in the exchange between Hera and Zeus preceding their love-making in which Hera pretends to be reluctant to sleep openly on the peaks of Ida and proposes that they go to the 'chamber' Hephaistos has built. In response, Zeus assures her they will not be seen where they are, for he will gather a 'golden cloud' about them. It is at this point that he embraces her and that the earth reacts by breaking forth in floral vegetation. In the passage just quoted from the *Republic*, Plato gives the content of this exchange-as-foreplay (and, on Hera's part, as-cunning) a definite moral significance, yet one that does not save Homer's text, constructing an ethically coded contrast between making love in an enclosure or 'chamber' and casually, 'on the ground', in order to stress the shameful shamelessness Homer has here, casually, depicted.

If Plato's moralisation indeed structures Milton's allusive use of the *Iliad* in the passage from *Paradise Lost* we are here examining, then its intertextual complexity is even greater than our discussion has so far suggested. Critics have frequently commented on the carefully structured opposition between prelapsarian eroticism and Book 8's post-lapsarian lust, and it has also been noted that in Book 9 Adam and Eve do not make it into their 'blissful bower'. As Fowler has remarked, the indefinite article 'a' in 'a shady bank' (9:1037) underlines the casual randomness of their choice of place.[25] Further, although this has not ever specifically been remarked, the passages in Books 4 and 8 that can be referred back to their 'Original' in Homer both have specific reference to the 'blissful bower'. The passage in Book 8 spiritualises Homer's scene by having the Earth give 'sign of gratulation' at the nuptial union of Adam and Eve in their 'nuptial bower'; the passage in Book 4 describes, specifically, the floor of the bower that the 'sovereign planter' has set apart for his creatures: 'underfoot the violet, / Crocus and hyacinth with rich inlay / Broidered the ground'. In Book 9, however . . . nature is somehow, seductively, in a potentially ensnaring manner, simply there: 'Flowers were the couch, / Pansies, and violets, and asphodel, / And hyacinth, Earth's freshest softest lap.'

Read in this way through Plato's mediating commentary, the main point of the Homeric allusions in Book 9 of *Paradise Lost* would now seem to be not the patriarchally structured polarity of male and female but the spiritually structured opposition between the sacred and the profane. The blissful bower, consecrated by the 'sovereign planter' for prelapsarian love-making, is the polar opposite of 'a shady bank, / Thick overlaid with verdant roof embowered'. Making love on the 'Broidered' floor of the blissful bower is thus also the polar opposite of Adam and Eve's *al fresco* love-making on 'Earth's freshest softest lap'. Indeed, it is tempting to think that the figures of Samson and Dalilah with her 'harlot-lap' were initially generated by the profane role in this structure of oppositions by 'Earth's freshest softest lap', the 'lap' – rather the two laps – here clearly signalling a lapse, *lapsus*, a fall, the Fall.

If 'lap(s)(e)' can be freed up as signifiers in this way, then the passage would seem to demonstrate in a pointed manner Johnson's remark that Milton saw nature 'through the spectacles of books'. But if it shows us Milton reading Homer through Plato's eyes, it probably also suggests a set of oppositions overlapping with that of the sacred and the profane. For Plato the sacred is of course associated with the realm of ideas, with the originals of which the realm of appearances and, *a fortiori*, artistic products are the profane and debased copies. Appropriated by *Paradise Lost*'s Christian Platonism, this becomes the opposition between a created or original sexual innocence and its fallen imitation, represented in Book 9. But the difference between original and copy, between Book 4's prelapsarian sexuality and its fallen counterpart in Book 9, is a difference produced in Book 9 by Milton's imitation of Homer's *Iliad*. And Milton's imitation of the scene of immortal love-making in the *Iliad* is ultimately mediated by Plato's critique of representation. What Book 9 of *Paradise Lost* would therefore appear to give us is an imitation of a scene in the *Iliad*, which, subjected by Plato to an attack on its shameful debasing of its divine originals, is itself presented as a debased or fallen version, bringing forth shame to its actors, of its original in Book 4. To say, as eighteenth-century commentators do, that Milton here imitates or copies Homer, is thus entirely to miss the logocentric critique of imitation that the scene, in this context, seems to constitute. Book 9's profane and self-implicated dramatic mimesis is radically dialectical, in that, by casting a Platonic doubt on the appropriateness of its own mimesis, it attempts to preserve its moralising discursive distance from the Fall.

But what do we do with the Samson simile now? This Platonic turn suggests a way of reading *Paradise Lost*'s allusions to the *Iliad* that leaves intact a non-sexist reading of the simile. If the *Republic* mediates Milton's use of Homer, then it would seem to provide us with a genuine *tertium quid*, one that permits us to acknowledge the presence of the potentially sexist allusive context but does not require that it signify as it has been thought to do. It could even be argued that Genesis and the *Republic* – or rather theology and philosophy – work together to effect a transformation (or *Aufhebung*) of the phallocentric intertext established by the *Iliad*, Judges and our fallen symbolic order, emptying the allusions of their representational and patriarchal content, and raising from the representational laps(e) a complex of abstract and spiritual significations.

V

Such a transformation or *Aufhebung*, by relying on Milton's Platonic and therefore logocentric critique of representation, would neatly illustrate Derrida's view that the Hegelian *Aufhebung* dramatises the capacity of logocentrism to recuperate itself. For that reason alone, the reading I have produced by means of this Platonic turn is open to interrogation. The reading's attractiveness is in part the result of its capacity to stake out stable grounds for the Samson simile's intelligibility. It can claim these grounds, however, only by suggesting that theological, philosophical and poetic discourses join forces in this passage from *Paradise Lost* to carve out a space in which abstract meanings appear as if in their original or unfallen transparency. And since the only guarantor of such a neutral, non-sexist transparency is the textual or authorial self-consciousness posited by critical discourse, it is really critical discourse itself that would finally have to be the unacknowledged fourth partner in the work of saving the text. Both textual self-consciousness and the critical discourse that seeks to posit such consciousness by effacing itself are, of course, idealist and ultimately phallogocentric constructs. So while it might be tempting to argue that *Paradise Lost* is not only fully awake to the implications of its masculinist codes but knowingly and subtly transforms them, to do so would be to posit a textual self-consciousness as transhistorically vigilant as the Father's all-seeing eye.

There are other, institutional grounds for turning against this Platonic turn, as well. It could easily be argued that to save Milton's text by means of idealist constructs is to make use of the dominant discourse of Milton criticism in the academy. But to save this particular text is also to come to the defence of Milton, the author, who can be made to appear in the light of this reading if not a proto-feminist, then at least a liberal humanist in the process of becoming one. There can be little doubt that the Milton establishment, perhaps especially in North America, the best-defended stronghold of liberal humanism, would heartily support such a defence. The rise in recent years of attacks on Milton by feminist literary critics has triggered a number of well-received apologies, which characteristically celebrate the egalitarian features of Milton's presentation of the marriage relationship in *Paradise Lost*, together with his representation of Eve as a character whose responsibility for her actions equals Adam's.[26] Yet as this brief account suggests, not only the defenders of the faith but the feminist 'opposition' (Joan Webber's term) as well have tended to conduct the debate without submitting its terms to any kind of ideological or historical analysis. As a consequence, the debate on Milton and sexual politics as it has taken shape over the last decade and a half has been severely restricted, both parties having been equally engaged with a highly individualised and ideologically charged figure of the author. The Milton of this debate is either appealed to as the patron saint of the companionate marriage and of the delicately imagined feminine sensibility, or stands darkly towering over us, the prototypical patriarch, the bad father of us all, and all our woe.

On such a battleground, to take up arms against a misogynistic misreading is clearly to risk becoming conscripted, willy nilly, to the cause of the father's defence. The risk obviously has to be taken, since the powerful and historically long-lived hold that sexist values have had on critical discourse on Milton has to be contested – whether that hold is exemplified in the case of the Samson simile's modern misreading, in that of the masculinist appropriations of Book 9's allusive use of the *Iliad*, or elsewhere. Yet because there are other determinations at work in the field of Milton and literary criticism, it is clear that a feminist discourse also wishing to contest the academy's dominant discourses cannot simply put a polemically inspired feminist interpretation in the place of a misogynistic misreading, and leave it at that.

I would therefore like to argue that the diverse elements of the passage as a whole the readings here produced have brought into focus should not – even if they could – be fused into a single and unproblematical reading. Not because indeterminacy is everywhere and at all times characteristic of linguistic or literary acts; nor because the endless proliferation of meaning better befits our late capitalist economy than does thriftiness. But on the grounds that the history of the reception of *Paradise Lost* is a history that cannot merely be transcended by the fresh production of new, definitive readings, being a history in which, institutionally and culturally, we still participate, as the contemporary debate on Milton and feminist issues clearly indicates. My analysis has indicated that in the past various critical discourses have sought to stabilise the passage in question by producing only those allusions or intertextual relations which can be mastered. Yet if the various discourses that have, historically, sought mastery over the text were themselves to be placed in intertextual relation with it, *and* in conflictual relation with any feminist counter-readings, as I have tried to do here, then *Paradise Lost* as a text whose meaning is somehow pre-given or authoritatively present would be lost to history by being given up to it. Intervening in that history, a feminist reading of the text we have been looking at would refuse to stabilise or recuperate it, thereby appropriating *Paradise Lost* by happily letting it go.

Notes

1. Biblical quotations are from the King James version.

2. Northrop Frye, *Fearful Symmetry* (Princeton, NJ: Princeton University Press, 1942), p. 362. To the best of my knowledge, B. Rajan is the only modern critic to provide anything like a reading that compares both Eve and Adam with Samson; but he does so by stressing a common, newly acquired 'blindness to the things of the spirit', *'Paradise Lost' and the Seventeenth Century Reader* (1497; repr. Ann Arbor, Michigan, 1967), p. 73. Typically incoherent in its unacknowledged shifts from plural to (androcentric) singular is Harry Blamire's commentary in *Milton's Creation* (London: Methuen, 1971), p. 237: 'They find their *eyes* indeed *opened* (1053), but not in the way anticipated (cf. 706–8, 985). They are opened to the recognition of their own darkened minds, to the disappearance of that "veil" (1054) of innocence that has "shadowed"

them from knowledge of evil. . . . Adam's waking to guilt is like Samson's waking from the lap of Dalilah, who, in his sleep, had cut off his hair and thereby deprived him of his strength. The correspondence underlines the concept of innocence as positive power, which it is important for the modern reader to sense. The loss of innocence is a virtual emasculation. "Shorn of strength . . . destitute and bare / Of all their virtue" (1062–3); this is their new condition.' E.M.W. Tillyard, in an edition of Books 9 and 10 for the *Harrap's English Classics* (London: Harrap Ltd, 1960), glosses the simile correctly: 'As Samson of the tribe of Dan woke to find his strength gone, so Adam and Eve woke to find their innocence gone' (p. 141). But editions published since that time stubbornly persist in the masculinist reading.

3. In line 1058 there is no stop after 'shame' in either of the original editions of *Paradise Lost*. Editors since Newton customarily provide one, however, often associating this personified 'shame' with Psalm cix: 29, 'Let mine adversaries be clothed with shame, and let them cover themselves with their own confusion, as with a mantle', and with *Samson Agonistes*, lines 841–2. Alastair Fowler, introducing a baroque variation on the misogynistic misreading, omits any stop after 'shame', offering among other explanations that 'Adam covers in response to Eve's guilty shame', *The Poems of John Milton*, ed. John Carey and Alastair Fowler (London: Longman, 1968), p. 917.

4. THOMAS NEWTON (ed.), *Paradise Regained and Samson Agonistes* (London, 1753), p. 277.

5. MICHEL FOUCAULT, 'What is an Author?', *Textual Strategies*, tr. and ed. Josué V. Harari (Ithaca, NY: Cornell University Press, 1979), p. 159. It should be said here that while making use of Foucault in this essay I do so accepting the Marxist critique frequently made of his work. The most acute and suggestive to my mind is Peter Dews's 'Power and Subjectivity in Foucault', *New Left Review* 44 (1984): 72–94.

6. *Poems of John Milton*, ed. Carey and Fowler, p. 918. JOHN R. KNOTT, Jr, *Milton's Pastoral Vision* (Chicago: University of Chicago Press, 1971), p. 124.

7. ROBERTA HAMILTON, *The Liberation of Women* (London: Allen & Unwin, 1978), pp. 22, 64–8. For a discussion of the distinctively Puritan development of this ideology see William Haller's influential 'Hail Wedded Love', *ELH* 13 (1947): 79–97, and 'The Puritan Art of Love' by Malleville and William Haller, *HLQ* 5 (1942): 235–72. Margo Todd argues convincingly for the importance of situating Protestant views in the context of humanist thought in 'Humanists, Puritans and the Spiritualized Household', *Church History* 49 (1980): 18–34.

8. For a reading, relying on these commentaries, of Eve's temptation in Book 9 of *Paradise Lost* and of the dramatic linearity of that book's action, see my 'Reading the Fall: Discourse and Drama in *Paradise Lost*', *ELR* 14 (1984): 199–229.

9. J. MARTIN EVANS (ed.), *John Milton, 'Paradise Lost': Books IX–X* for the *Cambridge Milton for Schools and Colleges*, gen. ed. J.B. Broadbent (Cambridge: Cambridge University Press, 1973), p. 33.

10. *Ibid.*, pp. 9–10.

11. *Ibid.*, pp. 167–8.

12. MICHEL FOUCAULT, *The History of Sexuality*, Vol. I, tr. Robert Hurley (New York: Random House, 1978), p. 66.

13. *The Westminster Confession of Faith* in *The Creed of Christendom*, ed. Philip Schaff (New York: Harper & Brothers, 1877), III, 615–17.

14. MILTON, *De Doctrina Christiana*, tr. John Carey, ed. Maurice Kelley, *Complete Prose*, 6:382 (Bk I. Ch. XI).

15. JOSEPH ADDISON, *The Spectator*, no. 351 (12 April 1712), ed. Gregory Smith (London: Oxford University Press, 1945; repr. 1973), 100–12.

16. THOMAS NEWTON (ed.), *Paradise Lost* (London, 1749), II, p. 201.

17. *Ibid.*, p. 202.

18. ALEXANDER POPE, *The Iliad of Homer*, ed. Maynard Mack, Vol. VII of *The Poems of Alexander Pope*, gen. ed. John Butt (London and New Haven, Conn.: Yale University Press, 1967), p. 193.

19. That among the upper classes an increasing emphasis upon the 'conjugal core' was accompanied by a strengthening of patriarchal powers is the influential thesis of Lawrence Stone in 'Part Three: The Restricted Patriarchal Nuclear Family 1550–1700', *The Family, Sex and Marriage in England 1500–1800* (London: Weidenfeld & Nicholson, 1977), pp. 123–218. See also Ruth Perry, *Women, Letters and the Novel* (New York: AMS Press, 1978), pp. 27–62.

20. *Iliad*, tr. Richmond Lattimore (Chicago and London: Harper & Row, 1951), p. 303. All further quotations from the *Iliad* are from this edition.

21. Pope, *Iliad*, p. 181.

22. *Ibid.*, p. 182.

23. *Ibid.*, p. 182.

24. PLATO, *The Republic*, III, 390, B–C, tr. Paul Shorey, Loeb Classical Library (London and Cambridge, Mass.: Harvard University Press, 1953), pp. 216–17.

25. FOWLER, *Milton*, p. 916.

26. Although this is not the place for a full bibliography, the following would qualify for membership in the feminist 'opposition': Marcia Landy, 'Kinship and the Role of Women in *Paradise Lost*', *Milton Studies* **4** (1972): 3–19; Sandra Gilbert, 'Patriarchal Poetry and Women Readers: Reflections on Milton's Bogey', *PMLA* **93** (1978): 368–82; Christine Froula, 'When Eve Reads Milton: Undoing the Canonical Economy', *Critical Inquiry* **10** (1983): 321–47. Among the defences are Barbara Lewalski's 'Milton and Women – Yet Once More', *Milton Studies* **6** (1974): 3–20; Joan Malory Webber's 'The Politics of Poetry: Feminism and *Paradise Lost*', *Milton Studies* **14** (1980): 21; and Diane Kelsey McColley's *Milton's Eve* (Urbana: University of Illinois Press, 1983). Although it, too, is engaged with the ideologically charged figure, the patriarch Milton, ' "Rational Burning": Milton on Sex and Marriage' by David Aers and Bob Hodge is an interesting attempt to deal with some of the contradictions articulated in Milton's writings (*Milton Studies* **13** (1979): 3–34).

13 Allegory and the Sublime in *Paradise Lost**

VICTORIA KAHN

Recent critics have analysed the Sin and Death episode in Book 2 of *Paradise Lost* in terms of its allusions to and revisions of Ovid, Spenser, and Scripture; and have usually understood the episode as dramatizing Milton's critique of allegory. They have thus tended to isolate the episode from the rest of the poem. In contrast, early readers of Milton viewed Sin and Death as examples of the grandeur or sublimity of *Paradise Lost* as a whole, at the same time that they noted Milton's transgressions of the generic constraints of epic in this episode. In this essay I argue for the programmatic rhetorical ambivalence of Satan's encounter with Sin and Death, and suggest that this ambivalence is central to Milton's meditation on linguistic difference as constitutive of human agency in *Paradise Lost*. The essay is located on the methodological cusp of rhetorical analysis and philosophical critique. In attempting to capture the philosophical implications of Milton's rhetorical ambivalence and indeterminacy, I have been influenced both by work on Milton's interest in the theological doctrine of 'things indifferent' (Barker; Fish), and by work on the literary and philosophical notion of the sublime as an unstable rhetorical structure that dramatizes the necessity of negation or difference to cognition and so implicitly stages a critique of mimetic theories of representation. I argue that in the Sin and Death episode Milton both dramatizes the structure of linguistic difference which is constitutive of human agency and stages a critique of his own narcissistic claims to justify the ways of God to men in this way.

---

* First published in this volume.

> *True madness lies primarily in immutability, in the inability of the thought to*
> *participate in the negativity in which thought – in contradistinction of fixed*
> *judgment – comes into its own.*

> (Horkheimer and Adorno)[1]

Ever since Addison and Johnson, critics have described Milton as the
poet of sublimity. Addison remarked in *The Spectator* that Milton's
'Genius was wonderfully turned to the Sublime [and] his Subject is the
noblest that could have entered into the thoughts of Man'; and David
Hume in his *History of England* wrote, 'It is certain that this author, when
in a happy mood and employed on a noble thought, is the most
wonderfully sublime of any poet in any language, Homer, and Lucretius,
and Tasso not excepted.' As for later readers of *Paradise Lost*, Books 1 and
2 provided many of the chief examples of the Miltonic sublime. In his
Philosophical Inquiry Burke gives Milton's description of 'the universe of
Death' in Book 2 as an instance of the sublime and Hugh Blair, in *Lectures
on Rhetoric and Belles Lettres*, describes the Satan of Book 1 as the sublime
figure par excellence:

> Here concur a variety of sources of the Sublime: the principal object
> eminently great; a high superior nature, fallen indeed, but erecting
> itself against distress; the grandeur of the principal object heightened,
> by associating it with so noble an idea as that of the sun suffering an
> eclipse; this picture shaded with all those images of change and
> trouble, of darkness and terror, which coincide so finely with the
> Sublime emotion; and the whole expressed in a style and versification,
> easy, natural, and simple, but magnificent. . . .[2]

Here, as in the first treatise on the subject, Longinus's *Peri Hypsos*, the
sublime is a term of highest praise. Yet there is one sublime episode in
Book 2 which has proved a consistent source of irritation to readers:
Satan's encounter with Sin and Death. Although the episode has the
sublime qualities of 'change and trouble, of darkness and terror,' the
allegory is regularly criticized from the eighteenth century on as
inappropriate to the otherwise non-allegorical epic. While admitting that
'the descriptive part of this allegory is . . . very strong and full of sublime
ideas,' Addison complains, 'I cannot think that persons of such a
chimerical existence [Sin and Death] are proper actors in an epic poem'
(*Spectator*, No. 309; No. 273). And Samuel Johnson echoes this view in his
Life of Milton: 'This unskilful allegory appears to me one of the greatest
faults of the poem.'[3]

Modern readers, in contrast, have preferred to see the 'fault' of
allegory as a deliberate rhetorical strategy. Yet, while defending the
appropriateness of the allegory of Sin and Death to the poem as a whole,

they have tended to deny its sublimity, arguing that the episode is a parody rather than a genuine instance of the sublime. Thus Anne Ferry has claimed that allegory represents a fallen mode of language,[4] and Maureen Quilligan writes:

> Allegory is the genre of the fallen world, for in a prelapsarian world, at one with God, there is no 'other' for language to work back to since there has been no fatal division. No distance, no divorce, no distaste between God and man, who has not yet known the coherence of good and evil in the rind of one apple tasted.[5]

Rather than being a form of inspired language or divine accommodation, allegory in this case would be a satanic version of the Word.

In the following pages I would like to suggest, in contrast to both eighteenth-century and modern critics, that the allegory of Sin and Death episode is both parodic and sublime, and that this deliberate rhetorical instability has implications for our reading of *Paradise Lost* as a whole. As we will see, the episode dramatizes the indeterminacy – or in seventeenth-century theological discourse, the indifference – of rhetorical figures (here, allegory) which is a condition of correct interpretation and free will.[6] In this light, distance and division are not simply a consequence of the fall but the structural precondition of prelapsarian experience as well. Attention to the generation of Sin as an event which glosses not only Ovid[7] and Spenser, but also Augustine and the Epistle of James, will allow us to read the episode not only as a deliberate exception to the non-allegorical poetic of *Paradise Lost*, but also as a genealogy of the poem as a whole; for the structure of linguistic difference which defines the parodic allegorical 'plot' of the episode also informs its sublime 'counterplot.'[8]

Before analyzing the Sin and Death episode in detail, it may be helpful to return for a moment to the ambivalent response of eighteenth-century readers, for this ambivalence captures something of the ironic structure of plot and counterplot I will be exploring below. Recently Leslie Moore and Steven Knapp have proposed related explanations for this response. Moore argues that in the eighteenth century the category of the sublime was often a way of discussing Milton's generic transgression or revision of the conventions of epic (11–13 and *passim*). In this light, the criticism of Milton's allegorical personification as a violation of epic would thus seem to be an attempt to delineate a proper or appropriate sublime – that of Satan in Books 1 and 2 or of Adam in Book 8 – one that can be integrated within the bounds of epic. In the critical discourse of the eighteenth century, Sin and Death are scapegoated in order to preserve the harmony or aesthetic proportion of *Paradise Lost*.

Knapp argues in a similar vein that eighteenth-century critics were uncomfortable with the allegorical personifications of Sin and Death because they dramatized the 'programmatic ambivalence' of the sublime. While Knapp insists that this eighteenth-century reading does not correspond to anything in 'Milton's own attitude toward personification,' I would like to suggest that his remarks do indeed describe the intended rhetorical effect of the Sin and Death episode. Commenting on the similarity between the sublime and the personified agency of allegorical figures, Knapp writes:

> the sublime depends on an ideal of perfect, self-originating agency that no one really expects or wants to fulfill. To 'experience' the sublime was not quite . . . to identify oneself with a transcendent ideal of pure subjective power, but rather to entertain that ideal as an abstract, fantastic, unattainable possibility. Kant, along with Burke and the English satirists, was aware of the intriguing proximity of *hypsos* to bathos, of subjective 'freedom' to a mad or comical inflation of the self. The sublime, as Kant explains it, is therefore programmatically ambivalent: it demands a simultaneous identification with and dissociation from images of ideal power. Unless the subject in some degree identifies with the ideal, the experience reduces to mere pretense. But total identification collapses the distinction between ideal and empirical agency and leads to a condition of 'rational raving' that Kant designated 'fanaticism.' (p. 3)

As we will see, Satan in the Sin and Death episode dramatizes the 'intriguing proximity of *hypsos* to bathos', of 'subjective "freedom" to a mad or comical inflation of the self'; and in so doing stages the extremes of total identification and total alienation which the reader of *Paradise Lost* must learn to avoid.

In the Sin and Death episode, Milton allies both these extremes with allegory at the same time that he provides an allegorical critique of allegory, in order to educate the reader to view rhetorical structures as indeterminate and thus finally less as things than as activities of discrimination and choice. In this episode, as in the poem as a whole, the poet's justification of the ways of God to men is inseparable from a meditation on linguistic mediation.

The Allegory of Sin and Death

The ambivalent critical reception of Sin and Death as both parodic and sublime registers the ambivalence dramatized in the episode itself and provides an important clue to Milton's rhetoric of things indifferent. As I have said, the episode is not simply allegorical but also constitutes an allegorical critique of allegory and thus dramatizes the indifference of this rhetorical mode. At the same time it implicates both thematically and intertextually the related questions of authority, obedience, antinomianism and rebellion in ways that are crucial for our understanding of prelapsarian Eden as well.

From the beginning the episode is presented to us as one with a high degree of self-reflexivity about its own allegorical procedures. Traditionally allegory was seen both as the representation of what is by nature obscure to human understanding and as itself an obscure form of representation. We can only know God or divine truths indirectly or allegorically but in accommodating these truths to human understanding, allegory also presents them under a veil or obscurely. Thus Demetrius in his *On Style* associates allegory with darkness and night, and Vossius writes that 'by its obscurity [allegory] resembles the darkness of night, which easily terrifies the fearful.'[9] The obscure representation of Sin and Death thus functions as a kind of allegorical parody of allegory. That is, in personifying the unknowable or unrecognizable, the descriptions should make Sin and Death clearer to us, but the descriptions themselves merely double the original obscurity of these terms. This is especially true of Death, 'the other shape/ If shape it might be called that shape had none' (2:666–7).

The parodic and self-reflexive dimension of the episode is manifest in other ways as well. On one level, Sin's description of her birth is a parody of God's generation of the Son, since the latter was traditionally allegorized as the birth of Athena during the Renaissance.[10] But while the traditional allegorization of the mythical allusion points to the divine counterplot, the passage also contains plot and counterplot on the literal level, as it were, of its allegorical figures. The passage is in the first instance a drama of recognition and misrecognition, of force and signification. Sin springs out of Satan's head as he and his fallen angels are joining together 'In bold conspiracy against Heav'n's King' (750–1). As Kenneth Knoespel informs us, the Hebrew word for sin, *pesha*, means rebellion. Thus the generation of Sin from Satan's conspiracy serves not only to dramatize etymology,[11] but also conversely to gloss the independent or self-regarding activity of the imagination, with its concomitant claim to unmediated agency, as sinful rebellion.[12] Finally, as a number of critics have remarked, the birth also 'gives rise to a linguistic event of its own' (Knoespel): 'amazement seiz'd/ All th'Host of Heav'n; back they recoil'd afraid/ At first, and call'd me *Sin*, and for a Sign/ Portentous held me' (758–61). Recognition of Sin is inseparable from a lack of recognition or, to put it another way, from a recognition of difference. Sin seems unfamiliar and this unfamiliarity is tied to recognizing Sin as a sign (of something else), a warning. It is familiarity or habit, here described as a narcissistic identification: 'Thyself in me thy perfect image viewing/ Becam'st enamor'd' (2:764–5), which leads to a misrecognition of sin's otherness, that is, to the deepest sin:[13] 'familiar grown,/ I pleas'd, and with attractive graces won/ The most averse . . .' (2:761–3).

We can begin to clarify the dialectical implications of this parody of allegory by examining Milton's biblical source. The genealogy of Sin and Death from lust derives from the Epistle of James, whose canonical status was controversial in the Renaissance not least of all because of its Pelagian or, in seventeenth-century discourse, Arminian argument for justification by works and thus for free will.[14] The passage reads:

> Let no man say when he is tempted, I am tempted of God: for God cannot be tempted with evil, neither tempteth he any man: But every man is tempted, when he is drawn away of his own lust, and enticed. Then when lust hath conceived, it bringeth forth sin: and sin, when it is finished, bringeth forth death.
>
> (1: 13–15)

In his preface to the epistle, Luther objected,

> Flatly against St Paul and all the rest of Scripture, [James] ascribes righteousness to works . . . [and] does nothing more than drive to the law and its works; He calls the law a 'law of liberty,' though St Paul calls it a law of slavery, of wrath, of death and of sin.[15]

As John Tanner has recently argued, however, it is precisely the Pelagian emphasis on individual responsibility which serves to condemn Satan in our eyes:[16] the autogeneration of Sin from Satan's forehead figures the responsibility of the sinner for his fall (as Adam says of man in Book 9 of *Paradise Lost*, 'within himself/ The danger lies, yet lies within his power:/ Against his will he can receive no harm' (9:347–9)); and Satan's failure to recognize Sin is a failure to recognize his own responsibility. Yet, according to Sin, when he does recognize her that recognition takes the form of enjoyment rather than use; and it is here that we begin to see the counterplot of Satan's claims to self-determination. What is Pelagian from one perspective turns out to be Augustinian or Lutheran from another.[17]

> familiar grown,
> I pleas'd, and with attractive graces won
> The most averse, thee chiefly, who full oft
> Thyself in me thy perfect image viewing
> Becam'st enamor'd, and such joy thou took'st

With me in secret, that my womb conceived
A growing burden.

(2: 761–8)

Satan's response to Sin suggests the familiar Augustinian distinction between signs which are to be used and those which are to be enjoyed. For Augustine 'all things are to be used (*uti*), that is, treated as though they were signs, God only to be enjoyed (*frui*), as the ultimate signification. To enjoy that which should be used is reification, or idolatry.'[18] Thus, while Sin's narrative of her generation might seem to suggest a necessary, organic, or unmediated relation between sign and signified, it also reveals the narcissism implicit in such assumptions. In this episode, in other words, allegory signifies a form of interpretation, and of self-reflection, which precludes genuine engagement with the text or the external world because it presupposes the signified from the outset. Allegory could thus be said to pander to the reader, to commodify truth and thus to obstruct the kind of rational exercise of the will which is the precondition of right reading and of virtue. In not leaving room for the reader's own activity, this pandering might just as easily be described as a kind of violence or coercion.[19] The allegory is thus one of force, of forced signification.

Satan's lust may tell us not only about Milton's Arminian belief in free will but about the dangers of antinomianism as well. It may be significant in this context that excessive allegorizing was associated with antinomian tendencies in the seventeenth century, and that antinomianism was often conflated with libertinism by its critics. James Turner writes, 'In mid-seventeenth-century polemic . . . radical "enthusiasm" was associated with the abuse of Genesis and the attempt to recover an Adamite relation to the body. This was supposed to involve either naturalistic sexual freedom or ascetic hatred of the flesh, and sometimes both at once. . . .'[20] At times such 'paradisal antinomianism' took the form of engaging in sex or sin in order to cast it out (87–8; a kind of parody of the Miltonic 'trial by what is contrary'). The incestuous coupling of Satan and Sin would thus figure in particular the antinomian abuse of the 'letter' or sign (2:760) with its attendant dangers of libertinism.[21] In contrast, prelapsarian Eden would represent the correct version of unfallen sexuality and of reading, where not allegory but innocence is the best 'shadow' or 'veil' (cf. 9:1054–5).

As an allegorical reader, then, Satan dismisses the sign (surface) for the psychological origin (genealogy) and so substitutes both structurally and thematically determinism for freedom, fate for faith and free will. Here too, 'fixed mind' (1:97) and force or compulsion coincide. Signs which should ideally point to something else simply point back to themselves. Despair is represented, in short, as the despair of referentiality.[22] The error of allegorical reading in *Paradise Lost* is thus, paradoxically, not to allow for error (wandering, the foraying out of uncloistered virtue). Satan's reading allows only for analysis, not for synthesis. At the same time, precisely because such analysis precludes genuine recognition of otherness, allegory here figures the danger of seduction by and idolatry of literature rather than, as it was traditionally presumed to do, providing armor against it. The episode could thus be said to perform its own immanent critique of the literary: the claim to unmediated imaginative activity is itself a form of violence, of reification and rebellion.

The Sublimity of Sin and Death

I would now like to turn to the way the Sin and Death episode itself functions as a thing indifferent, insofar as it articulates a rhetorical structure which has positive as well as negative implications or uses in the poem. If the episode criticizes the narcissism of allegory, it also suggests an alternative mode of reading the obscurity and failed referentiality we have noted in the representation of Sin and Death and in Sin's account of her encounter with Satan. Borrowing from the more appreciative critics of the poem beginning in the eighteenth century, we can describe this mode in terms of the rhetorical category of the sublime. Thus Edmund Burke, commenting on the line 'Rocks, caves, lakes, dens, bogs, fens and shades of death' (2:621), writes:

This idea of affection caused by a word ['death'], which nothing but a word could annex to the others, raises a very great degree of the sublime; and it is raised yet higher by what follows, a *'universe of death'*. Here are again two ideas not presentible but by language, and an union of them great and amazing beyond conception. Whoever attentively considers this passage in Milton . . . will find that it does not in general produce its end by raising the images of things, but by exciting a passion similar to that which real objects excite by other instruments.[23]

And Coleridge, commenting on the description of Death in *Paradise Lost*, writes in a similar vein:

The grandest efforts of poetry are where the imagination is called forth, not to produce a distinct form, but a strong working of the mind, still offering what is still repelled, and again creating what is again rejected; the result being what the poet wishes to impress, namely, the substitution of a sublime feeling of the unimaginable for a mere image.[24]

Burke's and Coleridge's comments nicely capture the ambivalence of the sublime. On the one hand, it seems as though the poet's deliberate failure of representation allows greater freedom to the reader's imagination; on the other hand, the reader's failure to imagine anything precisely serves to refer the reader to what is described by Coleridge as 'a sublime feeling of the unimaginable' but has been described by other theorists of the sublime as an identification with a higher power, one which transcends the faculties of perception and imagination. Luther's description of the law in his *Commentary on Galatians* would seem to exemplify this experience of the sublime: 'Wherefore this is the proper and absolute use of the law, by lightning, by tempest and by the sound of the trumpet (as in Mt Sinai) to terrify, and by thundering to beat down and rend in pieces that beast which is called the opinion of righteousness.'[25] The abasement of the sinner proves to be an uplifting experience insofar as it makes him aware of his own sinfulness and thus receptive to grace.

In our time, some critics have argued that in the experience of the sublime, reason 'stages' a failure of that form of representation which assumes an analogy between cognition and vision, understanding and the phenomenal world, in order to make room for the non-phenomenological activity of reading,[26] or – one might add – of prophecy in the seventeenth-century sense of exegesis.[27] The imagination fails to comprehend nature but this failure allows reason to recognize its independence from nature. As Donald Pease writes, 'Instead of locating the source of the sublime in its former locus, i.e. in external nature, the imagination redirects Reason to another locus, within Reason itself, where Reason can re-cognize astonishment as its own power to negate external nature.'[28] Accordingly, the failure of referentiality on one level thus allows for its recuperation on another. But it also simply displaces to this ostensibly higher level, 'within Reason itself,' the question of the authority of reason and the power of volition. Like allegory, the literary category of the sublime thus raises questions concerning the relation of free will and determinism which are central to Milton's theological and political concerns.[29]

While Luther's description of the effect of the law would seem to suggest that the sublime is a function of fallen experience, *Paradise Lost* shows that the structure of the sublime is constitutive of prelapsarian experience as well.[30] The fact that the allegory of Sin and Death can be described as both fallen or parodic and sublime is thus part of the larger argument of the poem. Yet, if the sublime exists in Eden, the poet still wants to distinguish between true and false versions of it. Thus, the distinction that Christianity has traditionally marked with the fall Milton places within Eden itself; though this does not mean that Adam and Eve are somehow fallen before their acts of disobedience. Rather, *Paradise Lost* shows that the structure of the prohibition not to eat of the Tree of Knowledge is the same as that of the law of postlapsarian experience (the prohibition is already a law); and that the differential structure articulated by the law is a condition of freedom as well as slavery. Whether the law is perceived as sublime or not is a function of reading, which in either case depends on the law in order to negate it. Milton's paradise, then, provides us with a phenomenology of consciousness – an account of the way consciousness constantly presupposes difference and at the same time, in so doing, negates and transcends it. So Milton's account of Eden is a metanarrative: a story about why we tell ourselves stories about an original fall, why we need both to posit a pristine state in which our ancestors were unfallen *and* locate the possibility of falling within that state.

The theological and aesthetic problem then is how to allow for difference in Eden while still preserving the distinction between pre- and postlapsarian experience. In this reading, allegory and sublimity name the coercive and enabling versions of the Christian's interpretive dilemma. The interpreter is confronted in both cases with a 'difficult ornament' or signifier which obscures or blocks access to the signified. Yet, in the first case the process of reading is codified and reified, while in the second there is a constant displacement or negation of any positive knowledge, a displacement which itself proves to be spiritually uplifting. We are made to 'judge of the sublime, not so much the object, as our state of mind in the estimation of it.'[31] My specific claim with reference to the description of Sin and Death is once again that the episode contains both these modes in the form of plot and counterplot. The episode does not simply represent the allegorical pole of reading, but criticizes it as well. In confronting the reader with the conflicting ethical possibilities of its indifferent rhetoric, the episode thus looks forward to dilemmas faced by Adam and Eve in Books 8 and 9 of *Paradise Lost*.

This point can be clarified if we return to the literary and linguistic strife dramatized in the description of Sin and Death. As Longinus recognized long ago, sublimity is achieved not simply in nature but also through the dramatization of literary combat, where the failure of recognition (of father by son) allows for struggle and identification. On the thematic level, the struggle between Satan and Death is an Oedipal struggle (cf. 11. 726–7; cf. also 790–800 on Death's rape of Sin), while rhetorically the episode enacts Milton's struggle with Spenser (in particular the figure of Errour in Book 1 of *The Faerie Queene*). And, in both cases, the apparent failure of mutual recognition allows for a deeper identification. In 711ff. Satan and Death engage each other in combat and

are identified in a simile which functions to conflate the antagonists just
as do the similes of epic combat in *The Faerie Queene*. Satan's seeing
without knowledge or recognition (743–4) is a parody of the sublime
experience. The 'failure of imagination' in his case is not represented
here as a failure to grasp in the imagination some indeterminate object,
so much as it is a failure to grasp that the indeterminate object is a
product of his own imagination. It is at this point that Sin articulates the
allegorical principle of causation. The structure of her narrative is worthy
of close attention because, like other moments in *Paradise Lost*, it seems to
problematize rather than fix the moment of original sin, the origin of the
fall.[32] In fact, her narration makes Sin both cause and effect of Satan's
rebellion:

> Hast thou forgot me then, and do I seem
> Now in thine eye so foul, once deem'd so fair
> In Heav'n, when at th' Assembly, and in sight
> Of all the Seraphim with thee combin'd
> In bold conspiracy against Heav'n's King,
> All on a sudden miserable pain
> Surpris'd thee, dim thine eyes, and dizzy swum
> In darkness, while thy head flames thick and fast
> Threw forth, till on the left side op'ning wide,
> Likest to thee in shape and count'nance bright,
> Then shining heav'nly fair, a Goddess arm'd
> Out of thy head I sprung . . .
>
> (2:747–58)

The syntactical ambiguity in lines 747–50 makes it seem as though Sin
had combined with Satan ('me . . . with thee combin'd') prior to her own
birth. Thus her own narration of her origin is proleptic: she is both
generated and self-generated.

   That this doubling and undermining of the narrative is positive as well
as negative can be clarified by returning to Luther's objections to the
Epistle of James. The Lutheran view of the law as a law of slavery
consequent upon the fall would seem to underlie any strict
differentiation between pre- and postlapsarian experience. While
Pelagius might suffice for a description of the original fall, as fallen
creatures we are incapable, according to Luther, of willing freely. Yet, in
Paradise Lost Milton takes issue with this Lutheran position. The fact that
Sin is first a sign means conversely that signs (linguistic mediation) allow
for the recognition of the possibility of sin. In glossing the genealogy of
Sin and Death in the Epistle of James, Milton's allegory thus suggests
that sin shares the linguistic structure of the sublime not only with the
law but with the prelapsarian prohibition.

Adam describes the prohibition in Book 4 in a way which helps us to see it as an example of the sublime since he explicitly ties its linguistic structure and its failed referentiality to the possibility of virtue. God 'requires,' he tells Eve,

> From us no other service than to keep
> This one, this easy charge, of all the Trees
> In Paradise that bear delicious fruit
> So various, not to taste that only Tree
> Of Knowledge, planted by the Tree of Life,
> So near grows Death to Life, whate'er Death is,
> Some dreadful thing no doubt; for well thou know'st
> God hath pronounc't it death to taste that Tree,
> The only sign of our obedience left
> Among so many signs of power and rule
> Conferr'd upon us, and Dominion giv'n
> Over all other Creatures that possess
> Earth, Air, and Sea. Then let us not think hard
> One easy prohibition, who enjoy
> Free leave so large to all things else, and choice
> Unlimited of manifold delights:
> But let us ever praise him, and extol
> His bounty, following our delightful task
> To prune these growing Plants, and tend these Flow'rs,
> Which were it toilsome, yet with thee were sweet.
>
> (4:420–39)

Here it is clear that while Adam does not understand the word 'death,' he does understand the prohibition as a test of obedience.[33] The partial obscurity of the prohibition is thus analogous to the obscurity of Sin and Death; in both cases it functions as a sublime obstacle, a boundary or limit. The sign is thus in a curious way performative rather than cognitive. It refers Adam and Eve to the limits of cognition, but recuperates this failure of cognition ('whate'er Death is/ Some dreadful thing no doubt') in the recognition of the task of obedience to God's word: 'for well thou know'st/ God hath pronounc't it death to taste that Tree.' As Milton intimates in the homophones of Raphael's later warning, 'Know to know no more' (4:775), knowledge is predicated on negation, on the knowledge of limits. Furthermore, this limit is of ethical as well as epistemological importance, for absolute knowledge would itself be coercive and thus preclude virtue. At the same time, it is clear that the prohibition itself is an obstacle, a limit which tempts one to 'think hard' – i.e., beyond the boundary it establishes; and to think that hard which formerly – i.e., without thought – was easy and so without virtue. Negation makes thought possible, at the same time that it makes the closure of absolute knowledge impossible, for us. But this impossibility is the condition of virtue. Just as the Mosaic law is given to fallen man to allow for the recognition of sin (12:187ff.), so the prohibition is given to Adam and Eve as a sign which, as it articulates difference, allows for genuine choice, reason, obedience. If the recognition of sin has the structure and effect (amazement) of the sublime by allowing one to recognize the condition from which one has fallen (i.e. to recognize difference), the prohibition is also a sign which by this very fact establishes the difference between force and signification.

In light of the preceding reflections on Sin and Death, Milton's narrative of prelapsarian events can be interpreted as an attempt to negotiate between two allegorical extremes: one in which everything is a function of the self, with the result that all experience is narcissistic; the other in which everything is a function of God and external circumstances, in which case experience – and education – are impossible. Disjunction between language and meaning has to exist in order for there to be interpretation and choice, at the same time that it must not be so radical that reading is impossible. Conversely, if reading is to be possible then the text must be conceived of as a thing indifferent in the precise sense that it offers an occasion for ethical deliberation.

I have argued that the Sin and Death episode is an exemplary instance of Milton's ambivalent or, in theological terms, indifferent rhetoric. In Sin's narration of her encounter with Satan we are offered an allegorical parody of allegory; and in the poet's description of Sin and Death we are offered what critics since the eighteenth century have called the Miltonic sublime. From one perspective (which we can identify with Sin's description of Satan's response), allegory implies a fallen mode of reading since it reifies signification and precludes any genuine encounter with otherness, any genuine exercise of deliberation and choice among possible meanings. From another perspective, the episode provides us with an allegorical critique of reading allegorically and so dramatizes the indifference of this rhetorical mode. From this second perspective, allegory shares with the sublime a structure of signification which characterizes pre- as well as postlapsarian experience. One burden of the episode is thus to show that signs, including prohibitions and laws, are not simply a consequence of the fall but the precondition of any genuine ethical choice: language itself is a thing indifferent which can be used well or badly.

Milton's recuperation of imperfect knowledge, including textual indeterminacy, as the condition of virtue is consonant with post-Kantian definitions of the sublime. As Neil Hertz has written, the sublime can be thought of as 'the story of Ethics coming to the rescue in a situation of cognitive distress.'[34] In this light, Milton's remark in *Areopagitica* –

'Reason is but choosing,' a remark which also describes the activity of the reader of *Paradise Lost* – is a sublime narrative in little: it posits the passage between epistemology and ethics. Faced with some kind of cognitive blockage or obscurity, the reader exercises ethical judgment and in so doing identifies with a higher power. The problem of course – and it is the problem of Reformation hermeneutics – is: how does one tell the difference between the Satanic self-aggrandizement of 'perfect, self-originating agency' (to recall to Knapp's remarks cited at the beginning of this essay) and those actions which do not simply claim to be but are obedient to a higher power? Here we return to those modern critics who suggest that, in the experience of the sublime, reason 'stages' a failure of the imagination in order narcissistically to 'discover itself freshly in an attitude of awe.'[35] Satan's narcissism in his encounter with Sin enacts this theatrical possibility. But the fact that the sublime can be staged or parodied, this also raises questions concerning Milton's own sublime rhetorical defence and education of the reader's ethical judgment. We know not only from the Sin and Death episode but also from the poet-narrator's self-descriptions, which frequently echo earlier descriptions of Satan, that Milton was himself sensitive to this dilemma. Milton stages the plot and counterplot of allegory and the sublime in the Sin and Death episode not only to engage Spenser in literary combat, or to begin to distinguish between legitimate and illegitimate dissent, reformation and rebellion, but also to meditate on the Satanic dimension of justifying the ways of God to men.

Notes

1. MAX HORKHEIMER and THEODOR W. ADORNO, *Dialectic of Enlightenment*, tr. John Cumming (New York, 1972), 194. A longer and earlier version of this paper occurs in *A Creative Imitation*, ed. David Quint *et al.* (Binghamton, MRTS, 1992).

2. JOSEPH ADDISON, *The Spectator* (London, 1729), No. 315 (3:111). Burke, Hume and Blair quoted in *Milton 1732–1801: The Critical Heritage*, ed. John T. Shawcross (London and Boston, 1972), 236, 237, 244.

3. SAMUEL JOHNSON, *Lives of the English Poets*, 2 vols (London, 1961), 1:110. See also Addison's *Spectator Papers*, No. 315; No. 357. On eighteenth-century discussions of sublimity in *Paradise Lost*, see Leslie E. Moore, *Beautiful Sublime: The Making of 'Paradise Lost,' 1701–34* (Stanford, CA, 1990); Dustin Griffin, *Regaining Paradise: Milton and the Eighteenth Century* (New York, 1986); and Steven Knapp, *Personification and the Sublime: Milton to Coleridge* (Cambridge, Mass., 1985). Knapp cites additional eighteenth-century critics who describe the allegory of Sin and Death as sublime on p. 52.

4. ANNE FERRY, *Milton's Epic Voice: The Narrator in 'Paradise Lost'* (Cambridge, Mass., 1963), 116–46.

5. MAUREEN QUILLIGAN, *Milton's Spenser: The Politics of Reading* (Ithaca and London, 1983), p. 95.

6. I use indifference here in the technical theological sense to refer to things or activities which are not essential to salvation and which may therefore be chosen or avoided, used well or badly at the discretion of the individual believer.

7. Satan's narcissism in the Sin and Death episode anticipates Eve's narcissism in Book 4 of *Paradise Lost* and shares with it an Ovidian subtext, *Metamorphoses*, 3:354, on Narcissus. On the relation of Ovid to Milton, see among others Richard Du Rocher, *Milton and Ovid* (Ithaca, NY, 1985).

8. I borrow these terms from Geoffrey H. Hartman, 'Milton's Counterplot' in *Beyond Formalism* (New Haven and London, 1970), pp. 113–123, esp. 115: 'Milton's feeling for this divine imperturbability, for God's omnipotent knowledge that the creation will outlive death and sin, when expressed in . . . an indirect manner, may be characterized as the counterplot. For it does not often work on the reader as an independent theme or subplot but lodges in the vital parts of the overt action, emerging from it like good from evil.'
   In considering the Sin and Death episode, I have benefited from the following works in addition to the ones already cited: Philip J. Gallagher, '"Real or Allegoric": The Ontology of Sin and Death in *Paradise Lost*', *ELR* 6 (1976): 317–35; John S. Tanner, '"Say First What Cause": Ricoeur and the Etiology of Evil in *Paradise Lost*', *PMLA* 103 (1988): 45–56; Stephen M. Fallon, 'Milton's Sin and Death: The Ontology of Allegory in *Paradise Lost*', *ELR* 17 (1987): 329–50; Ruth H. Lindeborg, 'Imagination, Inspiration and the Problem of Human Agency in *Paradise Lost*', unpublished paper.

9. Cited by DEBORA K. SHUGER, *Sacred Rhetoric: The Christian Grand Style in the English Renaissance* (Princeton, NJ, 1988), p. 160. The quotation is from *Gerardi Joannis Vossi commentariorum rhetoricorum, sive oratorium institutionum libri sex* (1606).

10. See the note to this passage by Alastair Fowler in his edition of *Paradise Lost* (New York, 1971).

11. On the Hebrew etymology of sin, see Kenneth Knoespel, 'The Limits of Allegory', *Milton Studies* 22 (1986), p. 82. Maureen Quilligan also discusses this passage in terms of etymological wordplay, but does not note the Hebrew meaning of sin. For the association of sin and sign, Merritt Hughes refers us to Dante's 'trapassar del segno' in *Paradiso* 26:115–17 ('Beyond Disobedience' in *Approaches to 'Paradise Lost'*, ed. C.A. Patrides [London, 1968], 188–9).

12. I was helped to see this point by the unpublished paper of Ruth H. Lindeborg. See also Maureen Quilligan's chapter, 'The Sin of Originality' in *Milton's Spenser*.

13. See Luther's remarks in his *Lectures on Genesis* (*Luther's Works*, ed. Jaroslav Pelikan [Saint Louis, 1955]), 1:166, on the sins which are so fully ingrained 'that they not only cannot be fully removed but are not even recognized as sin'.

14. On the identification of Pelagianism and Arminianism by seventeenth-century Calvinists, see for example A.S.P. Woodhouse (ed.), *Puritanism and Liberty* (London, 1938), p. 54.

15. 'Introduction to the Epistle of Saint James and Saint Jude' (1545) in *Works of Martin Luther* (Philadelphia, 1932), 6:478.

16. JOHN S. TANNER, '"Say First What Cause": Ricoeur and the Etiology of Evil in *Paradise Lost*'.

17. Tanner makes a similar point, though he does not comment on the significance of the allegorical form of Sin and Death in this context: 'Milton's myth thus exposes the irrationalism that lies at the core of ostensibly rational free-will explanations. It acknowledges that, at the deepest level, complete self-determination begins to look more like compulsion than free choice' (p. 49).

18. JOHN FRECCERO, *Dante: The Poetics of Conversion*, ed. Rachel Jacoff (Cambridge, Mass. and London, 1986), p. 108.

19. On the political dimension of allegory as a mode, see Joel Fineman, 'The Structure of Allegorical Desire' in *Allegory and Representation*, Selected Papers from the English Institute, 1979–80, n.s. 5, ed. Stephen Greenblatt (Baltimore and London, 1981), pp. 32–3:

    Allegory is always a hierarchizing mode, indicative of a timeless order, however subversively intended its contents might be. This is why allegory is 'the courtly figure,' as Puttenham called it, an inherently political and therefore religious trope, not because it flatters tactfully, but because in deferring to structure it insinuates the power of the structure, giving off what we can call the structural effect.

20. JAMES GRANTHAM TURNER, *One Flesh: Paradisal Marriage and Sexual Relations in the Age of Milton* (Oxford: Clarendon Press, 1987), p. 84.

21. Turner makes a similar point when he writes in a discussion of the allegorical interpretations of German mysticism and neoplatonism, 'Indeed, the grotesque figure of Sin [in *Paradise Lost*] . . . may parody the excesses of neo-Gnostic myth-making' (p. 155 and ff.).

22. In this context, see the interesting remarks by Joel Fineman in 'The Structure of Allegorical Desire'. Defining allegory in terms of Jakobson's 'poetic function', which 'projects the principle of equivalence from the axis of selection [*langue*] into the axis of combination [*parole*]' (p. 32), Fineman comments, 'This leaves us, however, with the paradox that allegory, which we normally think of as the most didactic and abstractly moral-mongering of poetic figures, is at the same time the most empty and concrete: on the one hand, a structure of differential oppositions abstracted from its constituent units; on the other, a clamor of signifiers signifying nothing but themselves' (34).

23. Quoted in *Milton 1732–1801: The Critical Heritage*, ed. John T. Shawcross (London and Boston, 1972), p. 236.

24. Quoted in Knapp, p. 8.

25. MARTIN LUTHER, *Commentary on Galatians* in *Martin Luther: Selections from his Writings*, ed. John Dillenberger (Garden City, NY, 1961), p. 141.

26. See THOMAS WEISKEL, *The Romantic Sublime* (Baltimore and London, 1976), pp. 40–1. See also NEIL HERTZ, 'The Notion of Blockage in the Literature of the Sublime' in *Psychoanalysis and the Question of the Text*, ed. Geoffrey H. Hartman (Baltimore, 1978), pp. 71–6; and STEVEN KNAPP, *Personification and the Sublime*, pp. 74ff.

27. See JOHN MILTON, *Christian Doctrine*, YP (6:582 and 584) (Book 1, Ch. 30). I am grateful to Victoria Silver for calling my attention to this definition of prophecy in the seventeenth century.

28. DONALD E. PEASE, 'Sublime Politics', *Boundary 2* **12/13** (1984): 264.

29. Cf. Jonathan Arac, 'The Media of Sublimity: Johnson and Lamb on *King Lear*', *Studies in Romanticism* **26** (1987): 209ff., on the sublime as allowing rebellion or

reinforcing conformity; and Ronald Paulson, 'Burke's Sublime and the Representation of Revolution' in *Culture and Politics: From Puritanism to the Enlightenment*, ed. Perez Zagorin (Berkeley, Los Angeles and London, 1980), pp. 241–69, esp. 248–52, on the political ambivalence of the sublime.

30. For a related argument, see SANFORD BUDICK, *The Dividing Muse: Images of Sacred Disjunction in Milton's Poetry* (New Haven and London, 1985), pp. 48, 73, 79.

31. IMMANUEL KANT, *Critique of Judgment*, cited by Raimonda Modiano, 'Humanism and the Comic Sublime: From Kant to Friedrich Theodor Vischer', *Studies in Romanticism* **26** (1987): 234.

32. See the remarks by Mary Ann Radzinowicz in 'The Politics of *Paradise Lost*' in *Politics of Discourse*, ed. Kevin Sharpe and Stephen N. Zwicker (Berkeley and Los Angeles, 1987), p. 217.

33. This is a traditional understanding of the prohibition. See Martin Luther, *Lectures on Genesis*, p. 154: 'It was God's intention that this command should provide man with an opportunity for obedience and outward worship, and that this tree would be a sort of sign by which man would give evidence that he was obeying God.' See also the gloss on this passage in the Geneva Bible, and *Paradise Lost* 3:93–5.

34. Hertz, p. 73.

35. Weiskel, p. 41.

14 The Father's House: *Samson Agonistes* in its Historical Moment*

JOHN GUILLORY

The following essay is one half of a diptych, the other half of which is entitled 'Dalila's House: *Samson Agonistes* and the Sexual Division of Labor' (published in *Rewriting the Renaissance: The Discourses of Sexual Division of Labor*, ed. Margaret W. Ferguson et al, Chicago: Chicago University Press, 1986). The two essays set out from a simple observation about the narrative structure of Milton's drama, the fact that Samson's crisis takes the form of a choice between several different houses in the poem. When Dalila offers Samson the option of returning with her to her house, she seems to stand for a domestic alternative to Samson's vocation, the possibility of withdrawal from his public role as Judge and scourge of the Philistines to the private domain of the household. Milton's drama stages this choice as the *conflict* between Samson's marriage and his vocation, a conflict which is only resolved by Samson's rejection of the former on behalf of the latter. In the essay on 'Dalila's House', I saw this resolution as making a kind of oblique argument for the legitimacy of divorce, potentially a new social practice corresponding to changes in the institution of marriage itself. In the essay on 'The Father's House', I attempted to look more closely at how Milton conceived of Samson's 'vocation' as a *public* practice, and here too I discovered the choice between two houses: between Manoa's house, to which Samson would return if he were to accept his father's ransom plan, and *God's* house, the 'father's house' to which Samson really does return when he once again takes up his divine vocation. Both essays on the houses in the poem provided me with an occasion for understanding the historical specificity of the 'vocation', a concept which is grounded in Protestant conceptions of the religious life, but

---

* Reprinted from *Re-Membering Milton: Essays on the Texts and Traditions*, ed. Mary Nyquist and Margaret W. Ferguson (New York and London: Methuen, 1987).

which is mutating into something more like our concept of the 'career', a kind of working life. It seemed to me that the historical moment of tension between these meanings of vocation was registered in the drama as the choice between Manoa's house and the father God's house. In both essays, then, I hoped to be able to read Milton's redaction of the biblical narrative of Samson in such a way as to demonstrate that Milton's drama expressed historical tensions for which no conceptual vocabulary yet existed in Milton's own time.

Life-narratives

The argument of this essay takes as its point of entry the long-standing conviction of Milton's readers that the narrative of *Samson Agonistes* does not yield to interpretation unless it can be made to stand quasi-allegorically for some other story whose constituent concerns and characters belong to the time and place of the drama's composition. The difficulty of producing this other narrative raises in an acute form the most general of theoretical questions concerning the historical specificity of any literary text; yet it may be that the very resistance to this specificity thrown up by the code-like narrative of *Samson* (extending even to the date of composition, which has never been fixed) is an interesting arena upon which to engage the theoretical question. I propose to read the narrative in its historical moment, but I do not mean that I shall decode the drama by establishing once again, or for the first time, its proper historical context. I intend rather to argue that the relation of text to contexts (as though to bring the historical 'background' a little closer) is a false problematic and has produced in this instance an illusion of narrative intelligibility. The problematic I would advance in its stead recognizes the text as itself a historical event, in the sense that Milton's choice of the Samson story is a determinate choice, not the neutral vehicle of meaning but an event whose significance is enabled and conditioned by a particular configuration of the total social formation.

The difference such a reading would make can be suggested by glancing briefly at the three contextual decodings of the narrative heretofore governing criticism. These are, first, a *political* context, in which Milton's redaction of the Samson story records a certain response to the failure of the Commonwealth and the restoration of the monarchy. Second, an *autobiographical* context, in which the life of Samson is identified with the professional, literary, or domestic life of Milton. And third, a *theological* context (currently the most favored), in which the narrative recapitulates the stages leading up to the 'regeneration' of the 'elect' Protestant.[1] None of these contextual readings, or their many variant or combined forms, is without explanatory power, nor are they mutually exclusive. Yet they produce their intelligible translations of the Samson story at the cost of isolating the dyad of text and context from the social formation within which both text and context are significant events. Here I would pose the question not to context but of *mediation* (scarcely a new concept, but one seldom enough employed in Renaissance criticism). The problematic of mediation, which addresses the relation between a field of cultural production and the whole of social life, has been developed most rigorously within a materialist concept of history and it is ultimately a materialist reading I shall attempt.

Nevertheless it will be necessary to begin with a rather more limited and specific hypothesis about mediation between social levels in the early modern period: Max Weber's still crucial argument in his *The Protestant Ethic and the Spirit of Capitalism*. Weber differs on some significant points with what would presumably be a thoroughly materialist account of the relation between religion and economy, but his work has provided the terms and evidence for virtually every concept of mediation specific to the early modern period and to Protestant Europe. For Weber the hinge of the social levels represented by Protestantism and capitalism is the practice of 'vocation,' which operates both as a focus of theological controversy and as a discourse on the working life. Weber traces this polyvalence to the early Reformation of 'good works' and the later emergence of a doctrine of election, a doctrine which in practice imposed a structure upon life itself. Calvin's God demanded 'not single good works but a life of good works combined into a unified system.'[2] Thus the Catholic organization of everyday life, wherein every moment is referred to eternity as the potential moment of death, is replaced by a *narratable* life, a structured life determined as 'elect' or 'reprobate' only as a whole. There is good prima-facie evidence for situating *Samson* as an intervention into this history in the very fact that current contextual decodings of the narrative have invariably sought out a context in which a life-narrative is at issue. Even the political reading of the drama is contingent upon the conventional figuring of the nation's history as the life of the heroic individual.[3]

At certain points Milton more openly attaches the life of Samson to the history of Protestant election or vocation, as when the Chorus, addressing God, says that Samson is

> Such as thou hast solemnly elected,
> With gifts and graces eminently adorned
> To some great work, thy glory
>
> (678–80)

Yet we know that in fact the sense of election in such a passage cannot be strictly Calvinist because Milton himself was a believer in the Arminian revision of Calvinist doctrine, which affirmed the freedom of the will over predestination. If at this moment the history of election appears in the margin of the drama merely as a problem of definition, or of the theological context, that impression will be dispelled as soon as we measure what is at stake in Milton's deployment of the received discourse. Such interventions take their place and have their effects within the long sequence of discursive practices by which the vocation is dislocated from the medieval ecclesiastical lexicon in order first to be identified with the radical Protestant concept of election, and later, in equally critical circumstances, to be extracted from its theological matrix. By the later eighteenth century the vocation functions as the key term in the bourgeois ideology of industriousness Weber finds exemplified in the writings of Benjamin Franklin. The current sense of vocation is therefore not the lineal descendant of some original discourse but the fossil record of successive upheavals. Its very sedimentation makes it capable of inflecting the working life both positively and negatively, as the déclassé 'vocational training,' or as the vocation which transcends the venal motives of careerism.

From works of law to works of faith: the Pauline doctrine enables for Calvinism the transformation of religious practice into a psychic economy, a spiritual accounting that constitutes the individual in a new way, over against the juridical constraints of the social, the 'law.' Clearly the homeostatic psychic economy of Calvinism permitted the achievements of the working life, in a fatal slippage from 'works' to 'work,' to be entered as credits in the ledger of the soul. Weber's study documents the emergence of this psychic economy, which he calls an 'ethic,' and which for him mediates between the major social structures of Protestantism and capitalism. I shall argue that the putative homeostasis of the individual psyche is geared to a *general* economy of social relations, an economy in which the vocation (in the sense of 'working life') is not merely a redundant conformation of a purely interior certainty, nor the state of faith merely the warm glow of material success. If the historical problem of the vocation can be conceived alternatively as the relation between an inaccessible inner state and a narratable life, then the problematic of mediation underlying Weber's study can be addressed as the question of how certain narratives – 'accounts' of individual lives – emerge and function within a specific historical conjuncture.

In the final section of this paper I hope to move on to the ground of materialism by locating the point at which the homeostatic economy of the psyche disintegrates and the vista of the general economy appears beyond the life of the individual. With reference to the narrative of *Samson*, this point is the moment of Samson's death, when his life becomes fully narratable, or when that life-narrative begins to circulate. From this retrospective vantage, it can be shown that the psychic economy generating the serial episodes of the life-narrative has all along been determined by a contradiction between the demands emanating from the poem's two fathers, Yahweh and Manoa; the distinction between these two fathers marks the *difference* between the psychic and the social. The Hebrew God demands a 'great work,' while the earthly father demands, as I shall show, 'labor in a calling.' Both demands can be identified with the concept of vocation, but this is no longer an instance of polyvalence so much as a contradiction. Samson arranges the disposition of his resources – the psychic, symbolic, or material capital represented by 'strength' – in order to satisfy the demands of both fathers; and this he is able to do not by a labor of production, but by a single, fantasmatic 'great work' of destruction.

Extraordinary Calling

To begin with Weber's question, then, is to set before us the task of fixing the typical thematization of the Samson story in Judges within the field of Protestant writings. Consider, for example, this text by the well-known theologian William Perkins, from *A Treatise of the Vocations, or Callings of Men*:

> And if we marke it well, the work of God shewes evidently to what dangers they are subject, that doe anything either without or against their callings. Sampson's strength lay not in his haire (as men commonly thinke) but because hee went out of his calling, by breaking the vow of a Nazarite, when he gave occasion to Dalilah to cut off his Haire, therefore he lost his strength; for God promised strength but with a commaundement, that hee should be a Nazarite to the end.[4]

Judges provides an illustrative tale of what happens when a man falls away from his calling; indeed, the calling is defined here by what diverges from it, just as it would seem to be defined in Milton's redaction. of the story. Yet this definition does not distinguish Samson from any other follower in the Nazarite path; he was called to much *more* than obedience to vows. In Perkins's text the story is partially depleted of its meaning in order that the situation of Samson might be read as normative. The same tactic of normalization is adopted by the marginal annotators of the Geneva Bible, who also interpret the narrative from Judges as a moral fable of 'vocation.' Such an allegory is developed during Samson's final moments, as here the uniqueness of his situation tends to escape the net of circumscriptive thematization. Hence, Samson's coerced 'sport' before the Philistine lords (16:25) calls forth this comment: 'Thus by Gods just judgements they are made slaves to infidels, which neglect their vocation in defending the faithful.' Not quite consistently, Samson between the pillars (16:29) is glossed: 'According to my vocation, which is to execute Gods judgements upon the wicked,' a statement that would seem to acknowledge a specific rather than a general concept of Samson's task. The more disturbing suicidal exclamation ('Let me die with the Philistines') is accompanied by a somewhat evasive return to a normative theme: 'He speaketh not this of despaire, but humbling himself for neglecting his office and the offense thereby given.' Samson's 'suicide,' which is conventionally explained away, is least of all compatible with a 'vocational' reading.

The texts from Perkins and the Geneva commentators, with which Milton would have been familiar, record an incapacity to fix a boundary between the two senses of vocation, as calling and as work. Yet such a distinction was frequently attempted, and it usually took the form adopted by Perkins in the following passage:

> The generall calling is the calling of Christianity, which is common to all that live in the Church of God. The particular, is that special calling that belongs to some particular men: as the calling of a Magistrate, the calling of a Minister, the calling of a father, of a childe, of a seruant, of a subiect, or any other calling that is common to all.
>
> (I:752)

Perkins' category of the special calling is scarcely exclusive, but it is evident from the remainder of the treatise that he is primarily interested in those callings which we would call 'occupations.' The relative poverty of Perkins' vocabulary reproduces the same paronomasia that is the subject of Weber's researches in *The Protestant Ethic and the Spirit of Capitalism*. The discursive problem to which Milton's version of the Samson story responds can now be more narrowly defined and examined: it concerns the distinction between general and particular vocation, as that unstable distinction conditions subsequent deviations from Calvinism.

Weber initially addresses this problem by tracing the emergence of the modern sense of *Beruf*, 'which undoubtedly goes linguistically back to Bible translations by Protestants' (207). His major example is Luther's translation of the apocryphal book of Jesus Sirach 11:20 as 'bleibe in deinem Beruf,' where the Vulgate has 'opus.' German Bibles had, formerly, 'Werk,' or 'Arbeit.' The Latin term synonymous with *Beruf* was of course *vocatio*, but that had referred to the *religious* life, particularly to the life of the cloister. Luther also translates a similar crucial verse, I Corinthians 7:20, as 'Let each man abide in that calling wherein he was called' (translating the New Testament *kleesis* as *Beruf*). More accurate translations would be, for the Latin, *status*, and the German, *Stand*. The alterations are small volleys in the polemics of Protestantism, aimed specifically at the *consilia evangelica* of the monks. The latter is replaced by a new 'valuation of the fulfillment of duty in worldly affairs' (80).

According to Weber, the sanctification of work did not necessarily imply its rationalization, which he associates with Calvinist rather than Lutheran forms of Reformation. In fact, Luther's sense of labor is in some ways thoroughly traditional; he believed, as Weber remarks, that 'the individual should remain once and for all in the station and calling in which God had placed him, and should restrain his worldly activity within the limits imposed by his established station in life' (85). Along with its newer resonances, *Beruf* retained the meaning of *status*. Luther's innovation might be simply irrelevant to any post-Calvinist conception of labor, were it not for the fact that he uses *Beruf* frequently also to mean 'the call to eternal salvation through God.' Calvin's sense of a 'call to eternal salvation' is only too clear; yet the machinery of predestination yields another distinction authorized by the cryptic final sentence of the marriage parable in Matthew: 'For many are called (*kleetos*) but few are chosen (*eklektos*).' This is the text by which Calvin expounds his distinction between a general and a special calling.

Whereas Luther had defined a special calling as the particular employment or labor of an individual life, Calvin identifies the same structural category with the *elect*. It might be supposed that the more radical and powerful Calvinist scheme would simply displace the Lutheran distinction, but that is not what happens. Weber shows that precisely the problem engendered by the discrimination of the elect from the reprobate is responsible for the retention of Luther's pun on *Beruf*: 'It was only as a result of the development which brought the interest in proof of salvation to the fore that Luther's concept was taken over and then strongly emphasized by [the Calvinists]' (210).

After Calvin, then, 'calling' and 'vocation' continue to be used indiscriminately on both sides of the distinction between *vocati* and *elecit*. The indeterminacy of this conceptual complex is the condition for the semantic link between Calvin's election, which has nothing to do, after all, with labor *per se*, and Luther's *Beruf*. Milton inherits these distinctions, along with their instability. An irresolvable ambiguity of terms is especially characteristic of the Arminian heresy, whose aim is scarcely to discard the technical apparatus of Calvinism; on the contrary, the terms remain in place, but their relations are altered, and another bifurcation appears. For Milton, as an Arminian, the distinction between *vocati* and *electi* cannot have quite the same force as it must for the Calvinist, since he no longer accepts a decree of reprobation. More than that, *De Doctrina* undertakes to remove election completely from its context of predestination; but then what content might it have? Would it not simply be absorbed by the secondary meanings of vocation, because, against its now conventional meaning, it would refer to *choosing* rather than *being chosen*? 'Whence I infer,' Milton writes, 'that "the elect" are the same as "believers", that the terms are synonymous' (VI:180). God chooses those who choose themselves. Milton has no need for a purely soteriological distinction between a general and a special election. All election is general: 'It seems, then, that predestination and election are not particular but only general: that is, they belong to all who believe in their hearts and persist in their belief' (VI:176). Finally Milton is careful to distinguish the general election from the idea of the particular, individual task: 'nor do I mean the election by which he chooses an individual for some employment [*ad munus*]' (VI:172).

But is the latter notion in any other way an example of election? Elsewhere in *De Doctrina* Milton refers to a similar idea as *special vocation*:

> Special vocation means that God, whenever he chooses, invites certain select individuals, either from the so-called elect or from the reprobate [*sive electos quos vocant sive reprobos*], more clearly and more insistently than is normal.
>
> (VI:455)

A distinction between election and vocation is very difficult to maintain, both here and in the chapter on 'Predestination.' Samson is unquestionably an example of 'special vocation,' like Abraham, called out of his house [*domo sua evocavit*] to do the work of God; but a much larger point emerges from this analysis: Milton's concept of special vocation is the *return* of election, the return of being chosen rather than choosing.

Unprofitable Servant

Samson, Manoa, and the Chorus allude frequently to Samson's unique calling, and it is these passages I hope to have located precisely within the region of theological controversy. I would now like to consider in

greater detail the key passage from *Samson*, with the intention of probing
the limits of Weber's conceptualization of the Protestant vocation:

> Nor do I name of men the common rout,
> That wandering loose about
> Grow up and perish, as the summer fly,
> Heads without name no more remembered,
> But such as thou has solemnly elected,
> With gifts and graces eminently adorned
> To some great work, thy glory,
> And people's safety, which in part they effect:
> Yet toward these, thus dignified, thou oft,
> Amidst their height of noon,
> Changest thy countenance and thy hand, with no regard
> Of highest favours past
> From thee on them, or them to thee of service.
>
> (674–86)

If election seems here to be an *ironic* predestination it is in this and
several other ways a transformation rather than a transcendence of the
Calvinist scheme. As a 'solemnly elected' individual, Samson stands
against not a spiritually reprobate majority but the *nameless*, 'the common
rout . . . Heads without name no more remembered.' The antinomies of
election and reprobation are redefined as election and *obscurity* – the
'invisible' church has become, precisely, the *most* visible. These 'elect' can
be figured as visibility itself; they are most conspicuous at 'their height of
noon.' The pressure of Milton's own obsession is evident here; certainly
he feared obscurity more than any discredited reprobation, but then he
has gone a long way toward identifying the one with the other. The
obsession of the drama with fame, itself an ethically suspect motive,
compounds with the Calvinist soteriology to produce a socially advanced
valuation of individual fate.

The homology of election and fame suggests a modification of election to
respond to a newly defined élite, one which *emerged* from the Calvinist
elect. Hence Milton is intent to dissociate Samson from a hereditary
nobility (171) just as much as from the common rout. In the biblical text
these discriminations are not made. At the same time, it is rather difficult
to specify any group to which Samson might belong as a representative
figure. It is easier to locate a referent for the obscure multitude in the
egregious interjection, 'That wandering loose about.' Such wandering is
not entailed by the distinction between those who are elected to a
conspicuous fame and those who are not. 'Wandering loose' implies a
hypothetical antithesis, a quality of fixity in the character of Samson, but

that idea is not to be found in the passage itself. Rather it generates a series of oppositions from beneath, operating as a covert thematic which is elsewhere openly acknowledged in the phallic narrative of Samson's castration by Dalila, signifying among other things a slackening of vocational rigidity. Resolute application to an ordained task is demanded by the 'special vocation' that Milton distinguishes from mere labor on the one hand, and predestination on the other.

'Special vocation' in the sense of the 'working life' is signalled by what is probably the most active subtext in the drama, the parable of the talents (Matt. 25:14–30). Milton has already linked both his blindness and his 'one talent' to this parable in Sonnet XIX, and it is unsurprisingly evoked by Samson, who possesses the singular talent of strength. Just as critical is an unmistakable affinity with the parable of the workers in the vineyard (Matt. 20:1–16); both parables conceive of the relation between God and man as that of a master-employer to a servant-employee. In *Samson*, any recollection of the parable of the workers in the vineyard would seem to cancel the elective assurance of the parable of the talents. Yet we hear in the protest of the Chorus against the (apparently) arbitrary master who remunerates his servants with ironic even-handedness ('just and unjust, alike seem miserable') the complaint of the workers in the vineyard. The contest of the two parables occurs more familiarly in Sonnet XIX: 'Doth God exact day-labour, light denied?' When Samson's 'one talent which is death to hide' does not yield a profit, his labor is mere wage-labor; he merely gets what he deserves. And getting what one deserves is of course the economic formula for *reprobation*, which can only be transcended by the absolute gift of election, the absolute transcendence of economy itself. The lament of the Chorus, '[Thou] throwest them lower than thou didst exalt them high,' is thus heavily charged with the same Calvinist irony that retroactively contaminates the parable of the workers in the vineyard: 'So the last will be first, and the first last.' The psychic economy governing Samson's 'special vocation' can be described as an attempt to affirm the economy of the parable of the talents against the economy of the parable of the workers in the vineyard (as though the economic form of talent/profit were not in fact mediated in the real world by the form of wage-labor).[5]

The logic of Milton's economy requires not the equal remuneration of labor but the production of a *profit*. We will see that for Samson, if that profit does not appear 'in the close,' labor is degraded to 'day-labour, light denied,' or worse, to 'idleness,' the condition of the 'common rout . . . wandering loose about.' That is to say, Samson will have no vocation. In its contempt of 'wandering,' the Chorus speaks in unison with Perkins and his colleagues, when they condemn 'rogues, beggars, vagabonds' for idleness, for not taking up a vocation in life.[6] Their vagrancy is of course a consequence of their mass expropriation, but the social fact of vagrancy is volatilized in the crucible of Puritan ethics and rematerializes as a schematic counterpart to the valorization of labor undertaken by all those theologians from Perkins to Baxter who imported the categories of election and vocation into the representation of everyday working life. Hence Samson prefers even a degraded form of labor, the 'servile toil' of the Philistine mill, to the idleness that is the antinomy of calling:

> To what can I be useful, wherein serve
> My nation, and the work from Heaven imposed,
> But to sit idle on the household hearth,
> A burdenous drone.
>
> (564–7)

Such a 'drone' could not be distinguished from the 'summer flies' dismissed by the Chorus. Samson's calling, which has consisted hitherto of isolated acts of destruction, is nevertheless an *occupation*. His vocational failure leaves him with nothing to do, an 'unprofitable servant' (Matt. 25:30) who has fallen out of his class and into the horde of the socially reprobate, the expropriated, the unemployed.

Intimate Impulse

Labor is the shadow cast by all of Samson's actions; yet the objective form of his vocation, his apparently random acts of destruction, prevents us from finally assimilating his narrative to a normative ideology. This problem, which is not accessible to a Weberian analysis, can be approached from another direction as the problem of the discrepancy between the demands of Samson's two fathers, God and Manoa. If Manoa disapproves of Samson's 'nuptial choices,' he also remains skeptical of those divinely inspired 'intimate impulses' which we know to be both the justification of Samson's object choices and the form taken by his calling. What does Manoa want of and for his son? The question might be rephrased to highlight Manoa's contemporaneity with Milton: 'What might the seventeenth-century middle-class father want of his male child?' Many things, of course, but at the least he might claim the right to control both marital and occupational choices. In his divorce tracts, Milton rejects the coerced choice of marriage partners as a 'savage inhumanity' (II:275). As for the second 'right,' the evidence (for example, of 'Ad Patrem') points to its rejection as well. On this point Milton was as usual advanced for his time. The period of transition is epitomized by one historian of the family, Jean-Louis Flandrin, as follows:

> In the sixteenth century, the only recognized vocation had been the religious one; apart from that, parents were left free to choose the occupations of their children. By the end of the seventeenth century, however, every estate had become a 'profession' and required a 'vocation,' which parents were forbidden to thwart.[7]

It would be very difficult to believe that this reversal was effected without trauma; we know that Milton's own father was perplexed by the occupational vagueness of his son's life. If Samson's activity scarcely has the appearance of an occupation, its structurally 'vocational' features are determined by the father's demand for a certain regular activity, for rational labor. At the same time, this activity must answer to the demand of the Father God, which Milton rather coyly implies is quite beyond Manoa's comprehension. This contradiction is focused (if not resolved) by the repetition of the 'intimate impulse,' a paradoxical rationalization of an act itself anarchic and eruptive.

In the antinomies governing the drama, the father, the law, rationality, and iterability must be ranged against God, transgression, irrationality, and a convulsive mode of action. Narrative repetition in *Samson* appears as singular, unstructured acts of impulsion, or as a 'compulsion to repeat.' Samson's marriages, his failures to contain his several secrets, his acts of destruction; everything must be done at least twice. Milton would have been sensitized to this pattern even by the current etymology of Samson's name, 'there the second time.' The narrative invokes a pervasive polarity between the law, as representative of social relations, and the impulse, as representative of an overruling psychic economy.

I would like to set this relation in apposition to several texts of Freud, with the intention of reconstructing that recurrent structure of ideology by which psychic economies, whether Calvinist, Freudian, or anything in between appropriate and displace the mechanism of the economic *per se*. A hypothetical 'psychic economy' governing the internal narrative of *Samson* therefore does not leave behind the prehistory of election, its complicity with Calvinist ideologies of labor, but rather follows the track of that ideology as it displaces the scene of action to the 'mind.' If Manoa can be seen to represent the familial interests of the contemporary bourgeoisie, it is Samson who refuses the representative function, who offers instead a unique and interesting *internal* drama. It will also be helpful to observe in the typical strategies of psychoanalysis the analogue of Samson's private justification of his public actions (founded upon a communication between himself and God); election is here performing the quasi-analytic function of inducing introspection, of displacing compulsion to a domain of interiority. Samson exhibits what Freud calls a *Schicksalszwang*, a 'fate compulsion,' described in *Beyond the Pleasure Principle* as 'being pursued by a malignant fate or possessed by some "daemonic" power.' The mythological terms are then smoothly translated into analytic language: 'but psychoanalysis has always taken the view that their fate is for the most part arranged by themselves and determined by early infantile experiences' (XVIII:21). In order to translate the *daemon* into *Zwang*, Freud overleaps several centuries, the whole period of the 'disenchantment of the world,' in which neither the *daemon* nor the *Zwang* are available terms of explanation. For Milton's Samson, it is an open question whether his fate is determined by an external agency or arranged by himself ('Whether prompted by God or by his own valour').[8] Fixing upon one or the other alternative will depend, precisely, upon whether and how external agencies are internalized, that is upon a *psychologizing* move. In his metapsychology, Freud attempts to demonstrate that the external *Zwang* is so transformed by the psychic economy as to become virtually supernumerary to its operation, reduced, as it were, from an agency of predestination to an impotent foreshadowing. I propose, then, something more than an analogy to this metapsychology: that if late Calvinist theology defines a psychic economy, the relation of economy to psyche, or of labor to election, can be theorized in a preliminary way as the relation of (external) *Zwang* to (internal) *Schicksal*.

Consider, for example, the analytic account of that external compulsion known as the 'law' given in *The Future of an Illusion*. In place of the Hebraic etiology of law as God-given, Freud posits as the founding institutions of civilization two forms of social coercion: 'But with the recognition that every civilization rests upon a compulsion to work [*Arbeitszwang*] and a renunciation of instinct [*Triebverzicht*], it has become clear that civilization cannot consist principally and solely in wealth itself and the means of acquiring it and the arrangement for its distribution' (XXI:10). The *Arbeitszwang* is soon left aside, since it is a universal necessity, and (at least at this point in the argument) does not undergo internalization. Freud is concerned only to explain the renunciation of instinct, and it is that 'external compulsion' (*äusserer Zwang*) which 'gradually becomes internalized' (XXXI:11).

In the major study to follow, *Civilization and its Discontents*, work appears again as a result mainly of the 'stress of necessity,' but in addition an attempt is made to articulate the two founding coercions of civilization in relation to a single defense mechanism, sublimation. Still, the most significant comment is relegated to a footnote:

It is not possible, within the limits of short survey, to discuss adequately the significance of work for the economics of the libido. No other technique for the conduct of life attaches the individual so firmly to reality as laying emphasis on work; for his work at least gives him a secure place in a portion of reality, in the human community. The possibility it offers of displacing a large amount of libidinal components, whether narcissistic, aggressive or even erotic, on to professional work and on to the human relations connected with it lends it a value by no means second to what it enjoys as something indispensable to the preservation and justification of existence in society. Professional activity is a source of special satisfaction if it is a freely chosen one – if, that is to say, by means of sublimation, it makes possible the use of existing inclinations, of persisting or constitutionally reinforced instinctual principles.

(XXI:80)

It is only rarely in Freud's work that the 'economics of the libido' touches upon the economy in the restricted sense, here as the re-entrance of libido into economy. Freud's note does not argue that work actually absorbs a considerable quantum of frustrated *erotic* libido – he only adds a tentative 'even erotic' to his list of possible sublimations. In this formulation, certain kinds of work, 'freely chosen activity,' provide the opportunity of sublimating *aggression*.[9] The activity resulting from such a sublimation can again be described as *Arbeitszwang*, but this would mean something new, an *internalized* compulsion. Joan Rivière, the translator of this work in the *Standard Edition*, gives us 'professional work' for the word *Berufsarbeit*, which should make very clear, historically, what kind of work Freud has in mind. The history sedimented in the word Freud employs recalls the same contradiction discovered in the Protestant *Beruf*, work as 'freely chosen activity' (vocation) and as being chosen (election).

Nevertheless the implications of this sedimented history are only ancillary to Freud's argument, which is concerned in the body of the text with accounting for the 'discontent' of that instinctual renunciation which is a consequence of aggression, the major derivative of the 'death drive.' The subtleties of the theory are less pertinent at the moment than the central thesis of an aggressivity placed in the service of the super-ego, which becomes a kind of breeder-reactor of renunciation and further aggression. It would seem that in this context the question of work would no longer be problematic, that the compulsion to repeat (*Wiederholungszwang*), as the major representative of the death-drive, would sum up every lesser example of compulsion. Nevertheless, the 'compulsion to work' does reappear later in the book, having ascended from the footnotes to a very prominent place in the argument – this time as a mythological complement to the sexual drive: 'The communal life of human beings had, therefore, a twofold foundation: the compulsion to work, which was created by external necessity, and the power of love. . . . Eros and Ananke have become the parents of human civilization too' (XXI:101). The identification of Ananke with the 'compulsion to work' (*der Zwang zur Arbeit*) is surprising; why is there no theoretical relation between this *external* necessity and the internal aggression that is everywhere else in Freud's later work the complement to Eros? Elsewhere the dyad is, as we know, Eros and Thanatos, the death-drive. The relation between Thanatos and Ananke can be brought to the fore by reconnecting the ligaments of the argument as follows: An internalized *Arbeitszwang* is the sublimation of aggression, which is a derivative of the death-drive, whose representative is the *Wiederholungszwang*. If work is indeed the sublimation of aggression according to the later theory of the drives, it is unfortunately also true that sublimation was never successfully integrated into the economic scheme of the metapsychology. It is just this failure of integration that allows Freud to idealize a certain kind of labor, the *Berufsarbeit*, and in fact to model the psychic economy of labor on two quite atypical examples, 'intellectual work' and 'artistic creation' (XXI:79). In this kind of labor, an *impossible* psychic economy obtains, one in which nothing is lost in expending energy.

If Calvinist theology can be said to function as a psychology, a system for inducing and representing psychic events, this psychology, like Freud's, also fails to represent labor except in idealized form, as extra-economic, as a sublimation or internalized *Ananke*. Indeed it is the conception of a *Zwang* subtending the ideology of the bourgeois vocation – a *compulsion to work* which is attested in myriad documents of the early modern bourgeoisie – that allows us to reconstruct something like a psychic economy of Calvinism. The *Berufsarbeit* of the Calvinist is also a sublimation of aggression (competition), which is a derivative of his fate (election), whose representative is the compulsion to repeat (as we shall see, accumulation of profit). Samson acts out the psychic economy of the Calvinist, but in a deviant form: his vocation is a *desublimation of aggression*, a crucial difference marking the discrepancy between the divine and earthly father's demands as the recto and verso of destruction and production.[10]

Like the bourgeois vocation, Samson's acts seem to escape the stress of necessity when they are no longer compelled from the outside, and this is to say that the individual is constituted as such ('Samson hath quit himself like Samson') at the moment when the vocation is proven, election confirmed. Of course the constitution of the individual as an autotelic mind, free in its interiority, completes a process of identification that is for Freud the original determinism of psychogenesis. 'Individuality' is a dialectical successor to the law of the Father, and it is asserted (as we know in Milton's case as well as Samson's) most conspicuously when the choice of vocation comes into conflict with the will of the Father. Clearly the choice of vocation can be made the terrain of renewed Oedipal conflict, but it is scarcely surprising that Freud has so little to say about this second battle between fathers and sons. The *Berufsarbeit* is always removed from the reductive reach of the metapsychology.

If the crucial point for Milton in placing Samson between the pillars is precisely his freedom ('Now of *my own accord* such other trial/I mean to show you of my strength, yet greater'), that freedom might nevertheless be read by the demystifying theory of either Calvin or Freud as the internalization of the law, the will of the Father. Milton is finally as undecided as Freud about the extent to which he will permit such a demystification, and thus the source of the 'rousing motions' is itself left undecided: 'And eyes fast fixed he stood, as one who prayed,/Or some great matter in his mind revolved.' The distance that produces the indeterminable option produces a fully privatized individual, who therefore acts of his 'own accord,' that is, in accord with his interiority. The Arminian heresy assumes a larger ideological function of identifying freedom with individuality. Such an identification is an unforeseen consequence of the very theology that administered so apparently final a rebuke to human volition. Late Calvinism, which typically weakens the doctrine of predestination to an ethic of self-determination, is locked into place as one possible ideological buttress of the bourgeois vocation. God wants us to do what we want to do.

We confront immediately what appears to be a contradiction, as the foregoing analysis would lead us to suppose that Samson's final act of freedom should be interpreted as internalization of the law, whereas by analogy with his marriage choices we may also regard the same moment between the pillars as a *dispensation*. Of course any declaration of freedom can be understood as, and reduced to, an internalized necessity, but I am inclined to take seriously the insertion of Samson's act into a category of dispensation. For once Milton has not defined freedom trivially as the alternative of obeying or disobeying the law, but rather located it in those hypothetical moments when the law is set aside. With this hypothesis in mind, we can be properly impressed that Samson is dispensed first from the law of endogamy (marriage within the tribe), and last from the corresponding prohibition in the ritual sphere, of participation in extra-tribal worship. He is dispensed from the *constituting prohibitions* of Hebraic culture. Milton poses, in heterodox theological terms, a radical question about the founding coercions of culture. It will not do, therefore, to recuperate the law wholly as an internalized necessity, by however sophisticated an articulation of an intervening 'third term,' a primal or symbolic father. There is an irreducible contradiction between the possible meanings of Samson's final act, as a determinate compulsion to repeat, and as the 'free' indulgence in the absence of the law, of what the law forbids to the individual – violence.

By the latter alternative I mean to confront the fact of aggression directly; it has for the most part been evaded in criticism of the drama, or reduced to the merely contingent circumstances of Samson's regeneration.[11] If the fact of legitimated aggression is as central to *Samson Agonistes* as it is to any revenge drama, that assumption of legitimacy must be read in the framework of a psychic economy as a fantasy of desublimation.[12] Such a fantasy is an exact inversion of the bourgeois ideology in which the *Berufsarbeit* is the sublimation of aggression. The concept of desublimation brings into focus that contradiction by virtue of which Samson's acts become the labor of violence, that is, both rational and dispensed from what will prove to be not the economics of the libido but a specific class rationality.

Symbolic Capital

The destruction of the Philistine lords serves the immediate purpose of seeming to overturn a relation of domination that has become structural in the perception of the dominated. As Milton knew, Philistia continued to rule until the period of the Kings. No national victory is claimed at the end of *Samson*. Rather Milton asserts the exemplary status of Samson's life and death, valued above even the providential history of the Israelites. The disappointed millennialism of the major works is thus countered by the consolation of the 'one just man,' a theme frequently enough evoked by collective failures. But what kind of consolation is this? How can it be said that an image of destruction compensates for the renewal of domination? The effective redress (an *imaginary* revenge) is possible because the image is an image of *excess*, of what would be called in the lexicon of contemporary ideology, 'terrorism.' The political allegory in *Samson Agonistes* mistakes the particular forms of domination (whatever they may be at the time of the play's composition) for an immutable structural domination from which there is no release except in fantasy. What emerges at the end of *Samson* is thus an intersubjective exchange, bypassing the polis, between Samson and the Hebrew youth who 'inflame their breasts/To matchless valour, and adventures high' with the memory of Samson's deed. The political has the status of an 'occasion' for the individual agon, a narrative condition which has successfully frustrated political interpretation of the drama, or opened it to the most facile of allegories. The historical moment of the drama, if it is indeed bounded by the failure of the Commonwealth, is also the moment of that class *victory* consolidated by the alliance of aristocratic and bourgeois property, when Weber's 'ethic' of individual success establishes ideological hegemony.

The narrative of *Samson Agonistes* acknowledges the victory of this class rationality by negating it in the fantasy of desublimation, of 'terrorism,' which is nothing other than an image of the abolition of all structural domination, the whole of political economy, in the face of its actual continuance.[13] Hence the law is dispensed, not abrogated. Milton's first and still in some respects his subtlest critic, Andrew Marvell, recognized just this terrorist hyperbole in his sly identification of Milton with the Samson of *Samson Agonistes:* '(So *Sampson* grop'd the Temple's Posts in spite)/The *World* o'erwhelming to revenge his sight' (italics mine). Samson's act of destruction extends beyond the Philistine temple to the world itself. 'Disestablishment' proceeds unchecked; all temples are demolished, all states, all societies.

That this complementary fantasy of destruction is itself a function of the social economy is attested by the final lines of the drama, where the 'servants' of the lord are dismissed, having drunk in the scene of destruction, with a greater accumulation ('acquist') of 'experience,' that is to say, a kind of usable *talent* as well as a *vocational* paradigm:

> His servants he with new acquist
> Of true experience from this great event
> With peace and consolation hath dismissed,
> And calm of mind, all passion spent.
>
> (1755–8)

The closing of the psychic account with both a surplus and an absolute expenditure argues that Milton's deepest protest was not against the Philistines (or the Stuarts) but against the very law of rational calculation, against the ceaseless counting of profit and loss. That protest is voiced by Peter in the first gospel: 'We have forsaken all, and followed thee; what shall we have therefore?' (Matt. 19:27). Calvin believed that Jesus answered Peter's question with the parable of the workers in the vineyard. This is of course not the answer that Milton would have wanted; he would surely have replied with the parable of the talents, by which he answered his own version of Peter's question, 'Doth God exact day-labour, light denied?' And it is surely the parable of the talents to which Milton returns in the Chorus's final speech. I propose now to translate the concept of desublimation into a more historically specific economic cognate, which would comprehend Milton's transformation of Matthew's 'talent' into what Pierre Bourdieu calls 'symbolic capital' (preeminently, 'honour' or 'fame').[14] Such a translation is intended not to reduce talent to capital but to recognize the specificity of that capital which goes by the name of talent.

The concept of 'symbolic capital' acknowledges the distance that has opened up in theory between the 'economy' in the restricted sense, and the general economy of such practices as the religious, the erotic, the aesthetic. Bourdieu does not describe the latter practices by analogy to the economy of production and exchange; on the contrary, he argues that 'a *restricted definition of economic interest* . . . is the historical product of capitalism' (177). There are important consequences in thus shifting the perspective upon economic interest from a restricted to a general 'economy of practices,' not the least of which is that the practice of Protestant vocation studied by Weber can be made more fully legible *as* a practice. For Bourdieu, a general theory of economic practice yields a concept of 'symbolic capital,' which is defined as '*credit*, in the widest sense of the word, i.e. a sort of advance which the group alone can grant those who give it the best material and symbolic *guarantees*' (181). The problem of the Calvinist *certitudo salutis*, of justification by *faith*, in so far as it is 'surreptitiously appropriated' in the agon of Samson's election, is expressed as an operation of symbolic capital: his final act is the conspicuous guarantee of that 'credit' which his group had been holding in abeyance, and which confirms the meaning of the sign of his election, his physical strength. Samson's symbolic capital is thus a complex structure of reciprocal interests (or 'credit') flowing between himself, his society, and his two fathers, Manoa and God. The restoration of credit, the actual 'regeneration' in the narrative, produces an immediate (posthumous) profit of 'honor' and 'fame,' and this profit is returned with Samson's body 'to his father's house.' As a form of symbolic capital, this honor or prestige might well be converted at some point into material capital. The interconvertibility of capital is attested in the narrative, although in the mode of denial, by a belated shadow plot of material capital, Manoa's plan to ransom Samson. Another kind of expenditure completes the circuit of exchange, the expenditure not of money but of the body itself ('dearly bought revenge').

The signal feature of the transaction defined by the sacrifice of the body can be identified, in Bourdieu's words, as 'the exhibition of symbolic capital . . . one of the mechanisms which (no doubt universally) make capital go to capital' (181). As an economic practice, Calvinist election is organized in exactly this way; it has its mystery of primitive accumulation, a primal decree of election, which is nothing other than the arrogation of symbolic capital. Such capital is 'exhibited' by the further accumulation of symbolic or material capital. Calvin's God declares, like the master of Matthew's parable, 'For unto every one that hath shall be given, and he shall have abundance' (25:29). Samson's election shares this much with its Calvinist precursor: strength returns to strength, election cannot be withdrawn. Nevertheless, the formula 'capital goes to capital' leaves out of the accounting the 'great work' itself, or the particular form of symbolic capital's exhibition. The distinction of Milton's redaction of Matthew's parable is not that it conforms to an economic paradigm but rather that it makes of the *denial* of rational calculation the most profitable of economic practices. As an economic figure for Samson's violent end, the image of the phoenix expresses this impossibly calculating denial of calculation: everything is sacrificed and everything is returned. More precisely, the phoenix represents an unlimited return (fame) upon an absolute investment (the body): 'though the body dies, the fame survives.' Here finally desublimation can be named for what it is, *spending*, the expenditure of 'energy' or 'libido' or 'capital.' Milton is able to acknowledge this expenditure by invoking its negative reflection in the stream of the narrative, the theory of tragic catharsis ('all passion spent'). Nevertheless the phoenix image, as the embodiment of that cathartic expenditure, does not tell us why we need not count the loss of the body as an absolute loss; rather, the infinitude of expenditure works a kind of mathematical magic: spending everything is getting everything.

At this point it becomes difficult, if also quite necessary, to distinguish categorically between desublimation and sublimation, especially as the latter is for Freud the patient, disciplined investment (*Besetzung*) of psychic capital in the form of desexualized libido. Investment, of material or symbolic capital, is also a mode of spending. The significance of spending as such in the history of economic exchange has been well established by Mauss and Bataille; primitive economic exchange is founded on 'expenditures,' gifts, sacrifices, ritual destructions. Hence it is possible to figure the transcendence of economic motives by recurring to the practice of the gift or the sacrifice, but this entails repressing the fact that these are economic transactions. The rational economy of capital accumulation is shadowed always by another, atavistic system of exchange. In Milton's *Samson*, the atavistic economy appears in the form of the narrative itself, the narrative of sacrifice, while the rational economy falls to the level of subtext and figuration. Samson's sacrifice is then both the repayment of a debt, his original 'credit,' and the *overpayment* of that debt. Only as such does it have the power to produce a profit, either for himself or the creditor.

Like desublimation, expenditure occupies a realm of fantasy set against the reality of rational calculation. The *discipline* of spending in the practice of investment makes all the difference historically; it has made a different world. That is not to say, however, that the fantasy of expenditure cannot be acted out, or that the acting out does not have real economic consequences. The transcendent economy of expenditure is not the survival of primitive exchange within an uncolonized territory of the capitalist economy; it is an atavism functionally integrated into the same economy. Just as investment seeks to conceal the labor that transforms capital into profit (in such 'surplus labor,' energy is absolutely expended), 'sacrifice' denies that what is absolutely lost or ritually destroyed can be expressed as an *economic* value. Hence the very body that Manoa intended to purchase from the Philistine is, when sacrificed, the occasion for no grief at all, no accounting of loss ('Nothing is here for tears'). Manoa's position is that of spokesman for the restricted economy. He will not recognize the secret table by which material and symbolic capital are converted into one another, the body converted into fame, or Matthew's 'talent' into Milton's. In this he makes possible a certain mystification Bourdieu describes as follows:

> Economic calculation has hitherto managed to appropriate the territory objectively surrendered to the remorseless logic of what Marx calls 'naked self-interest' only by setting aside a 'sacred' island miraculously spared by the 'icy waters of egotistical calculation' and left as a sanctuary for the priceless or worthless things it cannot assess.

(178)

That island has been for several hundred years the domain of art, but its appearance was prepared for by the segregation of the sacred itself, the religious life that Protestantism claimed to set apart not from everyday life but from the economic domain of legitimate self-interest. In the doctrine of election, the soul itself is beyond price, beyond any human effort to redeem it, and so relegated logically to the domain of the priceless or the worthless. At the same time Calvinism established a most rigorous program of psychic accounting, which, if it did not institute the discipline of everyday life, provided that discipline with its system of symbolic book-keeping.[15] In retrospect, it would seem that the logical relation between the priceless and the worthless is the mechanism by which the concept of vocation is reduced historically to the legitimation of the bourgeois vocation, the end of which is the constant accumulation of material or symbolic capital. Milton enacts this peculiar derivation not by idealizing productive labor, but by indulging a fantasy of release from the calculus of economic rationality, a fantasy taking the narrative form of violent expenditure or ritual destruction.

Self-sacrifice, exceeding the motive of revenge, is no less the meaning of Milton's identification with Samson than the *ressentiment* of blindness or defeat. The suicide of Samson is the proto-typical self-sacrifice of the artist, a fantasy capable of realization when there comes to prevail in late capitalism a relentless distinction between the worthlessness of the artist's life and the pricelessness of art. Post-artisanal 'artistic labor' is neither undervalued nor overvalued, but rather *unvalued*. In the life and death of Samson a paradigmatic life-narrative emerges, founded no doubt on the 'Christus Patiens' Milton never wrote, but sliding over that narrative, mutating into a new story, 'the life of the poet.' In this important sense, as Milton's readers have rightly intuited, Samson is a type not of Christ but of Milton, the Milton who, in Marx's famous phrase, 'produced *Paradise Lost* as the silkworm produces silk,' the inverted image of the figure who destroys the Philistines 'as an Eagle.'

Lodged between the narratives of saint and artist, the narrative of Samson's life records for Milton the transformation of the father's talents, the money-lender's material capital ('Fathers are wont to lay up for their sons'), into 'talent,' symbolic capital. The narrative that enacts this transformation has its historical moment on the threshold of the new order; no other story will do. In the determinate choice of the Samson story, the distinction between material and symbolic capital is magnified, projected onto the largest possible screen, the distinction between the conflicting demands of the two fathers, earthly and heavenly. So Milton himself scorns the material capital by which his career is made possible, while taking up as the deep paradigm of his poetic calling that relation between investment and profit which *was* his father's business. The poet reappears in his own narrative as the vocational double of the rational investor, the very figure with whom he is thought to have nothing in common. But 'relation stands': the poet is the 'son' of the scrivener, the life of expenditure and sacrifice is the complement of investment and accumulation. Like Samson, Milton makes a return, with interest, upon his father's investment: 'to himself and Father's house eternal fame.' But within the drama, with its fantasmatic doubling of paternal figures, the final recognition of 'talent' is reserved for the heavenly father, whose function is to foreshadow the accounting of those 'sacrifices' constitutive of the artist's life-narrative as he once reckoned the value of the saint's. Such value is supposed to be beyond measure, whether or not the products of the sacred island are exchanged in an antithetical mainland economy, at whatever price. By means of such narrative fictions, capital marks off the boundaries of an aesthetic kingdom, within which it reappears disguised as the opposite of itself.

Notes

1. *De Doctrina Christiana* defines regeneration as follows: 'Regeneration means that the old man is destroyed and that the inner man is regenerated through

the word and the spirit so that his whole mind is restored to the image of God, as if he were a new creature. Moreover, the whole man, both soul and body, is sanctified to God's service and to good works' (*YP*: 461). The linking of this passage to *Samson Agonistes* was made by William Riley Parker in *Milton's Debt to Greek Tragedy in Samson Agonistes* (Baltimore: Johns Hopkins University Press, 1937), 235ff., and elaborated in an essay by Arthur Barker, 'Structural and Doctrinal Pattern in Milton's Later Poems' in *Essays in English Literature from the Renaissance to the Victorian Age*, ed. Millar MacLure and F. W. Watt (Toronto: University of Toronto Press, 1964), pp. 169–94. In the last several decades, Samson's 'regeneration' has become a given of criticism; it is assumed to structure the narrative event where the context of *De Doctrina* is only distantly invoked.

2. MAX WEBER, *The Protestant Ethic and the Spirit of Capitalism*, tr. Talcott Parsons (New York: Scribner's, 1958), p. 117. The distinction Weber is making is crucial to his argument and should defuse the misunderstanding of his position on the question of the specific relation between Protestantism and capitalism. The 'structured life' is first of all an ideological practice, a retrospective or prospective working up of a life narrative out of life-experience. At the same time such a narrative represents a genuinely material practice, since it comes to constitute a condition (not a cause) for other practices as well. For an extended discussion of the Weber controversy, see GORDON MARSHALL, *In Search of the Spirit of Capitalism: An Essay on Max Weber's Protestant Ethic Thesis* (New York: Columbia University Press, 1982).

3. This is Milton's typical use of the Samson figure in his polemical prose, for example in the *First Defense* (IV:402), in *Areopagitica* (II:558) and the *Reason of Church-Government* (I:858).

4. WILLIAM PERKINS, *The Works of that Famous and Worthy Minister of Christ*, 3 vols (London: John Legatt, 1612), I:751.

5. Milton works out of such a poetic economy in the Preface to Book II of *The Reason of Church-Government* (I:801ff.), again founding his economy on the parable of the talents: 'remembering also that God even to a strictness requires the improvement of these his entrusted gifts'.

6. PERKINS, *op. cit.*, I:757: 'it is a Foule disorder in any Common-wealth, that there should be suffered rogues, beggars, vagabonds. . . . Againe, to wander up and downe from yeare to yeare to this end, to seeke & procure bodily maintenance, is no calling, but the life of a beast.'

7. JEAN-LOUIS FLANDRIN, *Families in Former Times: Kinship, Household, and Sexuality*, tr. Richard Southern (Cambridge: Cambridge University Press, 1979), p. 139.

8. The quotation is from the *First Defense* and reads in full: '[Samson] still made war single-handed on his masters, and, whether prompted by God or by his own valour, slew at one stroke not one but a host of his country's tyrants, having first made prayer to God for his aid' (IV:402).

9. All quotations from Freud are cited from the *Standard Edition of the Complete Psychological Works of Sigmund Freud*, ed. James Strachey *et al.*, 24 vols (London: Hogarth Press, 1953–74). Freud is speaking rather loosely in equating the narcissistic, the aggressive, and the erotic as libidinal components, and I am both criticizing and following this loose procedure in proposing a theoretical 'sublimation of aggression'. As the concept of sublimation is worked out in the earlier theory of the drives, it is always closely allied to a process of 'desexualization' in which, nevertheless, libidinal instincts are satisfied. The deficiency of that theory from an economic point of view is manifest and has

been frequently remarked (for example by Jean Laplanche and J.B. Pontalis in *The Language of Psychoanalysis*, tr. Donald Nicholson-Smith (New York: W.W. Norton, 1973), pp. 431–3; and by Jacques Lacan in *The Four Fundamental Concepts of Psycho-Analysis*, tr. Alan Sheridan (New York: W.W. Norton, 1977), pp. 165–6).

10. In the following argument I extrapolate from Marcuse's concept of 'repressive desublimation', elaborated in *One-Dimensional Man* (Boston: Beacon Press, 1964), and Jean Baudrillard's similar use of the term in *The Mirror of Production* (St Louis: Telos Press, 1975).

11. On this subject Kenneth Burke's discussion of the drama redresses the balance of criticism. See *A Rhetoric of Motives* (Berkeley: University of California Press, 1969), pp. 3ff. It should finally be possible to take up the question of why aggression, self or other directed, is so crucial to the drama as a motivated act of writing (language for use, as Burke would say).

12. In deploying the concept of desublimation, I do not mean conversely to credit the theoretical validity of sublimation in the Freudian metapsychology. On the contrary, sublimation names the same specifically ideological assemblage as Weber's 'rationalization'; sublimation names the disciplining of the drives in the service of what is 'finer and higher'. The theory of sublimation is therefore perfectly adequate to its ideological function, which is to prevent any form of the *Berufsarbeit* from being assimilated into the critique of culture-as-repression.

13. See BAUDRILLARD, *op. cit.*, p. 41: 'Although the concept of non-labor can thus be fantasized as the abolition of political economy, it is bound to fall back into the sphere of political economy as the sign, and only the sign, of its abolition.'

14. PIERRE BOURDIEU, *Outline of a Theory of Practice*, tr. Richard Nice (Cambridge: Cambridge University Press, 1977), pp. 171ff.

15. The 'spiritual accounting' metaphor is conventional, if also extremely popular with Protestant writers. My argument is intended to show that such accounting is not merely an economic metaphor – it represents an actual economic practice, the disposition of symbolic capital. The 'final account' to which Perkins refers, when 'the bill of our receipts and expenses' is drawn out (I:777), thus has its referent in practice not only in the Last Judgment, but also the everyday accounting to which Protestants subjected their souls in those diaries that were kept as faithfully as business ledgers. In *The Rise of Puritanism* (New York: Columbia University Press, 1938), William Haller quotes the typical diary of John Beadle, published in 1656: The godly man should 'keep a strict account of his effectual calling' (p. 96).

Notes on Authors

FRANCIS BARKER is a senior lecturer in literature at the University of Essex where he teaches Renaissance studies and contemporary critical theory. He has long been associated with the Essex Sociology of Literature project, and is a co-editor of its annual proceedings, including *1642: Literature and Power in the Seventeenth Century* (University of Essex, 1981) and *Uses of History: Marxism, Postmodernism and the Renaissance* (Manchester University Press, 1991). He is also a founding member of the Essex Early Modern Research Group. His current work in progress includes a forthcoming book on tragedy and history, *Signs of Invasion*, and a book of essays with the working title *The Culture of Violence*.

STANLEY FISH is Arts and Sciences Distinguished Professor of English and Law at Duke University. His early work centred on late medieval and Renaissance literature, by the 1970s he emerged as the leading exponent of American 'reader-response' criticism and more recently his writing has concentrated on legal theory. His publications include: *Surprised by Sin: The Reader in Paradise Lost* (St Martin's Press, 1967); *Is There a Text in this Class* (Cambridge: Harvard University Press, 1980); *John Skelton's Poetry* (Shoe String Press, 1980) and *Doing What Comes Naturally: Change, Rhetoric and the Practice of Theory in Literary and Legal Studies* (Oxford University Press, 1989).

CHRISTINE FROULA, Professor of English at Northwestern University, is the author of *A Guide to Ezra Pound's Selected Poems* (New Directions, 1983), *To Write Paradise: Style and Error in Pound's Cantos* (Yale University Press, 1984), *Joyce and Woolf: Gender, Culture, and Modernity* (1992), and articles on modernist writers, feminist theory, and the Western literary tradition. She is currently working on *Women Writers and Western Literature: Tradition and Transformation*.

JONATHAN GOLDBERG is the Sir William Osler Professor of English Literature at the Johns Hopkins University. With Stephen Orgel, he is the co-editor of the Oxford Authors *John Milton* (Oxford University Press, 1991). His most recent book is *Writing Matter: From the Hands of the English Renaissance* (Stanford University Press 1990). He is currently at work on *Sodomitries*, a book on Renaissance homosexuality.

JAMES GRANTHAM TURNER is Professor of English at the University of California, Berkeley. He co-edited *Politics, Poetics and Hermeneutics in Milton's Prose* for Cambridge University Press (1990), and has written, as well as numerous articles on seventeenth and eighteenth-century culture, *The Politics of Landscape: Rural Scenery and Society in English Poetry, 1630–1660* (Harvard University Press, 1979) and *One Flesh: Paradisal Marriage and Sexual Relations in the Age of Milton* (Oxford University Press, 1987), from which the extract in this volume is taken.

JOHN GUILLORY is Professor of English at The Johns Hopkins University. He is the author of *Poetic Authority: Spenser, Milton, and Literary History*. (Columbia University Press, 1983), as well as several essays in *Milton Studies*. He has just completed a book on the subject of the canon debate, entitled *Cultural Capital: The Problem of Literary Canon Formation*, forthcoming University of Chicago Press, 1993.

VICTORIA KAHN is Associate Professor of English at Princeton University. She is the author of *Rhetoric, Prudence and Skepticism in the Renaissance* (Cornell University Press, 1985) and of a forthcoming study of Machiavelli and Milton. She is also the co-editor with Albert Ascoli of the forthcoming *Machiavelli and the Discipline of Literature*.

WILLIAM MYERS is Senior Lecturer in English at Leicester University. He has a long-standing interest in the relations between politics, philosophy and literature. In addition to *Milton and Free Will*, his principal publications are *Dryden* (1973), *The Teaching of George Eliot* (1984), *Restoration and Revolution: Political, Social and Religious Writings 1660–1700* (Croom Helm, 1986) and *Evelyn Waugh and the Problem of Evil* (Faber and Faber, 1991). He is currently working on an edition of four plays by George Farquhar.

DAVID NORBROOK is Fellow and Tutor in English at Magdalen College and Lecturer in English at Oxford University. His publications, in addition to *Poetry and Politics in the English Renaissance*, include *The Penguin Book of Renaissance Verse* (with Henry Woudhuysen) and articles on Shakespeare and on Jacobean masques; he is currently working on republicanism and poetry in the 1640s and 1650s.

MARY NYQUIST teaches in Women's Studies, Literary Studies, and the Department of English at the University of Toronto. She is the author of articles on feminist theory, nineteenth-century women novelists, popular romance, and Milton. Co-editor with Margaret Ferguson of *Re-Membering Milton* (Methuen, 1987), she is completing a book provisionally called *Joyning Causes: Genesis, Gender, Discourse, Milton*.

ANNABEL PATTERSON is Professor of English and Literature at Duke University. She is the author of a number of books on Renaissance and seventeenth-century literature in its relation to history. These include *Marvell and the Civic Crown* (Princeton University Press, 1978); *Censorship and Interpretation* (Wisconsin University Press, 1984, repr. in paperback with a new introduction, 1990); *Pastoral and Ideology* (University of California Press and Oxford University Press, 1987); *Shakespeare and the Popular Voice* (Blackwell, 1989); and *Fables of Power* (Duke University Press, 1991.) A new volume of essays, *Reading Between the Lines*, to be published by the University of Wisconsin Press, shares some of the reception history recorded in the Introduction to this volume but places Milton's story in a longer history of 'The Good Old Cause'.

MARY ANN RADZINOWICZ is Jacob Gould Schurman Professor of English Emeritus at Cornell University. She is an Honoured Scholar of the Milton Society of America. Her publications include *Toward 'Samson Agonistes': The Growth of Milton's Mind* (Princeton University Press 1978) which received the James Holly Hanford Prize of the Milton Society, and *Milton's Epics and the Book of Psalms* (Princeton University Press, 1989). She has edited Book 8 of *Paradise Lost* for the Cambridge Milton for Schools and Colleges and the anthology entitled *American Colonial Prose: John Smith to Thomas Jefferson*, also for Cambridge University Press. She now lives in Ballyvaughan, County Clare, Republic of Ireland, where she is at work on a study of Milton's handling of biblical narrative as it changes down the course of his oeuvre.

MICHAEL WILDING is Reader in English at the University of Sydney and a Fellow of the Australian Academy of the Humanities. His critical works include *Milton's*

John Milton

'Paradise Lost' (Sydney University Press, 1969), Political Fictions (Routledge, 1980) and Dragon's Teeth (Clarendon Press, 1987). His novels include Living Together (University of Queensland Press, 1974), Pacific Highway (Hale & Iremonger, 1982) and The Paraguayan Experiment (1985) and his stories are collected in The Man of Slow Feeling (Penguin, 1985), Under Saturn (Black Swan, 1988) and Great Climate (Faber, 1990).

Further Reading

Note: for the reasons stated in my Introduction, that an eclectic use of the new criticisms and theories is more common than simple applications, the following organizational categories may be somewhat arbitrary.

From affective stylistics to deconstruction

BELSEY, CATHERINE, *John Milton: Language, Gender, Power* (Oxford: Basil Blackwell, 1988).

FISH, STANLEY, *Surprised by Sin: the Reader in Paradise Lost* (New York: St Martin's Press, 1967).

_____ 'Things and Actions Indifferent: The Temptation of Plot in *Paradise Regained*', *Milton Studies* **17** (1983): 163–85.

_____ 'Transmuting the Lump' in *Literature and History* ed. Gary Saul Morson (Stanford: Stanford University Press, 1986).

_____ 'Driving from the Letter: Truth and Indeterminacy in Milton's *Areopagitica*' in *Re-membering Milton: Essays on the Texts and Traditions*, ed. Mary Nyquist and Margaret W. Ferguson (New York and London: Methuen, 1987), pp. 234–54. A response to Christopher Kendrick's argument that includes the summation: 'Kendrick thematizes politics and ideological class struggle: I thematize theology and theologically derived aesthetics.' The essay also contains a massive footnote disputing Francis Barker's position on the tract.)

_____ 'Wanting a Supplement: The Question of Interpretation in Milton's Early Prose' in *Politics, Poetics and Hermeneutics in Milton's Prose*, ed. David Loewenstein and James Turner (Cambridge: Cambridge University Press, 1990), pp. 41–68.

SCHWARTZ, REGINA, *Remembering and Repeating: Biblical Creation in* Paradise Lost (Cambridge: Cambridge University Press, 1988).

SHOAF, R. A., *Milton, Poet of Duality* (New Haven: Yale University Press, 1985).

Ideology, history, politics

CORNS, THOMAS, 'Milton's Quest for Respectability', *Modern Language Review* **77** (1982): 769–79.

—— 'Ideology in the *Poemata* (1645)', *Milton Studies* **19** (1984).

—— '"Some Rousing Motions": The Plurality of Miltonic Ideology' in *Literature and the Civil War*, ed. Thomas Healy and Jonathan Sawday (Cambridge: Cambridge University Press, 1990).

GEISST, CHARLES R., *The Political Thought of John Milton* (Cambridge: Cambridge University Press, 1984).

HAMILTON, GARY, '*The History of Britain* and its Restoration Audience' in *Politics, Poetics and Hermeneutics in Milton's Prose*, pp. 241–55.

HILL, CHRISTOPHER, *Milton and the English Revolution* (New York: Faber, 1977).

—— *The Experience of Defeat: Milton and Some Contemporaries* (New York: Viking, 1984).

JAMESON, FREDRIC, 'Religion and ideology: A Political Reading of *Paradise Lost*' in *Literature, Politics and Theory*, ed. Francis Barker *et al.* (London: Methuen, 1986).

KENDRICK, CHRISTOPHER, *Milton: A Study in Ideology and Form* (London, 1986).

DAVID LOEWENSTEIN, *Milton and the Drama of History: Historical Vision, Iconoclasm, and the Literary Imagination* (Cambridge: Cambridge University Press, 1990). (Though concerned mostly with the prose tracts, this book also discusses the later books of *Paradise Lost*, as well as the relation of *Samson Agonistes* to Milton's earlier iconoclasm.)

MARCUS, LEAH, 'Milton's Anti-Laudian Masque' in *The Politics of Mirth: Jonson, Herrick, Milton, Marvell and the Defense of Old Holiday Pastimes* (Chicago and London: University of Chicago Press, 1986), pp. 169–202.

MILNER, ANDREW, *Milton and the Puritan Revolution: A Study in the Sociology of Literature* (Toyota, NJ: Barnes & Noble, 1981). (An account heavily influenced by Lucien Goldmann's sociological theory of literature, a blend of structuralism with Marxism.)

PATTERSON, ANNABEL, 'Forced Fingers: Milton's Early Poems and Ideological Constraint' in *The Muses Commonweale: Poetry and Politics in the Seventeenth Century*, ed. Claude Summers and Ted-Larry Pebworth (Columbus: University of Missouri Press, 1988), pp. 9–22.

RAPAPORT, HERMAN, *Milton and the Post Modern* (Lincoln: University of Nebraska Press, 1983). (Contains a sinister account of 'Milton and the State' designed to counter the Whig tradition of Milton as a defender of liberty.)

VENUTI, LAWRENCE, 'Political Criticism' in *Our Halcyon Dayes: English Prerevolutionary Texts and Postmodern Culture* (Madison: University of Wisconsin Press, 1989). (Contains a brief essay on Milton's *Eikonoklastes* as the conclusion to a study of Caroline culture.)

Feminist criticism or women-centred studies

AERS, DAVID and BOB HODGE, '"Rational Burning": Milton on Sex and Marriage', *Milton Studies* **13** (1979): 3–33.

FARWELL, MARILYN R., 'Eve, the Separation Scene, and the Renaissance idea of Androgyny', *Milton Studies* **16** (1982): 3–20.

FRESCH, CHERYL, 'The Hebraic Influence upon the Creation of Eve in *Paradise Lost*', *Milton Studies* **13** (1979): 181–9.

GILBERT, SANDRA, 'Patriarchal Poetry and Women Readers: Reflections on Milton's Bogey', *PMLA* **93** (1978): 368–82.

GUILLORY, JOHN, 'From the Superfluous to the Supernumerary: Reading Gender into *Paradise Lost*' in *Soliciting Interpretation: Literary Theory and Seventeenth-Century English Poetry*, ed. Elizabeth Harvey and Katharine Maus (Chicago and London: Chicago University Press, 1990), pp. 68–88.

HENDERSON, KATHERINE and BARBARA McMANUS (ed), *Half Humankind: Contexts* and *Texts of the Controversy about Women in England, 1540–1640* (Urbana: University of Illinois Press, 1985).

LEWALSKI, BARBARA, 'Milton on Women – Yet Once More', *Milton Studies* **6** (1974): 3–20

MACK, PHYLLIS, 'Women as Prophets during the English Civil War', *Feminist Studies* **8** (1982): 19–45.

MACLEAN, IAN, *The Renaissance Notion of Women* (Cambridge: Cambridge University Press, 1980).

McCOLLEY, DIANE, *Milton's Eve* (Urbana: University of Illinois Press, 1983).

MICHEL, ROBERT H., 'English Attitudes towards Women 1640–1700', *Canadian Journal of History* **13** (1978): 35–60.

NYQUIST, MARY, 'The Genesis of Gendered Subjectivity in the Divorce Tracts and in *Paradise Lost*' in *Re-membering Milton*, pp. 99–127.

SHULLENBERGER, WILLIAM, 'Wrestling with the Angel: *Paradise Lost* and Feminist Criticism', *Milton Quarterly* **20** (1986): 68–85.

WEBBER, JOAN 'The Politics of Poetry: Feminism and *Paradise Lost*', *Milton Studies* **14** (1980): 3–24.

WITTREICH, JOSEPH, *Feminist Milton* (Ithaca and London: Cornell University Press, 1987).

WOODBRIDGE, LINDA, *Women and the English Renaissance: Literature and the Nature of Womankind, 1540–1620* (Chicago: University of Illinois Press, 1984).

Psychoanalytic or psychological criticism

HALPERN, RICHARD, 'The Great Instauration: Imaginary Narratives in Milton's "Nativity Ode"' in *Re-membering Milton*, pp. 3–21.

KENDRICK, CHRISTOPHER, 'Milton and Sexuality: A Symptomatic Reading of *Comus*' in *Re-membering Milton*, pp. 43–73. (Kendrick describes this essay as moving 'from a psychoanalytic reading, which operates in the essential biographical context of what is sometimes called the young Milton's *chastity cult*; to a politico-cultural reading, set in the context of what Foucault calls the history of sexuality . . . to a socioeconomic reading, in which the chastity cult and generalized sexuality appear under the aspect of the reification imposed by emergent capitalism'.)

KERRIGAN, WILLIAM, *The Sacred Complex: On the Psychogenesis of Paradise Lost* (Cambridge, Mass.: Harvard University Press, 1983).

LE COMTE, EDWARD, *Milton and Sex* (New York: Columbia University Press, 1978).

Index